FRANTIC FRANK LANE

FRANTIC FRANK LANE

*Baseball's Ultimate
Wheeler-Dealer*

Bob Vanderberg

Foreword by Billy Pierce

McFarland & Company, Inc., Publishers
Jefferson, North Carolina, and London

LIBRARY OF CONGRESS CATALOGUING-IN-PUBLICATION DATA

Vanderberg, Bob, 1948–
    Frantic Frank Lane : baseball's ultimate wheeler-dealer /
Bob Vanderberg ; foreword by Billy Pierce.
        p.   cm.
    Includes bibliographical references and index.

    ISBN 978-0-7864-7018-1
    softcover : acid free paper ∞

    1. Lane, Frank, 1896–1981.   2. Baseball managers—
United States—Biography.   3. Baseball teams—United
States—History.   I. Lane, Frank, 1896–1981.   II. Title.
GV865.L3195V36 2013
796.357092 — dc23
[B]   2012049656

BRITISH LIBRARY CATALOGUING DATA ARE AVAILABLE

Front cover photograph: General manager of the Cleveland
Indians Frank Lane on the telephone at a hotel in New York City,
January 24, 1958. Lane, along with other baseball bigwigs, is
there for Major League Baseball talks (AP Photo/John Lindsay)

Manufactured in the United States of America

McFarland & Company, Inc., Publishers
    Box 611, Jefferson, North Carolina 28640
    www.mcfarlandpub.com

Table of Contents

Foreword by Billy Pierce

I cannot tell a lie. I wasn't always happy to be known as the first player ever acquired by Frank Lane as a major-league general manager. For the first few hours, days and weeks after hearing on Detroit radio that I had been traded from the Tigers to the White Sox on November 10, 1948, I wasn't happy at all. I mean, I remember seeing the White Sox in 1948, and they were a slow, old ballclub that lost 101 games. I remember Taffy Wright was in the outfield, 37 years old. Luke Appling, 41, was still playing short. There was Aaron Robinson, 33; Floyd Baker, 32, and Don Kolloway, 30. I'd look at this team and think, "Holy mackerel!" I remember once, while I was still with the Tigers, seeing a fly ball hit out to right field. Their outfielder took a step back, then came in, kinda slowed up and caught it on the first bounce. I thought, "Am I really seeing this?" Between that and the smell from the stockyards, that was one club I did not want to go to. But I went there and the older guys started moving out, and the year after that, Nellie Fox and Chico Carrasquel came. We got younger and faster and better. And Frank was the reason. He made all the deals. He changed the whole atmosphere.

The difference between the 1949 and 1948 White Sox was tremendous. Between 1948 and 1950, it was almost a completely new team. Frank did so many things around here to take a team that, shall we say, was not cherished by the fans, and remake it so that by '51 there were big crowds and the fans yelled "Go! Go!" What a change. And it wasn't like he brought guys here and then traded them a year later. I was here for 13 years. Nellie was here 14 years. Minnie Minoso was here off and on for a lot of years too. Sherm Lollar was here 12 years; "Jungle Jim" Rivera was here for 10.

A new ballplayer would come and talk to me when they'd first come to our club: "What about this general manager of yours? Can we trust him?" I'd tell him that, as far as I was concerned, I could trust him more than anyone I'd ever been around. "If he tells you something, it will happen." That's just the way it was. I remember in '54, the first year I'd ever had arm trouble. I was having a bad year. The year before, I won 18 games, threw seven shutouts and led the league in strikeouts. But now I was worried. "What's going to happen to me?" Frank came up to me one day and said, "Bill, don't worry

1

about anything. Your salary will be the same next year as this year. It's not going to get cut. You're taken care of." Well, what more can you ask? One time somebody way out on the West Coast was forging my name on things. A big restaurant or something was coming to the ballclub to sue me to get at my salary and pay "my" bill. Frank said, "We know Bill very well. If we hear from you again, we will sue *you.*" He stood up for me, and I didn't even know about it until about a year later.

People would ask me what it was like to be on a club with Frank Lane as the general manager in the days just before the old June 15 trade deadline. Frank wasn't happy unless he was active. So you always wondered who might be going. As often as things happened with Frank around, you never knew what was going to happen. If a trade wasn't made, there was always a rumor that it was going to be made. We had a lot of rumors. A lot. But if you didn't think about it, you know, something's wrong. One year (1952), June 15 was on a Sunday, and some of us had an outing planned at Ray Berres' cottage up in Wisconsin, near Kenosha, the next day, an open date. Frank made a trade with the Browns that Sunday night, so we had to say goodbye to Al Zarilla and Willie Miranda. But everyone else was relaxed the next morning. The deadline had passed; we were safe. And when we got home that night, Ken Holcombe was gone. He thought he had made it through the deadline. But Frank had made a waiver deal that afternoon and Kenny was on his way to St. Louis to join the Browns. He hadn't been safe after all.

One of my best friends when I first got here was Gordon Goldsberry. My wife and his wife got to be close friends. And bingo! A trade, and he's gone. And my wife felt terrible. She'd just lost her best friend. But as we say, that's baseball. And somehow baseball was always more fun when Frank Lane was around.

Walter Willam "Billy" Pierce was the first player acquired by Frank Lane as a major league general manager. Pierce went on to pitch for Chicago through 1961, winning 186 games, still a White Sox record for left-handers. He started three All-Star Games as a member of the White Sox, won 20 games in 1956 and 1957 and was named The Sporting News *Pitcher of the Year both years. He finished his career with 211 wins and a 3.27 earned-run average.*

Preface

They don't make them like Frank Lane anymore. A lot of people would say that's probably just as well. Those are the ones who swore at him. Yet there were many who swore by him. Then there was Frank Lane himself, who just swore — mostly at his own players. "His endless vitriol from the stands dropped like a thud on their egos," wrote *Sports Illustrated*'s Mark Kram in August 1968. "Lane, because of wonderfully creative swearing that effectively could clear whole areas of fans, often had to sit in the bleachers"— or in the right-field upper deck in Chicago or on the ballpark roof in St. Louis. When the game was over, though, Lane would be in the clubhouse, slapping his players on the back if they had won, providing encouragement had they lost.

He made close to 500 deals in his career, and while several didn't work out — most notably the Rocky Colavito-for-Harvey Kuenn shocker of April 1960 — he came out the winner far more often than not. His success, which at times he was not averse to pointing out, annoyed fellow general managers. To some of them, he was, as a political rival once described the great 19th Century English statesman Benjamin Disraeli, "a self-made man who worships his creator."[1] That sounds like something a wordsmith such as Bill Veeck might have said. But he did not. He almost always had only positive words for Lane.

"He was a remarkable guy, a dear, dear friend," Veeck said on the day Lane passed away. "He was a man who wasn't afraid to back up his judgment with action."[2] Veeck knew from experience. For thirty years, from Lane's seasons with the Chicago White Sox and Veeck's with the Cleveland Indians to the days when Veeck ran the White Sox and Lane made deals as a superscout with the then–California Angels, the two men made a number of trades. (Some of them more than once, as when slick Cuban shortstop Willie Miranda was moved from Chicago to St. Louis, then back again to Chicago 13 days later and finally back to St. Louis less than four months later.)

Lane and Veeck kidded each other, made deals with each other and joined forces in feuds — some serious and some not — with the mighty New York Yankees. Both men ran the White Sox during their careers and both also ran the Indians. As operators, though, Veeck won pennants and a world championship. Lane won neither. But that never bothered Frank. When he talked about his old friend, invariably he did so with a grin:

• "First of all, Bill is a merry rogue. I like him, but I know how far to trust him. I know him well enough that if he catches me, it's my own goddamn fault."

• "I prefer to disagree without being disagreeable. Well, Bill doesn't care."

• "Bill has done a great job as a promoter. Someone once asked me, 'Why don't you promote more?' I told him, 'My idea of promoting is getting one more run than the other team.' I wouldn't attempt to imitate Bill. But Bill spends more time and money advertising Bill than what it is he's selling."

• "Bill's not interested in perfection in his players. The only perfection Bill sees is what he sees in the mirror every morning."[3]

But this is a book about Frank Lane, not Bill Veeck. And here's hoping it leaves a smile on the reader's face, just as the following comments about "Frantic Frank" from Joe Garagiola have me smiling as I type them: "Lane was a general manager who not only was not afraid to make trades, but he was afraid *not* to. They used to say that the toughest job on any club Frank Lane was running belonged to the guy who had to take the team picture."[4]

A picture of Frank Lane is what this book attempts to present. It is the picture of a man who someday, certainly, should be enshrined at Cooperstown, alongside previously honored contemporaries such as Veeck, Branch Rickey, Larry MacPhail and George Weiss. Indeed, it is difficult to reconcile the presence there of men such as Bowie Kuhn, Tom Yawkey and Walter O'Malley with the absence of Frank Lane.

"I think Frank does belong in the Hall of Fame," Commissioner Allan "Bud" Selig, for whom Lane worked in 1971-72, declared recently.[5] "His impact on our sport and on so many franchises was really critical, and he was one of those individuals who, when you met, you would never forget. He was a remarkable human being."

Prologue: Chicago, June 1978

The hotel room door was slightly ajar, but the visitor, a young sports-writer keeping an appointment for an interview, knocked anyway. The room's occupant called out, "Come on in," and the visitor did just that, eager to meet the man to whom that voice belonged. And then, there he was, Frank C. Lane, general manager emeritus to a generation of baseball fans, the man who dealt home run champion Rocky Colavito for batting champ Harvey Kuenn and who almost traded Stan Musial. He was still in his pajamas at 10 A.M., telling his interviewer that he had only an hour or so, that he was heading over to Wrigley Field for that afternoon's ballgame and that he hoped his vis-itor wouldn't mind if their conversation were interrupted occasionally by the ringing of the phone.

Of course he wouldn't mind. Frank Lane was probably born with a phone attached to his ear, thought the visitor. Anyone who had pulled off close to 500 deals in his career, as Lane had, must have had a phone close by at all times. Even now the phone was among his closest friends, though he was no longer a general manager but a "superscout" for California Angels general manager Buzzie Bavasi and proud to be employed by "the Cowboy," Angels owner Gene Autry. "What I'm proudest of," said Lane, "is that just this last January I got a $15,000 raise. Well, damn few 79-year-olds in baseball are getting $15,000 raises."

There are damn few 79-year-olds in baseball, period, thought the inter-viewer, who suddenly recalled from his research that Frank had marked his 79th birthday three years earlier. But he wasn't about to interrupt. The phone would do that. Lane went on: "But I'm working for a hell of a guy. Gene Autry has been very good to me. And this job, it's interesting as hell. You know the news before it's news."

As if on cue, the phone rang. Charles O. Finley, Lane's boss in Kansas City for eight fun, but angst-filled, months in 1961 and at that moment still the owner of the A's, long since transplanted in Oakland, was on the other end. The two were talking deal, what with the 1978 trade deadline of June 15 just days away.

"Yes, Charlie, the Yankees want (Robin) Yount. They're offering (Mickey)

5

Rivers." Something Finley said made Lane laugh heartily. "You're probably correct. Anyway, I talked to Buzzie this morning, and here's what Gene is authorizing: We can give you Ken Brett and $400,000 for (Bob) Lacey, your lefthander. Yes. Brett's pitching tonight. Get back to me."

Lane hung up the phone and resumed discussing his job. "I've had higher-paying jobs, some of them where, with attendance bonuses, I was making $100,000 to $125,000 a year. But now, at my age, I'd pay to do this job. Only thing is, I die over every bleepin' ballgame. Like last night...." The Angels had lost 8–6 to Baltimore with one of their aces on the mound. "This Nolan Ryan. Goddamn stupid son of a bitch. Million-dollar arm, 10-cent head. And I know without even having been there what he's trying to do. He's trying to throw a curveball. Well, they're tickled to death when he doesn't throw 'em that fastball.

"And so they get 12 hits and seven runs off him in five innings. We get six runs for our $400,000 star and we can't win — something's wrong. But his arm must be bothering him now. They get 12 hits and seven runs off him, they're hitting the shit out of him."

About two and a half hours later, after more rants about Ryan and others, stories about some of the biggest names in baseball history, details of how he had swung some of his more controversial trades, why he had decided the designated-hitter rule — which he had championed as early as 1968 — long since had outlived its usefulness, plus two more calls from Finley, Lane looked at his watch. He, like his entranced listener, had lost track of the time. "Say, I have to get going. Do you have enough?"

He was assured that such was the case.

"Well, you have my number if you need more."

Sure enough, there were more conversations to follow in the weeks ahead. Lane talked about his hometown of Cincinnati and life in southwest Ohio; how, starting at age 18, he had played several years of semipro football — he was a tackle — for the Dayton Triangles, under the direction of future NFL coach Greasy Neale; and how he had played baseball — he was a first baseman — for a Class D ballclub in Marion, Ohio, a team owned by eventual U.S. President Warren G. Harding. Lane also had been a journalist, he said, serving time as sports editor of the *Cincinnati Commercial Tribune*, and even had tried his hand as a promoter: He once had brought the Chicago Bears and Red Grange to town for an exhibition game and presented a check for $5,800 to George Halas. He had been, too, a Big Ten football and basketball official for more than twenty years.

He also talked about going to night school to study law ("That was the extent of my proximity to college," he said, smiling). He explained how, by being in Cincinnati in the early 1930s, he'd had the good fortune of coming to know fellow basketball referee Larry MacPhail and Warren Giles, the men who ran the Reds, who had given him the job of traveling secretary, then promoted him to farm director and finally to assistant general manager. He said it was with the Reds and with MacPhail and Giles he learned how a winning team was built. Indeed, the Reds went from four straight last-place finishes (1931–34) to a pennant in 1939 and a world championship in 1940. And the Reds' farm system, which Lane had helped develop, churned out eight key members of the title teams: first baseman Frank McCormick, shortstop Billy

Commander Frank Lane poses with wife Selma and daughter Nadi circa 1944, during Lane's tour of duty in the U.S. Navy. Lane's duties at the bases where he served were to coordinate sports activates and oversee construction of athletic facilities for the sailors (courtesy Lane family).

Myers, right fielder Ival Goodman, center fielder Harry Craft and pitchers Johnny Vander Meer, Lee Grissom, Junior Thompson and Whitey Moore. Trades—oh, how he would grow to love trades—had brought Paul Derringer, Bucky Walters and Wally Berger and, much earlier, the great Ernie Lombardi.

When the United States entered World War I, not long after the Cincinnati club's success, MacPhail left for the New York Yankees and Lane enlisted in the Navy, where he attained the rank of commander. His duties were mainly to coordinate sports activities and oversee construction of athletic facilities for the sailors. Among them was future Yankee infielder Jerry Coleman. "He used to run us off the volleyball court so he and his wife could play," Coleman once recalled of Lane. "Then, later, he became my general manager at Kansas City in 1946."

By then, Lane said, MacPhail had invited him to join him in the front office of the Yankees both as GM of the organization's Kansas City Triple-A affiliate and as overseer of the western division of New York's vast farm system. He moved on in 1947 to the presidency of the American Association, a position he could have had for life. But he longed to experience the excitement of building a winner at the major-league level. He hoped against hope that such an opportunity might someday arise.

It came, he remembered, when the phone, that old friend of his, rang in his Columbus, Ohio, office on a late July day in 1948. The caller was Charles A. "Chuck" Comiskey II, the 22-year-old grandson of "the Old Roman," founder of the Chicago White Sox. Young Comiskey was just out of college and had been entrusted by his mother, Grace, the team president, with the task of straightening out a ballclub that was to finish 51–101 that season. Chuck, Lane remembered, said he'd like to discuss the White Sox with him some time in the next few weeks in Chicago. A date was agreed upon, the two met at a restaurant not too far from Midway Airport and, after some small talk, Comiskey cut to the chase:

"Frank, do you have any idea what I'm going to suggest to you?" Answered Lane: "No, I don't. But I have a good idea what I *hope* it is."

Comiskey then offered him the Sox's general manager job. Lane accepted, set up shop at Comiskey Park on November 1 and pronounced his office open for business. The newspapers paid scant attention, but he didn't mind. All that mattered was that he was running a major-league baseball team. And he was doing so in what was then the nation's second-largest city. The newspapers would be paying attention soon enough.

1

Getting Started in
Chicago, 1949–1950

The Great Awakening, as the mid–20th century turnaround of the Chicago White Sox is sometimes labeled by South Side old-timers, officially began November 1, 1948, when Frank C. Lane sat down for the first time in his new Comiskey Park office, propped his feet up on his desk and reached for the telephone. Nine days later, he made his first trade, landing a 21-year-old left-handed pitcher from the Detroit Tigers named Billy Pierce plus $10,000 for catcher Aaron Robinson, a former Yankee who was supposed to have been the key to Chicago's trade with New York the previous winter. That was the deal in which the White Sox gave up lefty Eddie Lopat, who had pitched outstanding baseball for putrid Chicago teams and soon would become a 20-game winner, a league earned-run average champion and a Sox-killer for the Yankees.

Lane's inaugural deal didn't exactly make Page 1 of the Chicago papers: Pierce, a Detroit native, had posted a 6.34 ERA in 1948 and, in 22 appearances as a Tiger, had allowed 47 hits and 58 walks in 55⅓ innings. Lane, though, was looking ahead five seasons, and he knew Pierce had been among the top high school pitching prospects in the nation a few years back, when he had been named MVP of the 1944 Connie Mack national all-star game in New York. Not only that, this was a chance to dump Robinson, who at 33 wasn't get any younger and surely wasn't getting any better. Lane followed that by selling longtime South Side outfield favorite Taffy Wright, then 37 years old, to the Philadelphia A's. Cash was beginning to move into the White Sox bank account, which had been all but depleted. Lane was enjoying this new gig. Thus, when some Chicago writers ran into Frank a little more than a week later, they were not going to convince him to change his mind about the job.

"I was refereeing an Indiana-at-Purdue football game," Lane said, thinking back to the November 20, 1948 renewal of the Old Oaken Bucket rivalry. "And John Carmichael (*Chicago Daily News* columnist) said to me, 'For Christ's sake, Frank, don't you know what you're getting yourself into? The ballclub's almost bankrupt, they've got no ballplayers.' ... And I said, 'John, listen: there are only 16 major-league general managers, and if it was a perfect job it wouldn't be open. Maybe no one else wants it, but I want it.'"[1]

When the 1949 season ended, he wanted it even more. He could look back on his first year with some satisfaction that the franchise was making progress and headed in the correct direction. True, the Sox had improved by only 12 victories (51–101 in '48 to 63–91 in '49), but home attendance had leaped from 777,844 in 1948 to 937,151 in 1949 — an increase of almost 160,000. There had been both positives and negatives. First, some of the negatives:

• Manager Jack Onslow: Lane had wanted to bring in Paul Richards from Detroit's Triple-A Buffalo farm club to manage the Sox, but the Comiskeys had promised the job to the 60-year-old Onslow, briefly a big-league catcher who had been successful while managing Waterloo and then Memphis in the Chicago farm system. So Lane bided his time and tried to make the best of a difficult situation. Three decades had passed, but Lane remembered Onslow well. "I inherited him. He loved me about as much as I loved him. A very unprepossessing guy. He's dead, and I didn't like him when he was alive, so I don't know why I should love him now that he's dead."[2] "Happy Jack" lasted the '49 season but was gone by the end of May 1950. Then, in his post-man-agerial days, he tried his hand at radio and opened his first show thusly: "Hello Jack Onslow, this is everybody speaking."[3]

• Lack of talent: Shortly after Lane took command at Comiskey Park, Lane remembered that "Chuck Comiskey had told me that we had a pretty good nucleus." So, to gauge interest in his players from the other 15 major-league teams, he put everyone on his 40-man roster on waivers. Only two were claimed: second baseman Cass Michaels and Howie Judson, a young pitcher from the University of Illinois. "So if we had a good nucleus," Lane said, "it was news to the other clubs."[4] Indeed, even though there were but eight teams in each league at that time, the Sox sent only one player to the All-Star Game at Ebbets Field — Michaels, who beat out Cleveland's Joe Gordon in the fan balloting. (Michaels went 0-for-2 but started one double play and was the middle man on another.) Michaels was batting .298 at the break and, after he collected three hits against Washington on July 15, the batting average of the 23-year-old blond-haired kid from Detroit never fell below .300 the remainder of that season, which he finished at .308 along with 101 walks, 27 doubles, 9 triples and 83 RBIs.

Michaels did not receive much assistance in the Sox lineup, however, outside of shortstop Luke Appling, who hit .301 at age 42; outfielder Dave Philley, who batted .298 (but had zero home runs); and former Yankee Steve Souchock, a Lane winter-meetings acquisition who batted just .234 but led the team with a grand total of seven homers! Injuries wrecked the rookie sea-sons of outfielders Gus Zernial (.318), a slugger up from the Pacific Coast

League, and Herb Adams (.293), a graduate of Oak Park-River Forest High School in Chicago's near west suburbs. Bill Wight, a lefty, led the pitching staff with a 15–13 won-lost mark, Randy Gumpert was 13–16 and Bob Kuzava 10–6. Young Pierce, meanwhile, finished his first full season 7–15, walking 112 in 171⅔ innings, but gave hope for the future with outings like his five-hit victories over Detroit on July 8 and Boston on August 25. Luck was not on the side of Judson, who posted a 1–14 record and received a ridiculously low 2.58 runs per game in offensive support from his teammates.

• "Home Run Lane": At Comiskey Park, Lane, hoping to create a little excitement as well as providing some aid for Zernial, had constructed a new five-foot-high, $5,000 wire fence, which reduced the home run distances from 440 feet in straightaway center field to 400 and from home plate to the foul poles from 352 to 332. The area between the permanent wall and the new fence was dubbed "Home Run Lane." It didn't exactly work out as planned. In the first eight games played at Comiskey Park in 1949, a total of 23 home runs were hit, but only eight by the home team. Worse, of the 11 homers landing in "Home Run Lane," only four were hit by the Sox. The madness reached its peak during the May 3–4 series against the light-hitting Washington Senators, the majority of whom thought of "homers" as inept umpires. The visitors struck seven long ones in the series opener and won 14–12 in 10 innings, then hit three more the next day to overcome a 7–0 deficit and win 8–7, despite the first and only home run of Sox third baseman Floyd Baker's career.

Jack Brickhouse, the late broadcaster who lived in the same Chicago North Side building as Lane, laughed as he recalled giving him a lift after that game. "The game was broken up by Mark Christman (brother of football great Paul), who was not exactly a Hall-of-Fame baseball player. So the Sox lose the ballgame, and the Yankees are coming into town next, from St. Louis. I'm driving Lane home, and he's boiling. He is just absolutely frying. We're driving up Lake Shore Drive past Oak Street Beach. I said, 'Frank, don't worry about it. Take your mind off it. Take a look at all those beautiful girls out there in their bathing suits. I'll do the driving, and you can do the looking.' But in order to see them, he had to look through another wire fence. He finally yelled, 'All I can see is that lousy fence! Can't even enjoy this!'

"And so now we get home, and about 1 o'clock in the morning, after he'd been stewing and fretting about it all night long, I guess you know he got poor Leo Dillon, the maintenance chief, out of bed and whipped that crew out there to that ballpark in the middle of the night. And that fence was *down* by the time the Yankees came out to the ballpark the next day. And Phil Rizzuto, who *never* hit any home runs, told me, 'Even I was licking my chops. Then we came out here and saw that fence was gone. We were really burned up.'"[5] Incidentally, Lane's action had more than the Yankees burned up. It prompted a new rule prohibiting the repositioning of outfield fences during the season.

• The loss of a rookie hotshot: Left fielder Zernial, 25, had hit .322 with 40 homers and 47 doubles and driven in 156 runs at Hollywood in the Pacific Coast League in 1948. At 6–2 and 220, he looked like a slugger. And in 1949, he started off playing like one, too. By May 28, he was hitting .355 and had 27 RBIs in his first 34 games. But that afternoon in Cleveland, making a diving catch on a sinking liner, he broke his collarbone and didn't start another game until August 21. The Sox were playing .500 ball at the time of the mishap; when "Ozark Ike" returned to the lineup, they were 49–66.

Still, there were these positives:

• Stunning the champs: The defending world champion Cleveland Indians came to town the weekend of May 13–15 for a scheduled four-game series that turned into a three-gamer when rain washed out Saturday's contest. Cleveland entered the series in third place, the Sox in fourth at 12–12, a game behind the Tribe. Friday night's game drew 36,914 and neither starting pitcher, future teammates Pierce and Early Wynn, lasted three innings. The Indians led 8–4 in the fifth when the home team suddenly erupted for five runs, the key hits—all with two outs—being a two-run double by Baker, a two-run pinch triple by Earl Rapp and, finally, an RBI single by Gordon Goldsberry off the legendary right-hander Satchel Paige. The Sox held on to win 11–10.

Then came Sunday's twin bill, played before a then-record Comiskey Park crowd of 53,325. The White Sox chased Bob Feller after two innings in the opener, Wight stopped the Tribe on five hits and Zernial and Michaels each had three hits and Michaels four RBIs in a 10–0 romp. In the second game, Goldsberry hit his first and last home run of 1949 to give Al Gettel a 2–0 victory. Lane, feeling a bit giddy, had the Comiskey Park home plate dug up and shipped to his good friend Bill Veeck, owner of the Indians, along with this message: "Put this on exhibit. Your guys didn't see it all day Sunday. Let them have a look at it." Two weeks later, the White Sox went to Cleveland for a weekend series. "Just before the game started," Lane remembered, "here comes the grounds crew, with a wheel barrel, to the home plate area. They had the home plate I'd sent him, still all wrapped up in ribbons, and they take out the old plate and put in the new one. And Veeck's team beat us three out of four."[6]

• The deal-a-day plan: From the season-opener through season's end, Lane made sure the sportswriters had reasons besides the ballgames to write about the White Sox. He had started slowly at the winter meetings, completing deals with Veeck's Indians (veteran left-handed pitcher Frank Papish for young lefties Ernie Groth and Bob Kuzava, who went on to a fairly successful career) and with the Yankees (outfielder Jim Delsing for outfielder/first base-man Steve Souchock, who had played for Lane at Kansas City). Lane also chose that venue to announce the purchase of 40-year-old reserve catcher Ray Berres from the Triple-A Milwaukee Brewers. Lane named him White Sox pitching coach, and Berres, a stickler for the mechanics of pitching, ended up serving the Sox brilliantly in that role for 20 years.

Once the regular season began, it seemed like the Sox were adding a new face every other day or so. Rapp, for instance, came from Detroit in early May for Don Kolloway, a local guy who lived in the south suburb of Blue Island. Pitcher Ed Klieman came from Washington late in the month, and then things got a bit more interesting as the deadline neared. Lane traded Rapp to Oakland of the Pacific Coast League for outfielder Catfish Metkovich, signed first baseman Charlie Kress, cut loose by Cincinnati, and signed high school shortstop Jim Baumer and high school pitcher Gus Keriazakos to ama-teur free-agent bonus contracts. In July, he bought catcher Eddie Malone from the Cubs and purchased left-handed pitcher Mickey Haefner from Washington. In August, he sent infielder Bobby Rhawn and cash to the Cubs for outfielder John Ostrowski on the 4th and, in a swap of right-handed reliev-ers on the 5th, sent Alex Carrasquel to the Tigers' Buffalo club for Luis Aloma. On the 6th, he rested. He would need that rest: The big deal was just weeks ahead.

• The beginning of a scouting staff: When Lane signed on with the Comiskeys, the ballclub's scouting staff was, for all intents and purposes, non-existent. "For a while there," he said, "I was my own scout. Then, when I could, I started hiring guys. I hired 'Sloppy' Thurston away from Cleveland, where he was making $9,000. I gave him $12,000, which was a hell of a salary back then for scouts. Most were making $4,000 or $5,000."[7] Thurston, a for-mer roommate of eventual Sox manager Al Lopez, covered California along with "Doc" Bennett, who was brought into the organization by Lane at about the same time. The pair was remarkably successful through the years in finding prospects for Lane and his successors. Thurston-Bennett "finds" included Earl Battey, Johnny Callison, Barry Latman, Jim Landis, Jim McAnany and many more.

• Fisticuffs in the clubhouse: This goes under the "positives" heading because of the ultimate result. The Sox were finishing up a doubleheader in St. Louis on Sunday, May 1. They won the first game 7–6 and had a seemingly safe 14–3 lead going into the last of the ninth in the nightcap. But then the Browns started hitting everything that first Bob Kuzava and then Randy Gumpert were throwing. Doubles here, triples there, and suddenly St. Louis had a man on third with two out and trailed just 14–11. Gumpert ended it by striking out Al Zarilla, but the real fun was just beginning. In the clubhouse,

Onslow sarcastically ripped into catcher Joe Tipton, second-guessing just about every pitch called by Tipton in the wild ninth. Tipton threw down his shin guards and went after Onslow, both men getting in a punch or two before they were separated. Onslow went to Lane and said Tipton had to go, and for once the two men were in agreement. But Lane had to wait until October 19 to find a taker, who turned out to be Athletics manager/owner Connie Mack. Mack acquired Tipton for a backup second baseman named Jacob Nelson Fox. The newcomer, who had batted .255 in 88 games in '49 and who was to celebrate his 22nd birthday on Christmas Day, was known only to a select few, Frank Lane among them. Years later, he said, "When I was still president of the American Association, I stopped off one night in Lincoln, Nebraska, and I saw their ballclub. And they had two little guys I loved as soon as I saw them. A left-handed pitcher and a second baseman with a huge chaw of tobacco in his left cheek. They were Bobby Shantz and Nellie Fox. I said right then and there, 'If I ever get to the big leagues, those are two guys I'm gonna get.' Well, I never got Shantz, but I did get Fox."[8]

• Chico *was* the man: In mid–September of '49, the renowned Brooklyn Dodgers front-office chief Branch Rickey dropped in on Lane and Chuck Comiskey on the South Side, obstensibly to watch a baseball game but actually to talk trade. Rickey had gotten wind of Lane's increasing interest in a spectacular Venezuelan shortstop, Alfonso Carrasquel, called "Chico," who played for the Dodgers' Fort Worth farm club in the Double-A Texas League. Lane had received glowing reports from friends in that league; indeed, one told Frank that the 21-year-old was "the greatest young shortstop I ever saw." Rickey studied the Sox that afternoon and saw more than one grounder get through the left side of the infield that had no business getting through. Time had long since caught up with 42-year-old Luke Appling. "Judas Priest, Frank," Rickey said when it was over, "you need a shortstop." Answered Lane, laughing: "That's a profound statement, Mr. Rickey. You've got all the shortstops in the world. Why don't you sell me one?"[9] Rickey kept with him a list of the Dodgers' best minor-league prospects, broken down by position, along with the dollar figure that Rickey had in mind if he were to sell them. "Bobby Morgan," Lane recalled, "was No. 1 on the list of shortstops. Rickey wanted $250,000 and three ballplayers for him. Down around No. 7 was Carrasquel: $50,000 and two ballplayers." He told Rickey he couldn't afford his top shortstops but would be interested in making an offer for Carrasquel. Rickey said if Lane made a fair offer, he would give up Carrasquel. The haggling began.[10]

Over the next two weeks, after listening to Rickey suggest other top Dodger minor-leaguers as trade targets for the White Sox — such as outfielder Irv Noren and infielder Danny O'Connell — Lane was able to infer that Rickey would let the Sox have Carrasquel only if they agreed to buy outfielder Sam

Brooklyn Dodgers front-office czar Branch Rickey is flanked by Frank Lane (left) and Chuck Comiskey during a September 1949 game at Chicago's Comiskey Park. Rickey had dropped by to gauge the level of interest the White Sox had in one of Rickey's minor-league shortstops, Venezuelan Alfonso "Chico" Carrasquel. Talks began that evening. By month's end, Chico belonged to the Sox. The two men in front are unidentified (photograph by Steve Marino, Sr.; courtesy Marino family).

Jethroe and pitcher Dan Bankhead, two African American prospects, in case a proposed deal with the Boston Braves broke down. For just the speedy Jethroe, who at Triple-A Montreal had hit .326 in 1949 with 34 doubles, 19 triples, 17 homers and an International League-record 89 stolen bases, the price tag was $150,000 and three players. Lane and Comiskey agreed they would like to have Jethroe, but they also realized they did not have that kind of money available to them. "We can't afford to buy both Jethroe and Carrasquel," Lane said to Comiskey, "and Carrasquel is the one we must have." Still, Frank feigned interest in Jethroe, all the while keeping his eye on the main objective. Lane then remembered that Rickey had indicated he wanted to get these minor-league sales completed by the end of September. He called Rickey in New York and said he was ready to announce the Carrasquel deal.

Rickey was stunned. "Do we have a deal?" he asked. Lane reminded him that Rickey had stated the White Sox could have Carrasquel if they made a fair offer. Lane's final offer had been pitcher Charlie Eisenmann and shortstop Fred Hancock and $25,000. Fair or not, the deal was accepted by Rickey, who then cleared his throat and said: "OK, let's get down to business on Jethroe." Lane's reply: "I'm not interested in Jethroe. Whatever gave you that idea?"[11]

The White Sox were beginning to assemble the pieces: a talented young lefty in Pierce, a possible starting second baseman in Fox, a potential All-Star shortstop in Carrasquel. But there was still a long way to go.

Frank Lane began warming up for the second season of the Comiskeys' version of The New Deal with an absolute steal at the winter meetings. On December 14, he sent right-hander Ed Klieman, who had worked just 33 innings over 18 games for the '49 Sox, to the Philadelphia A's for third baseman Hank Majeski, who had just turned 33 the day before but who in 1948 had helped the Athletics to a fourth-place finish with a .310 season that included 41 doubles and 120 runs batted in. Thus, Lane had given Jack Onslow an entirely new left side of the infield. Next came an upgrade behind the plate: Lane bought catcher Phil Masi, a graduate of Austin High School on Chicago's Far West Side, from Pittsburgh in February, a week before players were to begin arriving at the club's Pasadena training camp. Masi, in 1948, had caught in the World Series for the National League champion Boston Braves and was a .304 hitter as recently as 1947 and a three-time NL All-Star to boot. Majeski and Masi, two solid veterans, joined a healthy Gus Zernial plus holdovers Cass Michaels and Dave Philley. The pitching staff featured five left-handed starters, the majority young and talented: Pierce, Bill Wight, Bob Kuzava, Mickey Haefner and Bob Cain. On paper, anyway, the South Siders seemed much improved over 1949.

On the field, it was a rather different matter. The White Sox, opening at home against the sad St. Louis Browns, lost the opener, 5–3, and followed that up with a 6–1 defeat. It was off to Detroit, where the Tigers and Virgil Trucks beat them, 4–1, and Art Houtteman shut them out, 5–0. The Sox finally won a game, beating the host Tigers, 5–4, on April 23 as Pierce relieved Kuzava in the fifth and threw three-hit, scoreless ball the rest of the way. (That also was the day former Texas Christian running back Jim Busby made his big-league debut, playing center field and going 0 for 5 in the leadoff spot.) Then came a full week of weather-related cancellations. Finally, on April 30, the weather improved and Wight blanked Detroit, 5–0, in Chicago. The high point of the first few weeks came on a Thursday afternoon, May 4, in New York. Facing Eddie Lopat with two out and nobody on in the first inning, the Sox scored four times (Zernial and Carrasquel each drove home a run and catcher Ed Malone singled in a pair) and went on to romp 15–0 on 23 hits, including the first four of Busby's big-league career. Dave Philley, Luke Appling (playing first base), Carrasquel and Cain each had two hits; Majeski and Michaels added three apiece and Zernial joined the 23-year-old Busby with four. Cain, just 25, wound up with a five-hit shutout of the world champions.

That would be the most fun the Sox would have for weeks. The rout of New York gave them a 3–5 record. Soon they would be 6–20. The rest of the road trip produced two victories in 11 games; then the Sox came home and did even worse, losing the first six games of the homestand. Lane was ready to act, and when Bob Feller and the Indians downed Cain, 2–1, before just 9,879 on a Friday night at Comiskey Park, dropping the South Siders to 8–22, he went into action. First came the firing of Onslow after the game and the announcement that Red Corriden, one of the coaches, would replace "Happy Jack" as interim manager. Onslow, though he knew his ouster was inevitable and that the Sox would still be paying him not to manage, was bitter. "They won't second-guess me anymore," he said. "As far as I'm concerned, Lane can manage the club and Comiskey can coach at third base or any place he likes![12] I could say a lot of unpleasant things," he continued. "I could tell of the times I've had to take the rap for things which weren't my fault. I knew this was coming because I wasn't wanted here. And when you're not wanted, you don't stay long."[13]

Three days later, Lane announced the acquisition from Pittsburgh of lefty-swinging outfielder Marv Rickert, a .292 hitter for the Braves the season before. With Rickert on board, Busby, hitting .208, was sent down to Sacramento in the Pacific Coast League the same day. Then, on May 31, Lane completed a whopper, sending Michaels, Kuzava and reserve outfielder Johnny Ostrowski to Washington for a much-needed first baseman in Eddie Robinson, along with pitcher Ray Scarborough and second baseman Al Kozar. (Kozar was supposed to replace Michaels but ended up losing the starting job to Nellie Fox.) Ostrowski was asked for his reaction. Noting that he was of Polish extraction — as were Onslow, Kuzava and even Michaels (real name Kwietniewski) — Ostrowski said of Lane: "The son of a bitch just doesn't like Polacks."[14]

The firing of Onslow and the May 31st trade provided, as such things often do, a temporary spark, but this was a flawed team, despite the addition of Robinson, a left-handed power hitter to go with Zernial from the right side. Robinson would go on to bat .295 with 21 home runs while Zernial would break Zeke Bonura's club home run record of 27 by belting three out of the park (for a total of 29) during a season-closing twin bill with the visiting

Browns. Flawed though they were, the Sox did have their moments of success in 1950. Among the biggest was the three-game sweep of the Yankees June 13–15 at Comiskey Park that featured great drama. In the opener, played on a Tuesday night, a crowd of 42,970 cheered the Sox to a 6–5 ninth-inning victory. One day later, the Sox were one out from defeat when they mounted a four-run rally to pull out a 5–2 victory. The big blow was Philley's three-run homer off Joe Page. In the finale, Pierce outdueled Lopat, 5–0, while allowing only one hit, a leadoff single by Billy Johnson in the fifth.

In that game, Carrasquel opened the home first with a home run and added another hit later in the contest. That gave Chico six hits in 12 tries in the sweep of New York and upped his batting average to .285 and his on-base percentage to .385. On July 8, the Venezuelan embarked on a 24-game hitting streak that sent his batting average up to .303 before it was halted by Boston's Ellis Kinder on August 6 at Comiskey Park. He finished at .282. His fielding, however, was what grabbed everyone's attention. As far back as Opening Day in St. Louis, umpiring crew chief Tommy Connolly called a Carrasquel gem in the hole "one of the two or three greatest plays I ever saw."[15] Nonetheless, when the postseason awards were handed out, the AL Rookie of the Year trophy went to Yankees lefty Whitey Ford, who went 9–1 for the repeat world champs but didn't come up until July 1, made only 12 starts and appeared in a total of 20 games (to Carrasquel's 141).

Meanwhile, Lane had not taken the summer off. He landed catcher Gus Niarhos from the Yankees in late June, bought pitcher Lou Kretlow on waivers from the Browns and, in a historic move at the end of July, signed the White Sox's first African Americans: catcher Sam Hairston of the Indianapolis Clowns (in the Negro American League) and first baseman Bob Boyd of the Memphis Red Sox (same league). Both contributed to the White Sox in a big way. Boyd, before spending most of his career with Baltimore, was called up from Charleston in July 1953 and hit .297 while filling in for the injured Ferris Fain. Hairston worked in the Sox organization for decades as a player, coach, manager and scout, and his son Jerry, Sr., became the Sox's all-time leading pinch-hitter.

As he looked back on the 1950 season, the final 60–94 record and a dropoff in home attendance to 781,330 — almost back to 1948 figures — Lane had to be a tad discouraged. He knew he had to upgrade the pitching, land an imposing left-handed bat for the outfield, hope that the Fox kid at second base and the speedy Busby in center would improve and pray that Hank Majeski — who finished with a .309 average — would not lose the touch over the winter. Also, there was the matter of naming a new manager.

That came to pass on October 10, when Lane introduced to the press Paul Rapier Richards, 42, former major-league catcher, World Series hero,

The Lane family (Frank, Nadi and Selma) takes an off-season break at a dude ranch near Tucson, circa 1949 (courtesy Lane family).

minor-league manager and, at one time, an ambidextrous pitcher as well. Lane was a long-time admirer of Richards, who had become the manager of Atlanta in 1938. "He was the sort of guy who made you mad as an opponent but you wished you had nine like him playing for you," Lane said. "I followed Paul closely thereafter and finally made up my mind ... that if I ever had to hire a manager, Richards was my man. He won me mostly because of his insistence on speed and aggressiveness."[16]

After the meeting with the reporters, Richards went for a brief tour of the Comiskey Park dugout and clubhouse. On the wall outside the locker room was a sign, in old English lettering, that read: "Be a Good Loser." Richards reached up and ripped it off the wall and fired it into the nearest receptacle. "The housecleaning starts here," Richards said. "Maybe you can't help losing sometimes, but there's no law saying you have to accept defeat without doing something about it. If you're a good loser, you keep on losing."[17] The losing on Chicago's South Side was about to end.

2

The Go-Go Sox
Are Born, 1951–1952

Frank Lane was certain he had chosen, in Paul Richards, the right man to lead the White Sox. Years later, he told an interviewer: "One of the best deals I ever made was bringing Richards here to Chicago to manage." Then he grinned. "And he was great for me, because he'd go out and play golf and I'd stay in the office."[1] Now, with winter closing in and gotten his new manager signed to a two-year contract at $25,000 per season, Lane could concentrate his efforts on strengthening the roster he had presented to Richards.

First he selected relief pitcher Harry Dorish off the Triple-A Toronto roster and infielder Joe DeMaestri, then property of the Red Sox, from Double-A Birmingham in the minor-league draft. Then came the winter meetings in his home base of St. Petersburg, Florida, with Lane determined to land a lefty-swinging outfielder to give Richards a second strong hitter from the left side to go with Eddie Robinson. Red Sox right fielder Al Zarilla had hit .329, .277 and .325 and averaged 75 RBIs the last three seasons and was available—for pitching help. Lane packaged two pitchers coveted by the Yankees—lefty Bill Wight (10–16, 3.58 in 1950) and right-hander Ray Scarborough (13–18, 4.94)—and sent them to the Red Sox. In return, he received Zarilla and 34-year-old right-hander Joe Dobson, who had won 13, 18, 16, 14 and 15 games the previous five seasons for Boston and was the kind of staff workhorse every successful club must have. The Red Sox also tossed in left-handed pitcher Dick Littlefield, who spent most of his career modeling uniforms, in thanks, partly, to Lane. Littlefield was traded nine times in seven years; Lane twice traded for him and twice traded him away.

Following the announcement of the trade, the Yankees were hopping mad. For one thing, the Red Sox, their top rivals, had landed two pitchers that Yankees manager Casey Stengel had wanted. Also, just before the deal was made, Stengel and New York GM George Weiss had made a strong bid for Scarborough alone, offering Lane his choice of two outfielders—Gene Woodling or Cliff Mapes—plus two of these four pitchers: Joe Page, Tom Ferrick, Fred Sanford and Joe Ostrowski. But Lane went the Boston route instead, and then told the assembled members of the press the names of the players in the New York offer, which angered the Yankees even more. "When you suggest a deal," Stengel said, "you take it for granted the other side will keep the names secret, but Lane doesn't do that. It takes him an average of 15 minutes to tell everything.... I believe the time has come to do something abut making Lane shut his mouth." Another Yankee official added, "The only way to talk business with Lane is to get him in a room and make a deal on the spot. If the deal falls through, you have to gag him."[2]

Then, one day after the Zarilla deal, Lane swapped 33-year-old outfielder Mike McCormick, a right-handed hitter (.225 in 1950), to Washington for 34-year-old outfielder Ed Stewart, a left-handed hitter (.267 in 1950). This deal proved to be a big "W" for Lane: McCormick had been retired for two years by 1953, which is when Stewart went 10-for-34 (.294) as the White Sox's leading pinch-hitter.

Here's the Chicago White Sox 1952 Opening Day infield, all members of which were brought to Chicago by Frank Lane: from left, first baseman Eddie Robinson, acquired in May 1950 from Washington; second baseman Nellie Fox, acquired in October 1949 from the Philadelphia A's; shortstop Chico Carrasquel, acquired from the Brooklyn Dodgers' organization in September 1949; and 32-year-old rookie third baseman Hector Rodriguez, obtained in December 1951, also out of the Dodgers' system (author's collection).

Lane went back to Chicago confident he had made the Sox stronger. But Richards continued to urge him to do all he could to land a remarkably talented ballplayer who had thoroughly impressed him the summer before in the Pacific Coast League. The player was a black Cuban infielder-outfielder whose full name was Saturnino Orestes Arrieta Armas Minoso. Known by the nickname "Minnie," Minoso had played for San Diego, Cleveland's Triple-A affiliate, mostly as a third baseman but often too as an outfielder and, on occasion, a first baseman. In 169 games, he had hit .339 with 40 doubles, 10 triples, 20 home runs and 115 RBIs—not to mention 30 stolen bases. Because of three years in the Negro leagues and two more in San Diego, Minnie was 28 years old when Lane and Richards set their sights on him. But his exuberance and great speed made him look much younger. "Minoso," Richards kept saying to Lane. "Minoso's the guy." Lane, having heard tales of Minoso's shaky defense, always responded, "But he can't play anything." To which Richards countered, "Don't worry about him playing anything—I'll find a place for him. We'll just let him hit and run."[3]

Lane had approached Cleveland GM Hank Greenberg at the winter meetings and asked him if would be willing to deal Minoso. Greenberg said sure, but the price would have to include a good left-handed pitcher. Greenberg asked about Wight, but Lane was about to announce Wight's departure in the Zarilla transaction. Greenberg then asked for Billy Pierce, which ended the conversation but also caused Lane to contemplate the concept of a three-team trade in which the Tribe would wind up with a lefty. By Sunday, April 29, Lane finally had worked out a deal involving the White Sox, Cleveland and the Philadelphia A's, who in lefty Lou Brissie had the man Greenberg was seeking. Here's how it would work: the Indians were to send Minoso, pitcher Sam Zoldak and catcher Ray Murray to Philadelphia for Brissie; the A's would then send Minoso and outfielder Paul Lehner to Chicago for Dave Philley and slugger Gus Zernial, who was off to a .105 start but who would be reunited in Philadelphia with Jimmy Dykes, his manager at Hollywood in 1947 and '48 and one of his biggest admirers. Lane, Greenberg and A's GM Art Ehlers agreed they would release news of the trade on Monday, an open date on the schedule. But then Minoso himself nearly sabotaged the deal.

The Indians played a doubleheader that Sunday in St. Louis, and Minoso, batting third and playing first base due to an injury to Luke Easter, went 5-for-8 in the two games. He had a double and two singles and was hit by a pitch in the opener, then doubled twice, drove in a run and got drilled by a pitched ball again in Game 2. Lane, holed up in a New York City hotel and checking the wires for finals and box scores, almost had a heart attack when he saw the box scores from St. Louis: "I thought, 'Geez, if Greenberg hears that Minnie got all those hits, he'll never make the deal.' So I wanted to release the news a day early." In panic mode, Lane put through a call to Greenberg in Cleveland. Hank's wife answered. "She had no use for baseball and no use for anyone associated with baseball," Lane remembered, grinning. "Anyway, I said, 'I've got to get hold of Hank.' 'Well, Mr. Lane, he's out playing tennis.' 'Well, Hank and I have made this deal and we're releasing the news a day sooner.' I wanted to get it into print."[4]

Lane made three calls that Sunday afternoon to the Greenberg residence; the third time was the charm. "Finally," Lane said, "Hank comes in all out of breath and everything, and I say, 'Hank, I've gotten hold of your writers, Harry Jones and Gordon Cobbledick (of the *Cleveland Plain Dealer*), and they're gonna release the deal.' And Hank was anxious to get into the shower, so he gives the OK and we get it into print. Now Hank finds out within an hour that Minnie got five hits. And oh, was he hot. Although he never told me. But I know bleepin' well that he wouldn't have done the deal. Because later he said, 'Geez, that damn Lane—he got me with my pants down. I was in the shower.' Actually, of course, I got him before he got into the shower."[5]

The main thing was that Lane had gotten Minoso. Richards, whose ball-club had started well, was overjoyed. He made sure there was a warm welcome from his new teammates for the first black to play in a White Sox regular-season game and, to help Minoso deal with the media, he named relief pitcher Luis Aloma, a fellow Cuban, as Minnie's interpreter. Aloma was put to work after Minoso's first game, Tuesday, May 1, at Comiskey Park against the world champion New York Yankees and their ace right-hander, Vic Raschi. The Sox had lost the game, 8–3, and another rookie, 19-year old Mickey Mantle of New York had hit his first major-league home run off Gumpert. Nevertheless, something special had happened in the home half of the first inning. With one out, newcomer Paul Lehner singled to right and Minoso, wearing the uniform number (No. 9) that would be retired in his honor by the Sox 25 years later, swung at a Raschi pitch and drilled it over the bullpen fence in center field, 415 feet away, for the most dramatic debut by a White Sox player that anyone could remember. After the game, reporters crowded around Minnie's locker and asked their questions, with Aloma translating. Finally, one writer asked Minnie, "How are you going to play big-league ball with these guys if you can't speak English?" Minoso bypassed the interpreter and said, "Ball, bat, glove—she no speak English."[6]

Minnie did learn to speak enough English to get by that first year, although WGN-TV's Jack Brickhouse admitted to some trepidation on those occasions when Minoso appeared on the station's postgame show, "The Tenth Inning." "The first six times I interviewed Minoso on television, I don't think I understood one complete sentence," Brickhouse said. "I had to pretend that I understood what he was saying. I was real worried, too. You know, you say to yourself: 'I hope he's not using any bad language. I hope he's not advocating the overthrow of the government by force.' But whatever his answers were, he gave them so sincerely, with such a serious look on his face, and his eyes would light up — you just knew the sincerity was coming out of his ears."[7]

Meanwhile, though Minoso's bat might not have been able to speak English, it was speaking with authority. "The Cuban Comet," as he came to be known, went 2-for-4 in both Yankee games (May 1–2) and then continued hitting until, on Friday, June 8, with the Yankees arriving in town for a four-game weekend series, Minnie woke up and found that he was leading the American League in batting average at .366. Better still, his team was 32–11 and leading the second-place Yankees by 4½ games, the Red Sox by 6½ and the Indians by 8½. Minoso was also leading in on-base percentage (.482), runs scored (45) and triples (8) and was second in steals with nine (teammate and fellow rookie Jim Busby had 12) and in slugging percentage (his .612 mark just 10 points behind Sox first baseman Eddie Robinson's AL-best .622). Busby and Minnie, with their 21 steals combined, had topped by two the entire stolen-base total of 1950 Sox.

Lane had hit the jackpot with the Minoso deal. The Cuban energized an already improved team that had dropped that pair to the Yankees on May 1–2 but then had won 26 of its next 31 games. That stretch was highlighted by a 14-game winning streak — the Sox's longest since 1906 — and was particularly remarkable in that the first 11 wins were accomplished on the road. Fox's first big-league homer, a two-run shot off Boston's Scarborough just inside the Fenway Park right-field foul pole in the 11th inning, was the difference in the first one, on Tuesday, May 15. Lane, who during the game had traded Bob Cain to Detroit for right-hander Saul Rogovin (13–7 and 16–6 under Richards at Triple-A Buffalo in 1948 and '49), was reminded of Richards' innovative mind that day when, in the home ninth, Billy Pierce came in to relieve right-hander Harry Dorish and face the inning's first hitter, Ted Williams. Instead of departing the field, however, Dorish moved over to play third base. And after Pierce retired Williams on a popout, Richards removed Pierce, and Dorish returned to the mound, where he eventually picked up the "W."

The next afternoon, the Sox whipped Boston once again, 9–5, with two former Red Sox added during the winter doing the heavy lifting. Joe Dobson went the distance for the win and Al Zarilla drove in three runs, two with a bases-loaded double in a five-run first. Afterward, Lane announced yet another deal, this the purchase of former American League All-Star third baseman and base-stealing champ Bob Dillinger from the Pirates. All Dillinger did was hit safely in 20 of 21 games in a hot streak that helped send his batting average up to .396 by June 24. The next stop on the trip was in New York, where Eddie Stewart's seventh-inning grand slam was the game-winning blow in a 7–4 decision. There followed three triumphs in Washington, the finale a 9–8 thriller in which Dillinger collected three hits and Fox three hits and three RBIs, including yet another home run. After Randy Gumpert won 5–2 in Philadelphia, it was on to Cleveland for a four-game weekend series, and again the Sox turned on the offense. They totaled 23 runs in the four games against the league's deepest pitching staff: Pierce beat Bob Lemon, 6–4; Ken Holcombe shut out Mike Garcia and the Tribe 6–0; Dobson outlasted Early Wynn, 5–2, in Sunday's opener as the Sox used a 3-spot to break a 2–2 sixth-inning tie; and Howie Judson rode Zarilla's RBI double and home run to win the finale, 6–4.

The Sox returned to Chicago the next morning to find they had relegated the Korean War to the inside pages. Thousands of commuters at LaSalle Street Station greeted the team's train and received autographs from their new heroes. First-place New York was a mere game ahead of the Sox (and Chicago passed the Yankees that night by beating the St. Louis Browns, 4–2, while Boston downed New York, 3–2). Frank Lane could afford to relax a bit, but there was more work to do, more GMs to talk to, more newspapermen to charm, more youngsters to sign for future Sox pennant drives. Celebrations could wait, but, truth be told, inwardly Frank was celebrating the crowds his team would draw during this homestand: 34,856 for a Memorial Day doubleheader sweep of the Browns; 35,362 for a Sunday split with the Red Sox and 42,718 the next night for a twilight-night twin bill sweep of Boston, with fans chanting "Go! Go!" every time speedsters like Minoso and Busby reached base. Particularly pleasing about that evening was that Pierce had beaten ex-White Sox pitcher Ray Scarborough, 6–5, in the opener and then Rogovin had blanked the Red Sox, 2–0, with former Chicago lefty Bill Wight getting the loss. Lane's deals were making him look like a genius, so why not try some more?

Thus, on June 4, just before the twi-nighter with Boston, Lane had announced a three-way trade involving the Browns and the Athletics. First he sent Hank Majeski, seldom used thus far in '51 (.257 in just 12 games) to Philadelphia for Kermit Wahl, Philly's regular third baseman the season before. Then Lane shipped some cash plus Wahl and outfielder Paul Lehner, who had come to Chicago in the Minoso deal, to the St. Louis Browns for right-handed-hitting outfielder Don Lenhardt, a University of Illinois alum from downstate Alton, Illinois, who as a rookie in 1950 had batted .273 with 22 homers and 81 RBIs. The baseball world had to be impressed: Lane had given up zero necessary parts to obtain a consistent right-handed long-ball threat, something missing since the departure of Gus Zernial. But Lane was not through with his discussions with Browns boss Bill DeWitt. He had his sights on right-hander Ned Garver, 13–18 and 3.39 ERA for last-place St. Louis in '50 and already 8–3 in 1951 for an even worse Browns club. For

Garver, who would go on to win 20 games that season and might have made this new, exciting "Go-Go Sox" team a pennant-winner, Lane offered $250,000 and three players. He was turned down for the final time on June 15, the trading deadline.

On the field, the Sox-Yankees game on Friday night, June 8, drew a Comiskey Park record 53,940 fans, who saw Eddie Robinson crack a two-run homer, his 11th home run of the season, off Vic Raschi for an early lead before the Yanks rallied for a 4–2 triumph. The champs overwhelmed Pierce the next day, 10–5, before 24,726, and Eddie Lopat (9–1) outdueled Rogovin in Sunday's doubleheader opener, 2–1. Chicago did salvage the second game, as the remnants of a crowd of 52,054 cheered a four-run eighth-inning rally that snapped a 7–7 tie and featured — all with two outs — a single by Robinson that drove home a run, an RBI double by Lenhardt and a two-run single by Busby. Randy Gumpert, who was credited with the win, was now 5–0, but the White Sox's AL lead had been sliced to 2½ games over New York, 5½ over Boston and 7½ over Cleveland.

Sunday's throng had included a few too many rowdies for Casey Stengel's liking. Apparently in response to Gil McDougald's hard slide into the plate in the opener, a collision that forced Sox catcher Gus Niarhos out of the contest, fans in right field ganged up on rookie Mickey Mantle, peppering the right-field warning track with firecrackers, rolled-up newspapers, beer cups, flasks and even a few over-ripe sandwiches. "Foolish stunts like that might cut short a man's career or even cost him his eyesight," said Stengel, who called on the White Sox to do a better job security-wise. "Suppose one of those firecrackers had exploded right at Mantle's eye level?" Lane, who presumed Stengel was still upset because Frank had disclosed the names of the New York players in that proposed Sox-Yankee deal the past winter, reacted angrily: "I believe Stengel has enough of a job just managing the Yankees without trying to tell us how to run our ballpark."[8]

Meanwhile, back on the trade front, Ned Garver wasn't the only "name" player Lane failed to land at the deadline. With Zarilla slumping in the .240s after a quick beginning, Lane went shopping for another left-handed-hitting outfielder. One of his favorite targets, before and after '51, was the Athletics' Elmer Valo, a 30-year-old Czech native (real name Imrich Vallo) who swung from the left side, ripped line drives to all fields and, at all times, hustled. Valo was a consistent high-average hitter who invariably produced an on-base-percentage in the .400s. His problem, as far as Lane was concerned, was that he played well against the Sox, especially so when Lane and A's GM Art Ehlers were close to finalizing a deal involving Valo. The Sox just happened to be in Philadelphia on June 15 that year, but the pattern that had been established in past seasons was to continue.

"That darned Valo," Lane complained, "would get three or four hits and wreck the deal. This happened two or three different years." In this instance, Valo singled, doubled, walked twice and scored from first on Gus Zernial's 11th-inning double, separating the ball from Sox catcher Gus Niarhos in a home-plate collision. Another time, Valo forced the cancellation of a postgame trade announcement and press conference by hitting for the cycle and driving in three runs at Comiskey Park. "I'd call Ehlers and say, 'Let's announce the deal.' We'd *agreed* on it. I forget who we were going to give up, but it was someone agreeable to both teams. And he wanted to play for me. What the hell, he *knew* I was trying to get him. And I'd say, 'Well, go 0-for-4 sometime and I'll be able to get you.' But if ever there was a guy who'd give you 120 percent, it was Valo. He'd knock the fences down for you. What a hard-working son of a gun he was and what a good ballplayer he was. But Art Ehlers would say, 'Gee, Frank, you picked a bad time. I can't trade a guy who just went 4-for-5.' And at the time I was trying to get him that year, he was hitting about .250. And he wound up hitting over .300 (.302)." [9] Even without Valo or Garver, the Chicagoans were still on top at the All-Star break (at 49–29), but things were tight: the Red Sox were one game back, the Yankees two and the Indians four. Those four clubs dominated the AL All-Star roster, with Chicago landing two starters in Nelson Fox (hitting .325) and Chico Carrasquel (.283), who became the first Latin American player to start in the Midsummer Classic. Accompanying them to Detroit for the game were Minoso (.337 with an AL-best 12 triples), Robinson (.306, 16 homers, 70 RBIs), Busby (.319 and a league-leading 17 steals) and Gumpert (7–2).

Regular-season play resumed two nights later with the Sox hosting Boston for a pair under the lights. With 52,592 spectators watching, Mel Parnell shut out Chicago for eight innings before settling for a 3–2 triumph. Then, in a memorable nightcap, Rogovin pitched all 17 innings, only to lose 5–4 to Sox-killer Ellis Kinder (10 scoreless innings in relief) when Clyde Vollmer's fly to left scored Lou Boudreau from third. If that weren't enough, the two teams played a 19-inning affair the next night. This time, the White Sox fell behind 4–2 in the top of the 19th but won 5–4 when Eddie Stewart's bases-loaded single scored two runs for a 4–4 tie and Lenhardt followed with a deep sacrifice fly to left to send what remained of the original crowd of 25,211 home happy. The following afternoon, before 27,092, Ken Holcombe and the Sox had Boston and lefty Chuck Stobbs beaten 2–1 in the ninth until Bobby Doerr singled, Billy Goodman doubled and Vollmer singled to drive in both of them. Chicago loaded the bases in the bottom half, but Floyd Baker lined out to third to end it. Boston had taken over the AL lead by one game over the White Sox.

Jack Brickhouse, as was customary after day games, drove Lane home and, after dinner, the two tried to enjoy a few drinks. "Frank wasn't much for a drink — he didn't drink a lot," Brickhouse said. "He'd have one, maybe two in an entire evening after a tough ballgame. One time, we were in our favorite nightcap spot there on Diversey, where the fellows who owned the place were good friends of ours. And they kind of protected us a little bit. After all, Frank was a public figure. They let us sit in the back and wouldn't let too many people come back there and ask Frank a lot of questions. Sometimes it was unavoidable, and sometimes you enjoyed it, too. But once in a while, you'd like to have one by yourself. And anyway, that series with the Red Sox, when they lost three out of four — all tough ballgames, all hairline-decision games. And Lane — you could've lit a cigarette on the back of his neck after that series. We were having a nightcap, and some guy comes back to us and starts giving Lane a hard time. A real hard time. And Frank was in no mood for this one. We had to peel him off that guy."[10]

Lane likely was in an even worse mood the next afternoon, a Sunday, when the seventh-place Philadelphia A's swept the Sox, 3–1 and 5–0, in front of 26,793 head-scratching fans. The A's won the opener when pitcher Bob Hooper broke a scoreless tie by homering off Gumpert with two on and two out in the ninth; in the second game, the Sox managed only one hit off Sam Zoldak. Odds favored another A's win the next afternoon, with lefty ace Bobby Shantz going for Philly, but the Sox prevailed, 9–5, as Lenhardt collected a single, double and homer and drove in four runs. The Yankees were next to visit Comiskey Park, and Rogovin went another 10 innings to win, 4–3, on Tuesday night before 45,580.

The teams split the next two, and then came the series — a four-game weekend matchup with sixth-place Washington — that spelled the end of the 1951 pennant dream. The Sox were tied for the league lead with Boston, with New York and Cleveland each 1½ games back. Lou Kretlow, another of Richards' former Buffalo pitchers, had a 1–0 lead with two out and the bases empty in the top of the ninth. Eddie Yost singled to right, Gil Coan doubled to left to plate Yost and the Senators went on to win, 2–1 in 10. They also won Saturday and swept Sunday's doubleheader, leaving the Sox in fourth, 2½ games out of the lead. They never regained it, although they fought tenaciously the rest of the way. Lane did his part, adding outfielder Ray Coleman, a .280 hitter from the Browns; lefty Ross Grimsley, Sr., from the Brooklyn system and Rocky Nelson, a minor-league first baseman with a big bat — big, that is, in the minors.

Lane also got worked up enough during one contest to file a formal protest with the American League office. The date was Friday, July 27; the place, Yankee Stadium. Lane's club trailed 3–1 going into the ninth when, suddenly, in front of 50,125 mostly hostile fans, the White Sox came alive. In an inning that included a 26-minute rain delay, three pitching changes, various stalling tactics by Yankees manager Casey Stengel and the ejection of his usually quiet but now remarkably loquacious third baseman, Gil McDougald, the visitors scored three runs, two coming in on a bases-loaded single by 37-year-old pinch-hitter Bert Haas, 3-for-30 entering the evening. The bases were loaded with one out when the rains returned. The grounds crew took its time covering the field, but the umpires assured Paul Richards they would wait two hours if necessary in order to finish the game. Instead, they waited 1 hour and 10 minutes, until 12:32 A.M., by which time the rain had become a mere mist. And then they called it. The three ninth-inning Chicago runs were erased, the score reverted back to the last completed inning and the Sox had lost, 3–1. Richards was livid, as was Lane, who immediately sent his protest to the league office, asking that the game be replayed from the point it was halted. AL president Will Harridge tossed it out almost exactly a month later. By then, August 29, even Lane was thinking about 1952: The Sox were fourth, 11 games out of first place.

But when the season had ended and Chicago stood in fourth place, 81–73, Lane had to be thrilled with the progress made. The White Sox, with their first winning record since 1943, had surpassed the million mark in home attendance for the first time in their history, ending with 1,328,234, some 550,000 more than 1948. The hiring of Richards appeared to have been a master stroke. And almost all of Lane's player acquisitions—Pierce, Rogovin, Minoso, Fox, Carrasquel, Robinson and Dillinger (.301 in 89 games with Chicago) chief among them — had put together big years. One could argue, though, that the biggest years had been achieved by Paul Richards and the man who long ago had seen Richards' managerial potential — Frank Lane.

The White Sox, having taken some giant steps forward, were optimistic entering the "hot stove" season. Lane pulled off another three-team deal in November 1951 that had netted a solid regular catcher, Sherm Lollar, from the Browns and a steady utility infielder, Sam Dente, from the Senators. Also that month, he overpaid for impressive Red Sox lefty Chuck Stobbs, giving up Randy Gumpert and Don Lenhardt (neither of whom ever would have as good a season as they'd had in 1951). A month earlier, Lane had landed, in exchange for Floyd Baker, Washington shortstop Willie Miranda, an uncommonly weak hitter but a splendid fielder and possessor of a personality that lit up a clubhouse. Lane also acquired right-handers Marv Grissom and Hector "Skinny" Brown in a minor-league swap with Seattle and bought lefty Bill Kennedy from the Browns. In Lane's mind, though, the key deal was the one he announced in New York at the winter meetings: Rocky Nelson to the Dodgers' Montreal club for International League All-Star third baseman Hector Rodriguez, a gentlemanly fellow of undetermined years but said to be almost three years older than his fellow black Cuban, Minnie Minoso, who was alleged to be 28. "Hector the Line Drive Collector," as the nickname suggests, added another defensive weapon to the Sox infield and, Lane and Richards hoped, some offense and speed as well. Rodriguez was coming off a big year with Montreal: a .302 batting average with 28 doubles, 10 triples, 8 homers, 95 RBIs and 26 steals. No "Stop the presses" command was issued back in Chicago when Lane revealed that the Sox had brought Rodriguez into the fold but that didn't concern the GM. "I know nobody went into ecstacies when I got Fox from Philadelphia, either," he said. "Maybe by the end of the year they'll find out Rodriguez is a hell of a ballplayer." And then he added, "Rodriguez is married, has three kids and is a good family man. He'll be a good influence on Minnie."[11]

Unfortunately, 1952 was a season when Lane should have brought in someone to be a good influence on Chico Carrasquel. The shortstop reported late to spring camp and was overweight when he finally arrived. Recalled broadcaster Jack Brickhouse, years later: "He discovered the knife and the fork, and he slowed down a little bit."[12] Or, as Lane put it: "I think he only knew a couple of English words: probably 'steak' and 'money.'" An unidentified teammate went further: "The only English words Chico knows are 'filet mignon.'"[13]

This was to be a season of slow starts, inconsistency and disappointment. Lane was as active as ever, but even he was unable to figure out his streaky team. The inconsistency culminated when the Sox beat the Yankees three out of four beginning on June 20 and then immediately were swept three straight at home by Washington. The pitching was, for the most part, quite good, with Pierce, Rogovin, Joe Dobson and newcomer Marv Grissom leading the way. The offense was a different story. Minoso's start was painfully slow: he was hitting .233 on May 1 and .246 on Memorial Day. Jim Busby, in his first 16 games, went 5-for-39 for a .128 batting average and had zero extra-base hits and zero steals. Lane, impatient for the offense to get rolling, forgot all about Busby's fine 1951 rookie season and sent him to Washington for right fielder Sabath Anthony Mele, known as Sam because of his name's initials. Mele was leading the AL with a .429 average but he immediately stopped hitting, collecting just five hits in his first 41 Sox at-bats for a .122 average. He did not get above .200 until June 7. The Busby deal hurt the defense too, because Minoso, hardly a Gold Glover at that stage of his career, was asked to take over in center field after having had enough trouble in left.

Other slow starters were Carrasquel (hitting .195 on May 8), Fox (.263 on May 25), Lollar (.214 as late as June 8) and outfielder Ray Coleman (.141 on May 31). In the case of Rodriguez, even getting off to a fast start didn't help. He was hitting .380 on May 1 and was still at .306 on May 25 before he slipped into an 0-for-22 slide that brought him down to a .248 figure that was more in line with his teammates. Only Eddie Robinson, among the regulars, started fast and remained consistent (between .295 and .320) all season. And yet, Lane remained confident the White Sox, if he could deal for some help here and there, would contend. Two days before the June 15 deadline, in a break from trade talks, he told the *Chicago Tribune*'s Dave Condon, "We must have a Hank Bauer type of outfielder — a rough-and-ready ballplayer who has a fierce desire to win, plus great natural ability. Bauer and Bobby Shantz could bring us the pennant. Last winter, we offered $250,000 in cash and players for Shantz."[14]

Back to the phone went Lane, but his discussions with the A's concerning Shantz bore no fruit. Nor did his annual bid for Shantz's teammate, Elmer Valo. Lane did get a call back from Yankees GM George Weiss, but not the call he had hoped for. The Yankees, with young lefty Whitey Ford in military service, had expressed interest in Billy Pierce. Lane figured that Pierce, given his age (25) and his obvious potential, would bring a handsome return on the market. He was willing to part with Pierce and an outfielder — likely Ray Coleman or Al Zarilla — in exchange for Bauer, infielder Jerry Coleman and outfielder/first baseman Joe Collins. Recalled Lane: "Weiss called me up and said, 'Well, I'm gonna make you a deal.' I said, 'Who?' He mentioned a guy who was playing first base for their club in Birmingham. I said, 'That doesn't sound like Joe Collins to me.' He mentioned a guy named Frank Verdi, who was playing second base at Birmingham. 'Well, that doesn't sound like Jerry Coleman.' Then he mentioned the name of a guy they had playing left field at Binghamton. And I said, 'That doesn't sound like Hank Bauer.' He said, 'That's the closest you'll ever come to making a deal with me.' Which it was."[15]

Stymied on two fronts, Lane turned to his old friend down in St. Louis, Bill Veeck, with whom he had completed the Sherm Lollar deal and various lesser transactions that winter. On June 15, Lane moved Zarilla and Willie Miranda to the Browns for lefty-swinging outfielder Tom Wright and a third baseman named Leo Thomas, a former Yankee prospect who had batted .310 with 27 homers for Portland in the PCL the season before but thus far had produced just a .234 average and no home runs for the Browns in 34 games. Miranda was not gone long. When Carrasquel broke a finger during the Cubs-Sox Boys Benefit game on June 25, Veeck sent Miranda back to Chicago for the waiver price of $10,000. His travels did not end there. That October, Miranda and outfielder Hank Edwards went to the Browns for Joe DeMaestri (a Sox rookie in 1951) and the wild left-handed pitcher, Tommy Byrne. Said Lane: "We had Willie going back and forth like a yo-yo."[16] Miranda, a good-natured sort, didn't seem to mind. He enjoyed having Veeck as a boss, as much as he would enjoy playing under Casey Stengel with the Yankees in

1954. "But with Paul Richards on the White Sox," he said during a 1977 Comiskey Park visit, "it was all business. If Richards didn't like a player, he'd say, 'I'll send you so far down in the minors, even *The Sporting News* won't be able to find you.'"[17]

Somehow, despite Lane's inability to make a significant deal and his players' inability to score runs with any consistency, the White Sox stayed close to the top the remainder of June. And when Minoso hit his 10th home run of the season (he finished with 13), a solo blast to beat the Indians and Mike Garcia 3–2 at Cleveland on July 6, the last game before the All-Star break, the Sox were 44–34, in second place, 3½ games behind New York. Soon thereafter, however, the South Siders went into a July tailspin during which they dropped 11 of 13 to guarantee themselves also-ran status. The most devastating loss came at home on Tuesday night, July 29, less than 24 hours after Lane had announced the acquisition from the Browns of outfielder "Jungle Jim" Rivera — who had been Sox property in 1951 before his trade to St. Louis — along with catcher Darrell Johnson in exchange for outfielder Ray Coleman and catcher-outfielder J.W. Porter, the $65,000 bonus baby Lane had signed a year earlier.

Rivera, batting in the number two spot, singled and doubled off New York's Jim McDonald his first two trips, and his new teammates followed suit, especially Eddie Robinson. "Robby," batting .302 at game's start, singled in two runs in the first inning, belted a three-run homer (his 18th) in the fourth and singled home Minoso in the sixth (for his AL-leading 70th RBI) to stake Chicago and Pierce to a 7–0 lead in front of 38,967 fans. The Yankees scored three in the seventh off Pierce, but the score was still 7–3 as the ninth began, with relief ace Harry Dorish seemingly ready to nail down the victory. But with one out, Gene Woodling singled, Yogi Berra walked and pinch-hitter Johnny Mize singled in a run to make it 7–4. Lane was beginning to seethe up in his press-box perch. Young Kal Segrist grounded to Miranda at short, the runners moving up 90 feet. Chicago still led by three with two on and two out. The batter was rookie Jim Brideweser, who had replaced Phil Rizzuto at shortstop way back in the sixth inning. Years later, Pierce well remembered the night: "Ninth inning, I'm in the clubhouse, taking a shower, feeling good, listening to the game on the clubhouse radio. And an easy groundball was hit to Hector Rodriguez at third, and he booted it. And that set the stage for everything else."[18]

That grounder should have been the final out of the game, but instead the score was now 7–5, with runners on first and second. Because the next two Yankee batters — Joe Collins and Irv Noren — were left-handed, Paul Richards called in lefty Chuck Stobbs, who promptly walked them both, the second pass forcing in a run and leaving the bases filled with the Sox lead at

7–6. Next up was Mickey Mantle, the 20-year-old budding superstar. Mantle swung, and the ball was last seen headed for the far reaches of the upper deck in left-center field. It was now 10–7, and that would be the final score. For many years, The Mick called it "the most thrilling homer I ever hit in my life." "I'll never forget Mantle hittin' that home run," Robinson said. "It just disappeared into the darkness." Said Pierce: "Frank Lane was so mad, Rodriguez never played another game for us."[19]

Actually, he did. But the Cuban's playing time thereafter was cut substantially, and, in fact, on the very next day Lane called up third baseman Rocky Krsnich from Seattle of the Pacific Coast League. Rodriguez got into only five games in September, and, in October, Lane sent him to Syracuse of the International League. Lane did not forget Chuck Stobbs, either. He shipped him to Washington during the winter meetings and received 20-year-old right-hander Mike Fornieles in return. Rodriguez and Stobbs had been found wanting, particularly against the Yankees and in the clutch — to Lane, unpardonable sins. That pair would not be in White Sox uniforms when the club was ready to challenge for the pennant. It clearly was not ready yet.

If they were to become an elite team, Lane knew, the White Sox would need more protection in the lineup for Eddie Robinson, who hit .296 with 22 homers and 104 RBIs but had led the league with 11 intentional walks. They also would need more than 13 homers and 61 RBIs and a .281 average from Minoso, who produced those rather unimpressive numbers in '52. In addition, they would need more from Mele, who had hit just .259; from Lollar, who had finished at .240; and certainly from Carrasquel, who had batted .248 and was hardly the Chico of 1950 and '51 in the field. Other priorities included getting moving again on the basepaths, where their stolen-base total had slid from 99 to 61, and getting better defense in center field from Rivera, who seemed better suited for right field. Finally, the Sox would need Pierce (15–14, 2.58 in 1952), Rogovin (14–9, 3.85), Grissom (12–10, 3.74), Dobson (14–10, 2.51) and reliever Harry Dorish (2.47 ERA in 91 innings) to repeat their success, which in the case of Grissom (age 34) and Dobson (35) might be asking too much.

Yes, the White Sox, in sixth place and nine games out of first place on August 6, had rallied to repeat their 1951 record of 81–73 record and had moved up from fourth place to third. For that, though, they could thank Uncle Sam for calling back Ted Williams to active duty in the Korean War. Williams' presence surely would have meant at least five more victories in the standings, which would have left Boston tied with Chicago at 81–73. Lane, also aware that attendance had dropped off by 96,000 (to 1,231,675), decided a new approach was needed. The White Sox of 1953, he knew, would have to be better. And they would be.

3

Serious Contenders
at Last, 1953–1954

When the 1952 winter meetings wrapped up in early December in Phoenix, some might have assumed that Frank Lane had not even made the trip. After all, his White Sox had been extremely quiet on the trade front, and one had to wonder if perhaps "Frantic Frank" had fallen ill and decided to remain at his winter home in St. Petersburg, Florida. But he indeed had spent the week in Arizona and had carried on serious trade talks with several clubs, chiefly the Indians, with whom Lane had attempted to work out a Chico Carrasquel-for-Larry Doby blockbuster. However, the only discussions that bore fruit were those with Clark Griffith of the Washington Senators. On December 6, Lane and "Griff" jointly announced that 23-year-old Sox left-hander Chuck Stobbs, who had gone 7–12 in '52 and surrendered Mickey Mantle's memorable (to Lane, anyway) ninth-inning grand slam on July 29, was headed for Washington. In return, the White Sox were getting right-hander Miguel "Mike" Fornieles, a 20-year-old Cuban whom Lane had been watching for three winters during his off-season vacations in Havana.

Fornieles had broken in with the Senators that September by throwing a one-hit shutout against Philadelphia. A week later in Chicago, he pitched into the ninth before Sam Mele's pinch homer beat him 3–2. All told, in four games, Fornieles was 2–2, allowed 13 hits in 26 innings and posted a 1.38 ERA. "He's the finest 20-year-old pitching prospect I've seen," Lane gushed. "He has amazing control, an excellent curve, good speed, a baffling sinker and the poise of a veteran."[1]

But Lane had lots more on his mind than Mike Fornieles, including a contract squabble with his feisty second baseman. Nellie Fox, who had slipped slightly from his 1951 offensive form (.313 to .296, despite leading the league in hits with 192) but had actually cut his errors from 17 to 13 and led AL second basemen in putouts and assists, was upset with Lane's contract offer of $14,000, a mere $2,000 boost from his 1952 contract. He had sent back the contract and a copy unsigned. Five days after the Fornieles deal was announced, Lane sent Fox a letter that read, in part:

"Unless you inadvertently returned your contracts here unsigned under the impression that you had signed them, it appears to the writer that you have suddenly forgotten my generous method of dealing with you on salary.... I have always liked you very much personally. However, if I am to assume that your returning unsigned your contracts without the courtesy of a note in reply to a very friendly letter ... was intentional, then of course I will be forced to change my opinion.... Just singling out your 1952 play against the Red Sox ... I know of two games in succession in the 8th and 9th innings in which you dropped double-play balls when the White Sox were ahead ... and the errors cost us consecutive victories. Maybe the Red Sox is [sic] a jinx club for you, for the records indicate that in 22 games against that club, you drove in a total of but 2 runs.... Kindly sign the enclosed contracts and return them promptly. You can rest assured that you and I are not going to have any contractual difficulty.

"All good wishes.

"Sincerely,

(signed)

"FRANK C. LANE."[2]

Fox, in those days of the reserve clause, when the clubs had every advantage over the players, signed eventually, enabling Lane to move on to his next task. He had decided that, as splendid a player and teammate as Eddie Robinson was, he was being wasted, in a way, because there was nobody in the Sox batting order capable of providing real protection behind him. Hence, Robby's league-high 11 intentional passes in '52. Robinson's homer total had dropped from 29 to 22 in 1952; having celebrated another birthday, the 32-year-old Texan might fall off even further. And he was no magic act defensively around first base, either. In his mind, Lane was convinced that what his team needed was a fiery competitor who could lead with words and actions and, when necessary, as good a left hook as there was in baseball. That man was Ferris Fain, 31-year-old fancy-fielding first baseman of the Philadelphia A's and the American League's two-time defending batting champion. He was also the bane of the White Sox's existence, having scored a one-punch knockout of Saul Rogovin during a 1951 game at Comiskey Park, having sent Fox flying into short left-center with a vicious slide into second base in '52 and having batted .313 and .344 against Chicago the last two seasons.

Fain was asking for considerably more than the $27,500 the Macks had paid him in 1952. If Lane were to trade Robinson, among others, to Philly for Fain, how would his new teammates respond to him? Would hatchets be buried? Would Fain be as popular among his teammates as was Robinson? If the answers turned out to be positive, another issue still would remain. Because Fain was a singles and doubles hitter, the South Siders' power shortage would be even more pronounced if Lane went ahead with the deal. Who in that lineup, other than perhaps Minnie Minoso, might hit as many as even 15 home runs? But Lane, already working on a solution to that potential problem, had been talking for days with Boston Red Sox GM Joe Cronin about Vern "Junior" Stephens, the former star slugging shortstop of the Carmine Hose who had switched to third base as his age (and weight) increased. Stephens was 32 and, in an injury-plagued 1952 season, had hit just .254 in 92 games with seven home runs and 44 runs batted in. Lane, however, saw him as a better option than holdover Rocky Krsnich.

Lane was ready to act. First, on January 27, he decided the White Sox must have Ferris Fain as their first baseman. In the off-season's biggest trade, Lane landed Fain from Philadelphia in exchange for Robinson, infielder Joe DeMaestri and minor-league outfielder Eddie McGhee. Lane had enjoyed having "Robby" on the ballclub the past three seasons and believed a note of appreciation was the least he could send to his former employee down in Paris, Texas. Robinson sent Chicago writers a copy of the telegram, which

said: "Little did I believe when I was talking to you last week that I would today be notifying you of your assignment to the Athletics. It is with utmost reluctance that we sever our association with one of the finest gentlemen and athletes that it has been the privilege of the undersigned ever to have been associated with.... Best of luck, Frank C. Lane."[3]

Lane then had to spend the rest of the day denying reports out of New York that claimed the Sox were now going to pass Fain on to the Yankees in exchange for outfielder Hank Bauer and first baseman Joe Collins. "We didn't get Fain to trade him to the Yankees, nor

As much a fan as the most rabid paying customer, Frank Lane delivers some words of "encouragement" to one of his players from one of his favorite perches: the upper deck in right field at Comiskey Park. Opposing outfielders enjoyed his outbursts. Said Jimmy Piersall: "I used to listen to him, and I'd holler back up at him. And then I'd throw salt tablets up to him" (courtesy Lane family).

did we get him to prevent the Yankees from acquiring him. We got Fain because we think he'll help our ballclub.... We get a little weary now and then of the New York complex, that if there is a player available who could strengthen the Yankees he must automatically wind up in a Yankee uniform."[4]

When the Sox convened for spring training in El Centro, California, a few weeks later, the talk wasn't so much of the .344 and .327 averages put up by Fain the last two seasons, or of the way he recklessly charged the plate in bunt situations, of his overall stylish play around first base or of the fights he had started — and finished — on the field. Rather, it was more about the confidence the newcomer seemed to have passed on to his new teammates. Said Lane to Sport magazine's Al Stump: "He woke us up. I knew that, technically, he was the best first baseman in either league. What surprised me were his qualities as a leader. He's the kind who can pull a whole team up to his level and keep it there every day. Fain, I think, will turn out to be the smartest trade I ever made."[5]

That it was a smarter deal than the one that followed cannot be argued. On February 9, Lane sent three pitchers— right-handers Marv Grissom, Hector "Skinny" Brown and lefty reliever Bill Kennedy, 1952 regulars all — to the Red Sox for Stephens, rounding out, Lane and Paul Richards hoped, an infield that collectively would perform up to its members' All-Star credentials. Unfortunately for Chicago, Stephens had declined more than anyone could have predicted. "Junior" started 32 of the Sox's first 44 games, at which juncture his .204 batting average and subpar power numbers (one homer, 12 RBIs) left Richards no choice but to chain him to the bench.

Despite Stephens' failure, the White Sox opened the regular season by winning eight of their first 12 games and were 19–11 after a second straight dramatic triumph in New York on May 16. That afternoon, the Sox trailed 3–1 in the ninth inning with the bases loaded and two outs. Due up was Stephens, who had smacked 10 grand slams in his big-league career. Casey Stengel went to the mound, took the ball from starter Vic Raschi and waved in sidearming right-hander Ewell "The Whip" Blackwell, the former National League star. Richards, who knew more about Stephens' present capabilities than Stengel, intended to use a pinch-hitter for Junior, whether the man on the mound was Raschi or Blackwell. He summoned from the visitors' bullpen former Yankee pitcher Tommy Byrne, who threw and batted left-handed — and who at this point in his career was a better hitter than a pitcher. The count went to 2–2, and Byrne lined the next pitch into the right-field bleachers, about 25 rows up, for a grand slam that put the Sox lead up, 5–3. Even though Byrne's homer was not of the so-called "walk-off" variety, the entire Sox team came out of the dugout to greet him at the plate. "Everybody went crazy," recalled Byrne, who wouldn't be cheered again like that until his days as mayor of Wake Forest, N.C. "I remember Minoso jumping up on me and kissing me when I crossed home plate."[6]

Another early-season highlight was delivered by a pitcher who might have been White Sox property but, due to Lane's insistence, was not. Instead, Alva Lee "Bobo" Holloman, Jr., was a St. Louis Brown. Both Lane and Browns owner Bill Veeck had been given the same offer the previous October by Syracuse GM Gene Martin, a friend of both since their days in the minor leagues. Martin was attempting to sell, in what then was termed a conditional deal, two of his pitchers, Holloman and fellow right-hander Bob Keegan. Holloman, 30, had gone 16–7 with a 2.51 ERA for Syracuse in '52 but had walked 96 in just 183 innings; Keegan, 31, a veteran Yankee farmhand, was 20–11, 2.67, with 84 walks in 273 innings. Lane had first crack: If he selected one or the other, the Sox would pay Syracuse $1,500 at the time of the sale and $13,500 more if they kept the pitcher 30 days after the season opened. Recalled Lane: "He [Martin] offered me Holloman, and I said, 'No, I don't want that son of a bitch.'"[7] Instead he grabbed Keegan, who made the club in spring training but, as had been his pre- and early-season habit, developed a sore arm and spent the first six weeks of the campaign on the disabled list. Veeck, meanwhile, took Holloman, who was healthy but hardly effective. Through his first four games, all relief appearances, he had pitched 5 and one-third innings, allowed 10 hits and five earned runs and was carrying an 8.44 ERA.

Holloman complained to Veeck and Browns manager Marty Marion that he was a starting pitcher, not a reliever. The two caved and gave Bobo a start on May 6 at home against Philadelphia, in front of a Wednesday night "crowd" of 2,473. Holloman got two hits and drove in three runs, which was overshadowed by another accomplishment: He also became the first pitcher since 1892 to throw a no-hitter in his first big-league start. Not that he was dominating. He walked five batters and was touched for one vicious shot after another, all of them finding the gloves of St. Louis players. Veeck had mixed emotions: He could have some fun by tweaking Lane, but now, already strapped for cash in his final year as Brownies boss, he would almost be forced to keep Holloman and pay Syracuse the remaining $13,500. Being Bill Veeck, he did a little of both. First he told the sportswriters about the choices he and Lane had made the previous autumn.

According to Lane, Veeck's account went something like this: "Bill Veeck and Frank Lane both made the same conditional deal with Syracuse last fall. Chicago's Lane took Bob Keegan, who is on the disabled list at the present time. Veeck's choice, Bobo Holloman, just pitched a no-hitter. Mr. Lane can probably hear Veeck's laughter all the way up in Chicago." Lane added: "I called Bill up and said, 'You son of a bitch.' And he says, 'I'm over a barrel. How can I send back a guy who just pitched a no-hitter?' So he kept him.

And he had to pay Syracuse the $13,500. And that was the only complete game Bobo Holloman ever pitched in the major leagues."[8]

In his next five starts, Bobo lasted into the second, third, sixth, third and fifth innings before being led to safety. Veeck shipped his 3–7 record and 5.23 ERA on July 19 to Triple-A Toronto and received in return $7,500, enabling Bill to recoup at least some of the Holloman expenditure. As for Keegan, once he escaped the DL later in May, he settled in as a staff regular after a shaky beginning, finishing 7–5 with a 2.74 ERA in 22 games and then, after an 11–2 start the next season, winning a spot on the AL roster for the 1954 All-Star Game.

This, though, was still May 1953, and Keegan watched from the dugout, ineligible to aid his new teammates, who suddenly were in need of help. The White Sox were a respectable 25–17 at May's end, but then the Yankees arrived for a three-game midweek series on June 2 and swept it by scores of 4–3, 18–2 and 9–5 (in 10 innings). The Washington Senators were the Sox's next guests, and after they had administered 8–4 and 16–2 defeats, the struggling A's came to town and even they won two of three. Meanwhile the Yankees were in the midst of an 18-game winning streak. By the time former teammate "Skinny" Brown pitched Boston to a 4–3 triumph on, June 12, Chicago was 27–26, in fifth place and 13 games back of New York (38–11).

What had gone wrong? The hitting? Some White Sox hitters were certainly struggling. Nellie Fox, through the June 12th game, was batting .244, some 50 points below where he had figured to be; Ferris Fain was at .281, or 46 points below his '52 average; and Minnie Minoso, though batting .289, had hit just one home run and had 20 RBIs. But then, Sam Mele (.301), Jim Rivera (.279) and Chico Carrasquel (.270) were having acceptable years so far and the Sox was third in the American League in runs scored. The main problem, then, was the pitching. Only Billy Pierce among the starters and Harry Dorish among the relievers were having much success. The staff as a whole had allowed 255 runs; only seventh-place St. Louis and last-place Detroit had given up more. It was time again for Frank Lane, with the trading deadline three days away, to work his magic.

At this critical point, "The Trader" turned, as he had in the past and would in the future, to Bill Veeck, then in possession of veteran right-hander Virgil "Fire" Trucks, former big winner with Detroit and still throwing mid–90s heat at age 34. Lane knew that Veeck was more than appreciative of Frank's support for his plan to move the St. Louis Browns—either to Milwaukee or to Baltimore. In each case, the American League owners voted Veeck down. They simply did not want the brash but brilliant native son of Hinsdale, Illinois, in their exclusive club. Lane attempted to convince the other club owners that Veeck's presence could only strengthen the league, reminding them of the huge throngs that turned out at Cleveland's lakefront stadium during Veeck's ownership (1946–49) and the huge visitors-share checks they took home as result. Lane's pleas fell on deaf ears, but Veeck was listening. The two friends walked around their hotel in Tampa on the night of the Governor's Dinner on March 17 "until 3 or 4 in the morning," Lane remembered. "He said, 'I'll never forget you. If I can ever help you out....' 'Well, you have Virgil Trucks. I'd like first refusal if you ever decide to trade him.'" Veeck promised he would grant Lane his wish.[9]

Now, in June, two developments—besides the White Sox's mediocre showing to date—caused Lane to remember Veeck's promise of three months before. First, on June 4, the Cubs seized the Chicago newspaper headlines by acquiring slugger Ralph Kiner from Pittsburgh in a 10-player, $150,000 deal. Additionally, Sox starters Joe Dobson and Saul Rogovin, who had pitched so well the season before, were not doing so in 1953. Rogovin woke up on June 13 with a 2–8 record and an unsightly 6.02 ERA; Dobson was 4–4, 3.18, but was feeling shoulder pain and would make only nine more appearances, five of them starts, and work only 27 more innings that season.

Lane made an offer for Trucks, which Veeck okayed, pending approval from Lane's boss, Mrs. Grace Comiskey. "I said to Roy Egan [club board member and Mrs. Comiskey's lawyer], 'I've got to get Trucks.' Because we needed him and because we were battling the Cubs for ink in the Chicago papers as much as we were battling the Yankees and the other American League clubs. Roy said, 'What's it going to cost?' I said, 'Fifty thousand, and it's cheap at $50,000.' Because I knew that Veeck had gotten an offer of $100,000 and a ballplayer or two from Hank Greenberg (at Cleveland)."[10] The Comiskeys approved the expenditure, and off to the Browns went pitcher Lou Kretlow and catcher Darrell Johnson. To Chicago came Trucks and 36-year-old third baseman Bob Elliott, a former Boston Braves star for whom Lane tossed in $15,000. "That's something I'll never forget," Lane said of the deal. "When you did Veeck a favor and he made you a promise, he kept it. Trucks [47–26 in his 2½ years in Chicago] was worth about a million dollars a year to us for three straight years."[11]

Elliott, too, contributed far more than anyone could have anticipated, but the key was Trucks, who was about to lead the White Sox on a surge reminiscent of 1951. It began innocently enough, with Mike Fornieles turning in a complete game and Sherm Lollar belting a grand slam off Mickey McDermott for a 5–2 triumph over Boston on June 13, the day the Trucks deal was announced. Next afternoon, the Sox swept a doubleheader from Boston as both Billy Pierce and Sandy Consuegra, a smallish Cuban right-hander picked up by Lane from Washington in May, threw shutouts. Then came a trip to the east coast. First stop was Washington, where Chicago broke a 3–3 tie in the 11th, Elliott debuting with an RBI single that was followed by Ferris Fain's bases-loaded triple. After Rogovin lost 1–0 on Wednesday night, Trucks made his White Sox debut and led 2–1 entering the eighth but was tagged for three runs before being relieved. No worry. Chicago came up with six runs in the ninth, the key hits being two-run singles by Fain and Sam Mele. Next stop was Philadelphia, where the Sox won three of four, and then it was on to New York. On Tuesday night, in front of 46,756, Trucks went nine innings and fanned eight and the visitors pounded Allie Reynolds for nine runs and nine hits in six innings in an 11–3 victory. There was more fun the next afternoon, when the Sox scored five in the first inning of an 8–4 victory, as Rogovin won for only the third time that season. Elliott was the offensive hero with a bases-loaded triple. Next came the series finale and the latest piece of bizarre strategy from the fertile mind of Paul Richards, the celebrated Wizard of Waxahachie (Texas).

Yogi Berra homered off Billy Pierce with Joe Collins aboard in the last of the first for a quick 2–0 New York lead, but Fox hit the second of his three 1953 home runs, this one off Johnny Sain, to tie the game in the third. That half-inning ended with Fain getting tossed for arguing umpire Charlie Berry's third-strike call. Thus began a record parade of five White Sox first basemen in a single game: following Fain were Sherm Lollar, Freddie Marsh, Sam Mele and — this being a Richards-managed team — the pitcher, Pierce. Billy waited until the ninth inning for his turn, and by then he was leading 4–2, thanks to run-scoring singles by Rivera and Minnie Minoso in the top half. With right-handed hitter Hank Bauer scheduled to lead off, Richards brought in Harry Dorish to pitch and moved Pierce to first base. Casey Stengel then sent lefty-swinging Don Bollweg to hit for Bauer. Bollweg dropped a perfect bunt toward Pierce and beat it out. Next, Gil McDougald chopped one toward third, where Marsh was now playing. He charged the ball, picked it up and fired toward first, where Pierce had to reach into the runner's path to make the putout. Lane, sitting in a box seat near the visitors' dugout, was doing a slow burn. "McDougald avoided him," Lane recalled, years later. "But if that had been Bauer, Bauer would've cut his leg off. Bauer was known for that."[12]

In any case, the Yankees had a man at second with one out. Pierce went back to the mound, Dorish went to the clubhouse and Mele took over at first base. Gene Woodling drew a walk, and suddenly big Johnny Mize, batting for pitcher Sain, represented the winning run. Mize bounced to Fox, who got the force at second, and now came another pinch-hitter, Bill Renna, batting for Willie Miranda. Pierce struck out the right-handed batter and the Sox had won their ninth straight game at Yankee Stadium, dating back to the previous July 20. Lane, however, had a few words for his manager as they strolled off the field together. Before Lane could speak, Richards, more than pleased with the series sweep, the 8–2 start to the road trip and the team's 11th win in 13 games, wanted to talk first about his Pierce-to-first switch. "That must've had 'em laughing in Waxahachie. That must've had 'em rollin' in the aisles in Buffalo." Lane was not laughing. "We came damn close to losing a million-dollar pitcher," he said. Richards stopped in his tracks. "What do ya mean?" Lane responded, "If that had been Bauer running instead of McDougald, Bauer would've cut his leg off." Remembered Lane, chuckling: "He looked at me and said, 'Well, I knew that'd be too deep for you.'"[13]

The White Sox next visited Boston and the winning continued, the three-game sweep giving them an 11–2 mark for the Eastern excursion. Onetime Red Sox outfielder Tom Wright delivered a two-run pinch triple to win the Friday series opener, 5–3, on June 26, Minoso's two-run double with two out in the ninth was the decisive blow in Saturday's 6–5 triumph, and Minnie contributed four more hits and two RBIs Sunday as Trucks won again, 8–4, this time with relief help from Dorish, who lowered his ERA to 2.11. The team boarded its westbound train for Chicago, where they would play two nights later and lose to the St. Louis Browns. But that was just a glitch, as the Sox swept Detroit three straight. Then, after losing to Cleveland and Bob Feller 3–0 in the opener of a July 10th twi-nighter at Comiskey Park, Chicago enjoyed a 10-run seventh in the second game, capped by Minoso's three-run homer, to win 16–5 before 48,542. The White Sox won again, 5–4, the next day on Ed Stewart's pinch two-run single in the seventh off Early Wynn, then swept Sunday's twin bill, 14–2 behind Fornieles (7–2) and 3–1 behind Trucks (10–4). as 43,419 watched in disbelief.

Four more home victories over Washington on July 15–18, followed the Cleveland series, with Fain among the heroes of Saturday's finale, when he went 5-for-5. The amazing White Sox had won 29 of their last 35 games to pass Cleveland and move into second place, four games back of the mighty Yankees, against whom the White Sox were 7–4 on the season and who just happened to be coming into town next. The Sox (.636) owned the second-best winning percentage in baseball, trailing New York (.686) and just edging Brooklyn (.635). Just about everyone in the lineup and on the pitching staff had made contributions in the 35 contests since June 12. New man Trucks had gone 6–0 and Fornieles 5–0, Pierce 5–2 and Dorish 4–1.

Minoso had batted .375 with seven home runs and 44 RBIs in the 35 games, while Elliott had hit .348, Fox .345, Lollar .303 and Fain .297. And then there was Sam Mele, who ran off a 22-game hitting streak beginning June 27 and ending July 19, when Vic Raschi put a halt to it. During the streak, Mele was 29-for-84, a .345 clip, drove in 19 runs, clubbed five homers and raised his batting average to an even .300. All 10 of the above-mentioned players had been brought in by Lane, nine via the trade route.

The Yankees came to town next for a Sunday doubleheader on July 19 that attracted a record 54,215 people. The team disappointed the huge crowd by getting two runs and 10 hits all afternoon off Eddie Lopat and Vic Raschi. Losses by scores of 6–2 and 3–0 dropped the White Sox back to six games behind New York.

Only Sam Mele showed up offensively, going 3-for-3 in the opener with a single, a triple and a home run. As the weeks went on, he seemed determined, perhaps too much so, to post a .300 batting average for the first time in his career. "I'd never gloat over a deal," Lane claimed, much later, "but I said to Richards, 'Well, maybe I got one right for once.' And Paul said, 'Well, Frantic, don't start feeling too good over that deal. I'm a little fearful.'" Lane was a bit taken aback. Mele was hitting .300 and was to fluctuate between .290 and .312 for the next few weeks. Why be fearful? "Tell you what you do," Richards told Lane. "After the game starts, come on down by the dugout and just observe what you observe." Lane did not understand why Richards wanted him to study Mele in the dugout rather than on the field. Nonetheless, he made his way below the stands and to the runway leading to the Sox dugout. Then he spotted Mele, on the bench, trying to light a cigarette, dropping it once or twice before finally getting it lit. "He was so goddamn anxious," Lane said. "But Paul was a little more experienced in Sam's ups and downs, and he said, 'Sam is so afraid he's gonna hit .300 that I guarantee you he *won't* hit .300.' Well, Sam hit .274."[14]

And that was 18 points higher than the league's batting champ of 1951 and '52 ended up hitting in 1953. Ferris Fain, who had finally gotten his average up to .287 on July 18, went into a 5-for-40 tailspin from July 24 through August 2nd that dropped him to a very non-champion-like .269. After the Sunday, August 2nd game in Washington — a 1–0 loss to Walt Masterson — Fain went out to dinner and followed that up with a visit to a couple of Maryland night spots. At the Romano Inn in Colmar Manor, Maryland, he was dancing with a young woman when a man named James Judge asked to cut in. Fain and the girl ignored the request, and quiet words soon became louder until the two men decided to go at it with fisticuffs. One punch caught Fain between the eyes, but another one, this a left hook thrown by Fain, decked his opponent, who lost six teeth in the fracas. Police were called, peace was restored and Fain went to a nearby hospital to have his swollen left hand X-rayed. Judge, meanwhile, ended up filing a $50,000 damage suit for assault and battery against the player that, after Fain's lawyer counter-sued, was eventually settled out of court. The Sox fined Fain three days' salary (he was making about $35,000 a year), but worse news was that the first baseman had broken a bone in his left hand and would miss almost a month. "Yes," he said, smiling, "I am announcing my retirement from the ring."[15]

Rest assured Lane wasn't smiling. "Fain didn't take very good care of himself, to say the least," he said 25 years after the incident. "He spent more time in the nightclub than he did on the ballfield. I remember being in the clubhouse before a Sunday doubleheader at Comiskey Park. And I looked over at Ferris, and he was sitting in front of his locker, his head down, looking at the floor. And I said to him, 'Let me see ya.' Geez, you could've chinned yourself on his eyeballs. So I go over to Richards and I said, 'For Christ's sake, don't play that son of a bitch today.' Oh, it was a blistering hot day. Richards says, 'Well, it serves him right.'"[16]

Fain's absence gave Lane and Richards a chance to see what they had in the former Negro American League batting champ, Bob Boyd. Called up from Charleston in late July along with former Kansas City Monarchs pitching star Connie Johnson, Boyd took over at first base, stepped right into Fain's No. 2 spot in the batting order and hit .343 in his first two weeks. That solid start included a 7-for-13 weekend in New York August 7–9, when the White Sox lost three of four and fell seven games back to douse any yet-flickering hopes of a pennant in 1953. (Incidentally, Boyd delivered a one-out double in the ninth inning of the series' third game to break up a no-hit bid by ex–Sox lefty Bob Kuzava.) finished the season at .297 and his strong showing had Richards thinking seriously about making a full-time left fielder out of him in 1954, moving Minnie Minoso back to third base and hoping for a return to normalcy at first base by Fain.

Lane was thinking, too, about an offer from Clarence Miles, who soon would be finalizing the purchase of the St. Louis Browns from Bill Veeck and thus become owner of the new Baltimore Orioles. Miles was quite interested in making Lane his new GM, and Lane was willing to listen. How serious Frank was is open to question, but the offer became a moot point when Mrs. Comiskey held him to his White Sox contract. Still, Miles' bid gave Lane leverage to gain a new seven-year contract from Mrs. Comiskey intended to keep him in Chicago through 1960.[17]

On the field, meanwhile, the White Sox were playing out the string, dropping out of second place and settling in again in third place. No one, though, could blame the slump of the season's final two months (17–13 in August and 11–13 in September) on Sandy Consuegra, who though losing a pair of 1–0 games at Yankee Stadium closed on a high note, allowing only 10 runs (nine earned) in his final 52 two-thirds innings (a 1.54 ERA). Nor could anyone blame Pierce, who threw a two-hit shutout at Washington August 3, a three-hit shutout at New York August 9, a six-hit shutout August 14 at Detroit and a four-hit shutout at home against New York August 30, at which point his earned run average was 2.16. Billy finished with an 18–12 record, a 2.72 ERA and seven shutouts. He was also the AL strikeout king with 186.

Virgil Trucks was blameless as well. Lane's prize 1953 acquisition ended up 20–10 and posted a 2.93 ERA and five shutouts.

Other players also had strong seasons. Chico Carrasquel regained the leadoff spot in September and finished with a .279 batting average and was the Chico of 1950 and '51 at shortstop. Nellie Fox struggled in the .260s during August before closing at .285 with a career-high 72 RBIs. Minoso rebounded from the 1952 slump year by hitting .313 with 15 home runs, 104 runs scored and 104 runs batted in and led the league in steals (25) for the third consecutive season. The White Sox final record of 89–65 was the franchise's best since 1920. This was, however, still a third-place team. Frank Lane was ready to work all winter on making it a first-place team.

Before the 1954 White Sox gathered in their new spring-training home, Al Lopez Field in Tampa, Florida, Frank Lane had been busy putting some finishing touches on what both he and Paul Richards believed could be the best team in the American League. First, from the minors, he had brought in two new pitchers: 26-year-old lefty Jack Harshman, a converted first baseman who had won 23 games at Double-A Nashville in '53, and former Yankee Don Johnson, a 27-year-old right-hander coming off a 15–12, 2.67 season at Triple-A Toronto. At the winter meetings, Lane had added appreciably to the Chicago bench, landing lefty-swinging outfielder Willard Marshall from Cincinnati for three players, of whom only Saul Rogovin was notable, and purchasing infielder Cass Michaels, whom he had traded away in May 1950, from the Philadelphia A's.

Next, Lane sent Sam Mele, who had turned 31, to the new Baltimore club for 27-year-old center fielder Johnny Groth, a graduate of Chicago's Latin High School whose presence would allow Jim Rivera to move from center field to right, where he was much more accomplished and comfortable. Finally, Lane got Minnie Minoso's name on a contract that called for a 1954 salary of $27,000, a raise of $5,000 over his '53 deal but still considerably less than the $35,000 figure suggested by Minnie's army of financial advisers (read "extended family and hangers-on") back in Cuba, folks who enjoyed the fruits of Minoso's labor and the comfort of his new home outside Havana. "There are 13 or 14 relatives living there," Lane said, "all figuring that since Minnie is working, why should *they* work?"[18]

The season opened with three straight defeats, two at home to Cleveland and also the Baltimore Orioles' home opener, the first major-league game in Baltimore since 1902. In that historic affair, Virgil Trucks was outdueled by smoke-throwing Bob Turley, 3–1. Richards soon scrapped his plan to put Bob Boyd in left and Minoso at third, and then the White Sox started rolling, winning eight of nine. After a loss, the pitching staff posted three straight shutouts, one apiece by Bob Keegan, Trucks and Johnson. Tough losses (4–3 and 3–2) to the Yankees were followed by eight straight triumphs, and, during that stretch, Lane made one of the boldest moves of the Chicago portion of his career. He sent infielder Grady Hatton and, depending on reports, either $100,000 or $125,000 to last-place Boston, where Red Sox owner Tom Yawkey had been throwing money around for years in an attempt to buy a winner. The White Sox, in return, received another former AL batting champ, 31-year-old George Kell, holder of a .311 lifetime batting average. Kell had hit at least .300 in eight straight seasons and was an excellent fielding third baseman as well. Never mind that the move upped the Sox payroll to $408,000, fourth in baseball behind the Yankees, Indians and Dodgers. Never mind that Cass Michaels, who had been playing third base, was batting .347. The White Sox were going for the big prize.

"We have been happy with the play of Cass Michaels at third base thus far this season," Lane said, "but we couldn't pass up the opportunity to add one of the game's top stars to the White Sox roster. Kell will give us more right-handed hitting and excellent defense at third base."[19] Red Sox GM Joe Cronin sounded almost happy to have lost a perennial All-Star. "The offer was so good," he said, "we couldn't turn it down. For a change, the money comes to Tom Yawkey instead of him giving it."[20]

The White Sox were happy to make the expenditure. Now they had an All-Star infield with Ferris Fain, Nellie Fox, Chico Carrasquel and Kell. They had one of the league's top three players in Minoso. Groth, Rivera and catcher Sherm Lollar were respected major league veterans. The pitching looked solid with Trucks, Keegan, Sandy Consuegra, Billy Pierce, Harry Dorish, Mike Fornieles and newcomers Harshman and Johnson. There was, however cause for concern about Pierce, who had come down with a sore arm during spring training that was to plague him throughout a rather mediocre season.

A deep bench got a bit deeper with the May 24th signing of 37-year-old Chicago native Phil Cavarretta, fired as Cubs player-manager just before the club broke camp. ("Cavvy" would wind up hitting .316, helping out at first base, in the outfield and as a pinch batter.) Then, just before the Sox opened a four-game series on June 11 at Yankee Stadium, Lane made one final deal involving two other teams. First he sent pitcher Gus Keriazakos, the onetime bonus baby, and $20,000 to Washington for reliever Sonny Dixon. Then he dealt Dixon, rookie outfielder Bill Wilson and another $20,000 to the Athletics for ex-Sox outfielder Eddie McGhee and lefty Morrie Martin, a hero of the Battle of the Bulge who had gone 11–4 for the A's in 1953 and, by season's end, had recorded an ERA of 2.06 in a Chicago uniform.

Entering the series, the White Sox were 35–16, a game ahead of Cleveland and 4½ up on New York. Minoso was hitting .338 with an AL-best 53 RBIs,

Fox was at .321, Fain at .315 (with 38 RBIs, fourth in the league), Groth at .306, Rivera at .288 and Lollar at .276. Among the pitching leaders were Keegan, tops in the AL with nine wins, and Trucks with eight; Pierce was second with 60 strikeouts and Trucks fourth with 56; and Keegan was fourth in ERA at 2.23. The White Sox were first in runs scored and had given up the fewest. Kell, who had gotten off to a slow start, was in the neighborhood of .250, but everyone knew he would start hitting soon. All in all, this was a fine ballclub. On this weekend, however, the team began to lose a little of its swagger. The Yankees' Allie Reynolds won 3–2 Friday night before 44,445, Whitey Ford beat Jack Harshman 2–0 on Saturday and Eddie Lopat beat Consuegra 4–2 in Sunday's first game before Trucks shut out the hosts 8–0 to salvage the finale in front of 60,070.

A weekend later, the scene shifted to Chicago. Rookie pitcher Bob Grim stunned 45,216 by driving in four runs with a single and home run as New York held on to win, 7–6, on Friday night; Consuegra blanked the visitors, 3–0, on Saturday; and on a threatening Sunday, 37,075 watched the Yankees pound Pierce and an assortment of relievers 16–6 before Keegan won 7–3 in the second game. By nightfall, the Sox were 40–22, in second place, four games behind red-hot Cleveland and a game ahead of New York.

The following Sunday, there was further reason for worry. Fain, hitting .302 with 51 RBIs in 65 games, tore knee ligaments in a collision at the plate with Boston catcher Sammy White. A week later, he was declared lost for the season. That Friday, July 2, Kell wrenched a knee during the first of four straight one-run losses at Cleveland and was lost until August 6. (When he returned, he showed he had been missed by going 17-for-44 — a .386 average — and driving in 13 runs in his first 14 games back.)

The four defeats in Cleveland included one that involved another example of Paul Richards' curious brand of strategy. Consuegra, seeking to improve his record to 11–2, took a 3–2 lead into the last of the eighth inning of the third game, played on an unseasonably cool Saturday night. Due up first was Larry Doby, the lefty slugger who had homered off Consuegra the previous at-bat. Therefore Richards brought in lefty Morrie Martin to face Doby and moved Consuegra to third base. Trying to stay warm, Consuegra slipped on his jacket and prepared for play to resume. "But the umpires refused to let Sandy play third with the jacket on," Lane remembered. "They made him take the jacket off."[21] Consuegra did so, and Martin went to work on Doby, who eventually flied out to right. Out came Richards, who took out Martin, called Freddie Marsh from the dugout to play third base and brought Consuegra back to pitch. Sandy was just preparing to get in his warmup throws when the plate umpire, John Stevens, said, "No warmups! Play ball!" Richards was beside himself. Never before in any of his pitcher-to-infield-to-pitcher moves had the hurler not been allowed to warm up again. In any case, the next two batters were right-handed, Al Rosen and Wally Westlake. Consuegra, still not loose, managed to get Rosen on a grounder to short, but Westlake hit the next pitch deep into the left-field seats to tie the game. The Sox eventually lost in 15 innings.[22]

But Lane, who had grown a bit weary of some of Richards' more intricate maneuvers, was not entirely displeased with the umpire's ruling against Consuegra's wish to loosen up. He said a bit later, "Sometimes I long for the days when baseball wasn't the complicated game that Paul seems to make it. I've come to the conclusion that some of the nutty things Casey Stengel did and got away with has everyone else trying to see if he can do something nuttier in the interests of strategy. I don't think this game was ever designed to be this bewildering."[23]

The White Sox proved to be somewhat bewildering themselves the very next weekend. Written off after the Cleveland debacle and the injuries to Kell and Fain, the Sox awaited another four-game series with league-leading Cleveland, this one at Comiskey Park, on the eve of the All-Star break. Despite their 50–31 record, the Sox were seven games off the pace and they even trailed the second-place Yankees by three games. A split would do Chicago no good, but a sweep seemed too much to ask for. Nevertheless, the Sox rallied for four in the seventh and Keegan beat the Tribe 8–3 Friday in front of 43,740. Harshman and Consuegra then outpitched Wynn on Saturday, 3-0. In Sunday's opener, Minoso hit a two-run homer in the first inning off Ray Narleski and Pierce two-hit Cleveland, 3–0, with 45,466 watching. In the second game, 6-foot-7-inch bonus-baby first baseman Ron Jackson's three-run homer off Bob Lemon in the third inning of propelled Trucks to an 8–2 victory—and the implausible four-game sweep.

So the Sox were third, three games back, as seven of their number headed to the All-Star Game at the home of the AL leaders, the Cleveland Indians, who held a half-game edge on the Yankees. The seven All-Stars in White Sox uniforms were Minoso and Carrasquel, voted in as starters, along with Fox, Lollar, Keegan, Trucks and Consuegra. Two others, Fain and Kell, made the team but were forced out by injury. Fox delivered the tie-breaking, game-winning single in the eighth and Trucks came on in relief and nailed down the AL's 11–9 victory.

The second half of the 1954 season had its share of highlights. Harshman provided two of them, with a club-record 16-strikeout performance at Boston July 25, and a 16-inning, 1–0 decision over Detroit on August 13. Trucks contributed a terrific five-hit, 4–0 victory over the Yankees in front of a record Comiskey Park weeknight crowd of 53,067 on July 27. There was also an eight-game winning streak. Nevertheless, no matter how well the Sox played—and they were 40–29 (.580 ball) after the break—they had no chance to catch Cleveland. The Indians finished 111–43 (but went just 11–11 vs. Chicago). Even the Yankees, who won 103, couldn't get closer than 3½ games during the final four weeks.

Lane had to be pleased with the final record of 94–60 and the performances of Minoso, who had his greatest year (.320, 19 homers, 29 doubles, 18 triples, 116 RBIs), Fox (.319), Carrasquel (a career-high 12 homers and 106 runs scored), Trucks (19–12, 2.79, AL-leading five shutouts), Consuegra (16–3 for an AL-best .842 winning percentage) and Harshman (14–8, 2.95, four shutouts in his rookie year). Lane was not pleased that his manager, Paul Richards, had accepted an offer from Baltimore with two weeks left in the season to become both the Orioles' field manager and general manager. Late in August, with his two-year deal about to run out, Richards had asked for a three-year contract extension from the Comiskeys. The offer from Baltimore was there for the taking.

"I'd hate to see him leave," said Trucks, speaking for many of his teammates. "He's the greatest manager I've ever played under."[24] Lane, despite occasional disagreements with his manager, did not want him to depart, either. "I don't blame anyone else for wanting Richards. But we want to keep him. He has done a grand job. I might say that if Paul is lured away, it will not be because he is underpaid by the Sox. Only Casey Stengel draws a bigger paycheck among the league's managers, and I'm sure Richards' salary will be increased in our new offer."[25] Stengel was getting $75,000 per season from the Yankees; Richards was said to be receiving $30,000 plus a "nickel-a-head" bonus for each paid admission above one million. That meant his 1954 bonus (for final attendance of 1,231,629) was to have been $11,581.45, for a total take of $41,000-plus. However, the Baltimore pitch was too enticing to resist. Even so, Lane wished to assure Paul that he had not brought former Cardinals star and manager Marty Marion on board as the team's first-base coach the previous winter to undermine Richards. "I know you're probably suspicious," Frank said. "Not at all," Richards said. "Marty's done a hell of a job for me."[26]

He was destined to do a marvelous job for Frank Lane in 1955. And Richards was to do similarly well in building the Orioles into a consistent contender by 1960. He did it with terrific scouting, proper use of the resources made available to him and, having worked under Lane and seen him in action for four years, the occasional big trade. To be sure, the first deal Richards pulled off sent standout Orioles pitcher Bob Turley, Don "Mr. Perfect" Larsen and Billy Hunter to New York in exchange for catchers Gus Triandos and Hal Smith, hard-hitting Gene Woodling and old friend Willie Miranda. All told, Richards' monster deal with the Yankees numbered 18 players. When the trade was announced in late November, somewhere Frank Lane had to be smiling. Eighteen players? Even he had never done a deal *that* big. But then he realized that Bob Turley was now a Yankee. The smile went away.

4

The Race Heats Up, and
So Does Lane, 1955

Marty Marion, to be sure, had his doubters. The White Sox, the unbelievers said, almost certainly would take a tumble in the standings in 1955 with the tough, tall Texan, Paul Richards, having left for Baltimore. The players, Marion's detractors claimed, would walk all over the new manager, a nice guy and a terrific shortstop who had teamed with Stan Musial, Enos Slaughter and Red Schoendienst to form the core of the great St. Louis Cardinals clubs of the '40s. Marion did not take long to show that, if need be, he could be just as tough as Richards.

Early in spring training, he learned which players didn't necessarily give it their all at all times. To get their attention, he gave increased playing time to backups as well as potential *heirs apparent*. Chico Carrasquel, for instance, found himself sitting while his countryman and eventual replacement, 21-year-old Luis Aparicio, received opportunities to show his abundant talents. Aparicio had played only one year in the minors, at Class B Waterloo in 1954, but he had hit .282 there and stolen 35 bases in 94 games. Like Minnie Minoso some years earlier, Aparicio represented another behind-the-scenes victory by Frank Lane over his Cleveland counterpart, Hank Greenberg. Lane had first learned of Aparicio from Eduardo Moncada, sports editor of *El Mundo*, a Caracas newspaper. Moncada's rave reviews sounded implausible, but Carrasquel, who had seen Aparicio play dozens of times, assured Lane they were true. Lane finally sent scouts, who likewise were astounded by the youngster's play but also reported that the Indians were close to signing him. Lane still had a shot, however: The Aparicio family wanted $10,000 for Luis' signature on a contract. And, at the time, any player who signed for more than $4,000 was considered a "bonus baby" and had to spend two years with the parent club before he could be sent to the minors for seasoning. While Greenberg waited for the Aparicios to lower their demand, Lane struck. "Acting as vice president of our Waterloo club," he remembered, "I signed him to a contract worth $4,000. Then, later, I gave him a bonus of $6,000 for reporting to Waterloo. See, it was just another way to skin a cat."[1]

And it was another terrific deal by Lane, who had made plenty of news at the December 1954 winter meetings in New York. Having already made a minor-league purchase in September, that of right-hander Dick Donovan (18–8, 2.69 at Double-A Atlanta in '54), he turned to the trading market for more help — but not before laughing off a trade rumor reported by Washington writers. This one claimed Lane was ready to send Minnie Minoso, George Kell and Johnny Groth to the Senators for third baseman Eddie Yost, outfielders Roy Sievers and Tommy Umphlett and lefty Mickey McDermott. "If we trade Minnie," Lane said, "we might as well trade Lane."[2] Then, on December 6, he swung two deals involving 13 players. First, admitting by this action that the Ferris Fain trade was not the smartest of his career after all, Lane sent Fain and two minor leaguers to Detroit for three players: 6-foot-5-inch first baseman Walt Dropo, 1950 AL Rookie of the Year while with the Red Sox; Bob Nieman, an outfielder with a solid bat; and Ted Gray, a left-handed pitcher with a sore left arm. Later that day, Lane got together with Richards and dealt him catcher Matt Batts, infielder Freddie Marsh and pitchers Don Johnson and Don Ferrarese (18–15 at Oakland in the Pacific Coast League) for catcher Clint Courtney, infielder Jim Brideweser and reliever Bob Chakales. The deals had given Lane and Marion more depth and, in Dropo and Nieman, two potentially dangerous hitters from the right side. It also gave the army of newspapermen on hand something to write about. In fact, when the annual convention had wrapped up a couple days later, Harold Rosenthal, a baseball writer with the *New York Herald-Tribune*, filed the following lead:

"There's a unanimity among the baseball writers in nominating Frank Lane, general manager of the White Sox, as their pin-up boy of 1954. Without him, the major league meetings would have been a washout. Without his two hectic deals in a single day generating some excitement and a generous use of black ink, the annual winter conclaves in New York would have been a journalistic waste of time."[3] Said Lane, by way of explaining his reason for being aggressive: "The first time you relax your vigilance, that's when you miss out." Years later, he said, "I never preened myself on being so smart. It's just that while some of these other guys were out being entertained, I was working. That's why I would always say that my success, if I had any, was 10 percent inspiration and 90 percent perspiration."[4]

Lane, as the 1955 season dawned, was more and more becoming a voice commanding attention throughout baseball. He was chairman of the AL's realignment committee, charged with studying the possibilities of a 10-team league and potential home cities for expansion teams. Clearly affected by the previous August's beaning of White Sox infielder Cass Michaels, whose career had been ended by the injury, Lane was leading the campaign to require batters to wear protective helmets. He also was proposing a rule change whereby a batter hit by a pitch would receive two bases instead of one.

But to Lane, the deal was always the thing. In two more transactions before the start of the season, Lane acquiesced to Marty Marion's wishes by signing former Cardinals lefty Al Brazle, who had just celebrated his 41st birthday, and purchased speedy outfielder Lloyd Merriman from Cincinnati. Brazle was released during camp, and Lane, in an attempt to help the Cubs fill their hole in center field, sold Merriman to the North Siders the day after the season opened. Merriman had fanned as a pinch-hitter during the Opening Day loss at Cleveland in his only at-bat in a Sox uniform. Also, rumors circulated in spring camps throughout both Florida and Arizona that Lane, not completely confident that George Kell's knee could hold up for even 100 games, was in the market for a third baseman. Possibilities, some writers claimed, were Eddie Yost of Washington and second-year man Jim Finigan of Kansas City.

Kell, however, wasn't about to go anywhere. After an injury-marred 1954 season in which he hit just .276, he was to play a major role in 1955, leading the Sox in batting average (.312) and runs batted in (81) and going on a tear with the bat when his team needed it most. The White Sox were 32–19 and 2½ games back of first-place New York on June 13, an off date, and Kell, more often than not the Sox cleanup hitter, was batting just .243 with four home runs and 24 RBIs. However, from June 15 through July 27, Kell collected 56 hits in 144 at-bats for a .389 average. In July alone, he hit at a .413 clip, this during the period the Sox clawed back from a six-game deficit at the All-Star break to seize the AL lead by month's end.

Also missing in action in the first half was Minnie Minoso, who began slowly before getting his average up to .278 going into the May 18 game at Yankee Stadium. He had done nothing spectacular thus far, save for going 4-for-6 with two doubles and a homer, five runs scored and five driven in during the record-tying 29–6 rout of the A's on April 23 in Kansas City.[5] On this May afternoon, Minnie suffered a hairline fracture to his skull after being beaned by New York's Bob Grim and missed 16 days. He wasn't the same until July. By June 17, he was down to .226. and at the All-Star break, he was batting .254 with two home runs and just 28 RBIs. To beef up the offense until Minoso could snap out of it, Lane attempted to construct a three-team trade at the June 15 deadline that would have brought Roy Sievers to Chicago, but the deal fell apart.

Another struggling Chicago outfielder was center fielder Jim Busby, brought back from Washington on June 7 in what, on paper, looked like one of Lane's best deals, despite Busby's .230 batting average thus far. To the Senators went Bob Chakales (1.46 ERA over just 12 one-third innings), Johnny

Groth (hitting .338 in limited action) and catcher Clint Courtney (.378 in just 19 of the team's 47 games). Courtney had landed on Marion's wrong side during an Eastern trip in May. Marion, demonstrating again that he could be tough if necessary, walked into the clubhouse in Baltimore before one game and announced: "Those four guys who were out after curfew last night — I want you in my office right now." Four players arrived within a few minutes. "That'll cost each of you $200," Marion began. Just then, the door opened and in walked Courtney. Said Marion: "That'll be $200 for you, too, Courtney. I can't help it if you're so dumb you can't count to four."[6] In exchange for Courtney, Groth and Chakales, back to Comiskey Park came Busby, who had hit .312 and .298 the previous two seasons and who, coupled with Minoso and Jim Rivera, gave the White Sox baseball's fastest outfield. "I wanted Jim back," Lane recalled, "because he had helped himself in learning to hit the curveball. He was always a great outfielder. But Jim wouldn't have been available if he hadn't been hitting .230."[7] Everyone anticipated, though, that Busby would start to hit eventually. He did not. Marion had made him the new leadoff man, but when that failed, the manager decided that Minoso was the man for the job.

After the All-Star break, the White Sox won six of their first eight games, but Minoso was still in his slump. That's when Marion made him the leadoff man. Over the next 29 games, one of them a tie, Chicago was 19–9 and Minoso hit .317 with 23 runs scored and 15 driven in. Restored to the number three hole, he then went on a 23-game hitting streak from August 9 through August 30, during which he went 40-for-95 (.421) and moved his batting average up to a more typical .293. With Minoso and Kell now clicking together, with Dropo, Nieman and Sherm Lollar providing occasional power, with their superb defense up the middle and their new-found confidence against the Yankees (4–2 vs. New York in July, 9–9 vs. the Yanks on the season with four meetings to go), the White Sox finally were in a pennant race to stay. The differences from Lane's previous Sox clubs were several: better overall depth, the veteran leadership of Kell, the performance of first-year pitcher Donovan, the clutch hitting of 35-year-old veteran Bob Kennedy and the consistent brilliance of Billy Pierce. Some of these were on display during Game 2 of the Sunday, August 28 Sox-Yankees doubleheader, played in 95-degree temperatures in front of 50,990 sweaty patrons, the season's biggest crowd at Comiskey Park.

The Yankees had won the opener, 6–1, with Whitey Ford giving the Sox nothing to hit and Mickey Mantle giving Chicago right-hander Connie Johnson nothing but trouble — in particular his 34th home run, a three-run blast. New York now led Lane's club by 1½ games, and Pierce was set to face Bob Turley in the nightcap, a game Chicago had to have. Marion switched his lineup around, starting Kennedy in right field and in the fifth spot in the batting order. Kennedy, a native of Chicago's South Side who first came to the majors with the White Sox in 1939, had come through with big hits ever since Lane had taken him off Paul Richards' hands at Baltimore on May 30.

"I got him on Memorial Day — got him on waivers," Lane recalled in 1978. "He was hitting .143. And Mrs. Comiskey remembered Bob Kennedy from when he'd been here before. I think the waiver price was $15,000. And Mrs. Comiskey said to me, 'What are you doing with that old man? He's hitting about .140 and that's about his age.' And I said, 'Mrs. Comiskey, he's an old pro. You wait and see.'"[8]

She didn't have to wait long. From June 1 to season's end, Kennedy hit .304 in a Chicago uniform with nine homers and 43 RBIs in 214 at-bats and was Mr. Clutch most of that summer. But he was saving his biggest contribution for this all-important match with the Yankees. (As Lane himself once said, "Anytime we'd beat the Yankees one game it was like beating somebody else three.") In the home half of the first inning, Kell singled to center with one out and Minnie Minoso walked. Walt Dropo, 3-for-4 with a home run in the opener, went down swinging. Up stepped Kennedy. "He popped a foul," Lane said, "about 20 feet to the right of my box. My box was just to the right of Mrs. Comiskey's. And Yogi Berra came toward the wall for the popup, and he muffed it. And the next pitch Kennedy hits into the upper deck for three runs. I yelled over, 'How do you like that old man now?'"[9]

Soon Lane was up in the air-conditioned comfort of his office, having invited *Chicago Tribune* columnist Dave Condon to follow the rest of the game via Jack Brickhouse's telecast on *WGN-TV*. Condon was in for a treat. On the screen, a pop fly fell between Nellie Fox, shortstop Jim Brideweser and center fielder Jim Busby for a cheap hit to open the New York third. "Did you see that?" barked Lane, pointing at the screen. "The bleepin' Yankees have so many power hitters they can't use them all, and then we hand them a gift."[10] Lane was concerned about the 5-foot-10-inch, 160-pound Pierce having to throw extra pitches on such a sultry day. But Pierce was enjoying the most consistent season of his career: He was to finish 15–10, including four 1–0 defeats, and would lead the majors with a 1.97 ERA. Here he retired Hank Bauer on an easy fly to Minoso in left and then fanned Gil McDougald. Lane relaxed, but not for long.

Minoso led off the Sox third with a hit to right and moved up on Dropo's groundout to second baseman McDougald. Now Kennedy grounded to Jerry Coleman at short; for some reason, Minoso took off for third, where he was an easy out, Andy Carey slapping the tag on Minnie after taking Coleman's throw. Lane was furious. "What's Minnie trying to do? He was out by 15 feet! That could cost us a run. Suppose [Sherm] Lollar gets a hit here. Minnie scores and it's 4–0." Sure enough, Lollar lined a single to left. "There's a hit. See? If Minnie stays at second, we have another run. I'll believe in miracles if we win this game."

Yogi Berra opened the fourth with a double and scored on Bill Skowron's infield out to make it 3–1, and Brideweser's error in the seventh set up New York's second run. When Pierce walked Hank Bauer to load the bases in that same inning, Marty Marion, accompanied by a choir of boos, went to the mound, took the ball from Pierce and waved in his top reliever, Dixie Howell, a 35-year-old right-hander whom Lane had plucked off the Double-A Memphis roster in early June. Howell's task was to finish things for Pierce; his immediate task was retiring McDougald. "Howell has to give us everything he has," Lane told Condon, "but he usually does that. Only what Howell has isn't as good as what Pierce has."

It was good enough to get McDougald, who lined the ball right at Busby in center to end the threat. Condon got up to leave for the Sox clubhouse, but Lane would have nothing of it. "No you don't!" Frantic Frank all but hollered. "You stay and sweat it out." That's what they did, along with 50,000 other folks. Soon it was the ninth. Elston Howard grounded to Fox for the first out, and then, batting for Carey, came Eddie Robinson, the left-handed power hitter who had reached Comiskey's right-field seats with regularity during his three years on the South Side. On the TV, Jack Brickhouse mentioned that Robinson was an ex–White Sox and a great Chicago favorite. "Robinson will be 'a great Chicago favorite' if he just flies out," snapped Lane. Seconds later, Robby fouled out to Kennedy, who had switched to third base in the seventh. Now came another lefty pinch-hitter, Joe Collins. Howell was a sinkerballer; Collins was a low-ball hitter. This could be trouble. A shot just foul down the right-field line brought from Lane an audible gasp. "Could've been a home run," said Frank. "A homer will tie it, but it wouldn't if Minoso had stayed on second and given us a fourth run...."

Collins swung and drove the ball off the wall in deep right-center for a double. Said Lane: "Now they'll send up Noren." Noren, another left-handed hitter, had batted .319 the year before but was down to .245 at the moment. Still, he was a Yankee, it was the ninth inning and the Yankees were down by a run. That usually meant danger. Lane held his breath. Noren ripped one on a line to left field, but Minoso snared it. The game was over, and the deficit was a mere half-game. "Well, we won," Lane, suddenly calm, said to Condon. Then he added, "Did you notice back there when Casey Stengel started to come out of the dugout to squawk? Why don't they keep Stengel in the cage, where he belongs? Casey gets too excited about these games."

The final act in the increasingly chilly Frank Lane-Chuck Comiskey relationship was about to be played out, as was the white-hot pennant race. The

Boston Red Sox were in town for a two-game series before the White Sox were to leave for a four-game set in Cleveland, followed by 15 more road games. This was the trip that would tell the tale. But first things first: Virgil Trucks vs. Tom Brewer on Tuesday night, August 30, before 41,166 people. The standings showed the Yankees leading the White Sox by a half-game, Cleveland by one game and the Red Sox by 3½.

Cleveland had beaten Baltimore earlier that evening, and the Yankees were about to lose, 4–3, in Kansas City. The White Sox, with a victory, would move into first place by a half-game. The pressure was great, as was the action on the field. A sample: Boston led 5–4 in the top of the sixth with two out, Sammy White at second base and Grady Hatton facing Dixie Howell, on in relief of another reliever, Harry Byrd. Hatton laced a hit to right for what all present figured would be the Red Sox's sixth run. But Jim Rivera, the AL leader in outfield assists, charged the ball and fired a perfect one-hop throw to catcher Sherm Lollar, who tagged White for the third out. It would be an understatement to say that the on-deck hitter, Jimmy Piersall, took issue with the call by plate umpire Larry Napp. Piersall, who had overcome a nervous breakdown to return to the diamond a couple of years earlier, jumped up and down, screamed at Napp, kicked sand all over the umpire, and, all in all, put on quite a show for the big crowd. In the end, though, White was still out.

The White Sox had assumed that Piersall, no stranger to ejections, had been thrown out of the game. But Napp, knowing Piersall's psychological history, had overlooked his histrionics and allowed Piersall to remain. The White Sox, especially Lollar, who among Chicago personnel had been the closest witness to the Piersall performance, let Napp know how they felt about his failure to toss Piersall. Napp walked over to the home team's dugout between innings and gave the heave-ho gesture. No one knew who the victim was until backup catcher Les Moss took Lollar's spot behind the plate. Lane was outraged. "He threw Lollar out because he was mad at Piersall," Lane said, decades later, of Napp. "And our only other catcher was Moss, and he had a damaged left thumb — it was all bandaged up."[11]

Meanwhile, upstairs in the press box, columnist Jack Mabley, then with the now-defunct *Chicago Daily News*, was sitting next to Chuck Comiskey. Lane was a few seats away. "Comiskey had no use for me because the Chicago press was so good to me," Frank claimed. "But I worked my ass off for [the Comiskeys]. When I started, the club was all but bankrupt, and when I left there was $3 million in the bank and the club was good enough to win the pennant in '59. So Chuck says, 'Hey, Mr. GM, why don't you do something about the umpiring?' And I said, 'Why don't *you* do something about it? You're the vice president of this bleepin' ballclub.' Chuck was always great at telling you what to do. He didn't know shit from apple butter. So, anyway, before I knew it, from that press box, in about three minutes I'm down there by the American League box, where Cal Hubbard, the supervisor of umpires, is sitting with Mr. [Will] Harridge, the league president. I said, 'Hey, Cal, we're in this goddamn league too. Your umpire keeps Piersall in the game and throws Lollar out? Goddamn it, I don't like it.'[12]

"And the fans around there, they're yelling, 'That's right, Frankie, you tell 'em!' And that's when I realized I'd made a horrible mistake. Here's the league president — I didn't give a shit about Hubbard — but Harridge was one of my favorite people. A fine, fine gentleman. Now meanwhile, Mabley is writing this thing: 'Lane's conduct is terrible,' and so on. Comiskey was feeding him, see? Comiskey was mad because I was running the bleepin' ballclub. In fact, his father-in-law, Frank Curran, used to say, 'Well, does Lane own this ballclub or do you own it?' Chuck had lied to him, said he was supposed to be the next president. Said it was in [his mother's] will, but it wasn't. It was never in the will that he would be president. Anyway, Mabley writes this column: 'Comiskey is very irate with Lane and with Lane's language.' He couldn't tell what I was saying. I'm downstairs, they're up in the press box and there were 40,000 people in the park. So I thought, 'You son of a bitch — I've taken this team from the bottom to first place on August 30. And this is the thanks I get.' So that's what precipitated my leaving."[13]

As for the ballgame, the White Sox won 7–5, scoring three in the sixth on George Kell's two-run triple and Minnie Minoso's RBI single. First-place Chicago won the next afternoon, as well, when Rivera belted a pair of two-run homers for a 4–2 triumph. Then it was on to Cleveland for four games with the defending AL champs. The Sox lost the final three, but the off-the-field intrigue was also attracting attention. Word of Lane's trip to the AL box reached the ears of commissioner Ford Frick, who fined the Sox executive $500 for "conduct unbecoming a baseball official." When Lane asked Frick the identity of the person who had told him of the incident, he said, "A friend."[14] He suspected immediately it had been Chuck Comiskey.

Said Lane: "I remember [*Chicago Daily News* lead sports columnist] John Carmichael went to Mrs. Comiskey and asked, 'What about this fuss between Frank Lane and Chuck. What are you gonna do about it?' And she said, 'Chuck's my son and I love him, but he couldn't run a peanut stand. Frank Lane is the boss.' So her comments were published and I thought, 'Well, this is a bad thing, because it looks like I am coming between mother and son.' So I called her up from Cleveland and said, 'Sweetheart, I appreciate your allegiance and loyalty, but you've made it necessary for me to leave.' 'Oh, don't give me that crap,' she says. 'You wanted to get away anyway.' 'No, I didn't. Otherwise I wouldn't have signed that seven-year contract.' See, I was in the second year of a seven-year contract, through 1960. But I was getting sick and tired of wet-nursing Chuck. And I had liked Chuck like a son. When I first took the job, Mrs. Comiskey said, 'I want you to be a father to this guy.' And Chuck was great with me. Never second-guessed me or anything else. But it got to where his father-in-law would say, 'We thought we were marrying the next president of the White Sox.' And it kinda got under Chuck's skin. And I'd had two or three offers elsewhere, so I thought, 'Well, here's the time to get out.' So that's the reason I went down to St. Louis."[15]

For several days he insisted that no deal had been struck with the Cardinals, although no one actually believed him. Backing up his claim, however, was the long-distance phone call he took in the White Sox dugout before the final night game of the season, September 23 against Kansas City. It was from his daughter, Nadi, then 16 and on the staff of her high school newspaper in St. Petersburg. "Are you going to St. Louis, Daddy?" she asked. His wife, Selma, cut in: "Don't tell her, Frank. She wants a scoop for the paper." Lane told her he honestly did not yet know for sure. There was no "exclusive" for Nadi.[16]

Had some things turned out differently, Lane might not have left for Missouri. The White Sox might have won the 1955 pennant, or they might have finished closer than five games behind the Yankees (their final deficit), had Dick Donovan not undergone an emergency appendectomy on July 30, when his won-lost record stood at 13–4. The rookie missed three weeks and was not the same pitcher when he returned: He finished 15–9.

It was a late-season 19-game road swing that produced only eight wins that really did in the 1955 White Sox. They lost the final three games on the first stop, Cleveland, as Early Wynn beat Pierce, 6–1, on Saturday, September 3, and then Bob Lemon and Mike Garcia each won 5–3 on Sunday, with Ray Narleski saving both games. Chicago was now 1½ games behind first-place Cleveland, which led New York by a half-game. A fourth straight defeat came in the opener of a Labor Day twin bill at Detroit before Bob Keegan blanked the Tigers 3–0 to earn a split. Because the other contenders also split, Chicago remained 1½ games out. The Sox could only win one of two games in Washington, winning 4–3 on September 7 but then, unable to hold a 4–1 lead, dropping a 5–4 decision the next afternoon.

That one was perhaps the most crucial defeat of them all. The White Sox, entering this contest, were 17–4 vs. Washington on the season and 9–1 at Griffith Stadium, where they had outscored the Senators, 42–17. That meant little this particular afternoon. Chicago's 4–1 lead became 4–3 when Mickey Vernon hit a two-run homer off starter Virgil Trucks in the sixth. Then, with one on and one out in the seventh and a left-handed pinch-hitter, pitcher Mickey McDermott, coming up, Marion switched to lefty Morrie Martin, tough on lefties and, because of his screwball, just as tough on right-handed batters. The Senators now made their change: right-handed hitter Tommy Umphlett, batting all of .204 on the year, replaced McDermott. Even had the .204 average been .304 and that day's gathering of 2,437 fans had been 42,437, Martin wasn't one to get rattled easily. A combat engineer during World War II, he had experienced amphibious landings in North Africa and Sicily and at Omaha Beach on D-Day, was wounded twice in the Battle of the Bulge, had his leg saved from amputation by 150 shots of penicillin, had been left for dead when the house in which he and two fellow GIs were hiding collapsed after a shelling and, finally, had been awarded two Purple Hearts.[17] Certainly Tommy Umphlett was no problem — except for this time. Martin, whom Lane later acquired twice more when he was running the Cardinals and then the Indians, gave up a single to center that sent Jose Valdivielso from first base to third. Next up was Eddie Yost, who began the day hitting .221. Yost lined a base hit to left, the game was tied, runners were at the corners and Martin had retreated to the dugout. Relief pitcher Harry Byrd, Lane's lone 1955 trade-deadline pickup, came on to face 5-foot-4-inch, 145-pound rookie outfielder Ernie Oravetz, who muscled up and lifted a flyball deep enough to center field to drive in the go-ahead run. Pedro Ramos stopped the White Sox in the final two innings, and the deficit now was 2½ games.

It became 3½ the next afternoon in Yankee Stadium, where Joe Collins victimized Donovan for a three-run homer and one with the bases empty, both balls driven over the inviting right-field fence. New York was up, 4–0. In the ninth, the White Sox, narrowed the gap to 5–4 and had two runners on base with two out before Walt Dropo, who had hammered Yankee pitching all year, finished an 0-for-5 day with a roller to second baseman Billy Martin. Yet it was Dropo whose bases-loaded, two-out single in the ninth the next day that scored the tying and go-ahead runs in a 9–8 victory for Chicago, which had trailed 6-1 in the second inning. (For the year, Dropo, Frank Lane's top off-season acquisition, hit .373 against the Yankees with six homers and 18 RBIs.) Even with this victory, though, the Sox remained 3½ back of Cleveland and two behind New York. They got no closer.

Did Lane think the White Sox should have won the pennant during his tenure? He listed the possible years and then gave his reasons for answering in the negative.

• 1953: New York's 18-game winning streak helped end things early. Lane hadn't expected Ferris Fain, defending AL batting champion, to hit .256, nor had he anticipated that Joe Dobson and Saul Rogovin would lose it so suddenly in the same season.

• 1954: AL champ Cleveland won a record 111 games, and yet the Sox split their season series with the Tribe. Lane's club simply couldn't withstand

Big Walt Dropo, one of six players acquired in one day by Frank Lane at the December 1954 winter meetings, is welcomed at home plate by fellow newcomer Bob Nieman (18) and previous Lane imports Minnie Minoso (9) and Nellie Fox after his grand slam off Cleveland's Ray Narleski on April 16, 1955. Not pictured is George Kell, who also scored on Dropo's blast. Nieman followed with a homer of his own for the final run in Chicago's 9–4 victory (author's collection).

injuries to All-Star first baseman Fain, All-Star third baseman Kell and the arm woes of Pierce, who suffered through a rare down season.

• 1955: Pierce's greatest year, the fastest outfield in the majors (Minoso, Busby, Rivera), a fine comeback year for Kell and terrific, unexpected contributions from so many: Donovan, Howell, Kennedy, Connie Johnson, and Bob Nieman. Surely Lane must have thought there was a chance this season, especially with the Sox leading the league heading into the Labor Day weekend. But no: "If you don't see it on the field, don't wish for it," he said. "We had a good ballclub, but we just didn't have quite enough — unless we got a lot of lucky breaks. And Mr. Rickey used to say, 'There's no such thing as luck; luck is the residue of design.' Well, I had the design, but I didn't have the ballplayers. If Pierce had been twins, we might've won."[18]

The final weekend of the '55 season was an emotional time for Lane. The Sox were home to face Kansas City in a season-closing three-game series. On Friday night, the fans below him in the press box rose as one for a standing ovation, and Lane responded by waving to "my public," as he called them. The Sox joined the farewell festivities by scoring four runs in the first inning and five more in the second, two on Bob Kennedy's homer off former Sox bonus baby Gus Keriazakos, to whom Lane had once given $65,000. "We made a mistake on him," Lane acknowledged. "But when you make a mistake, admit it. Don't keep your mistake on the ballclub."[19]

Presently the eighth inning arrived, and Nellie Fox tripled to drive in the 10th Chicago run. "That's my boy!" yelled Lane, who nearly six years before had brought "Little Nell" to Chicago. Now batting was Minnie Minoso, another one of Lane's finest acquisitions. "C'mon, Minnie. You've only had three walks and a single.... There it goes!"[20] Minnie had just belted an Art Ceccarelli pitch into the upper deck in left for two more runs. After the 12–4 romp was over, Lane said he was going to go down to the White Sox clubhouse before the next afternoon's game and, at the request of the players, address the team. The room was packed. Lane posed for photos with Fox and Billy Pierce, roommates and early examples of Lane larceny. Then Frank asked for silence and, his eyes moist, began his remarks. "I'm very proud of all of you. You're a grand bunch, in my book. During the season, I have died a thousand deaths with you and thrilled to your great comebacks in games which had seemed lost. If I've seemed critical of you, and I know I have, it's because I wanted you to win so badly."[21]

He had more to say, but his voice, cracking, betrayed him and he decided to call it quits. The clubhouse then burst into loud applause as the players paid homage to their boss. They then went out and whipped the A's again, 4–0, for Dick Donovan's 15th win of the season and followed suit the next day when Pierce (15–10) blanked Kansas City, 5–0, to give the White Sox a final record of 91–63, five games off the Yankees' winning pace and two games worse than Cleveland. On the way out of the ballpark, scores of fans approached Lane and wished him the best — in St. Louis or wherever he wound up. Frank was touched. "They're the greatest, these White Sox fans," he said. "How I hate to leave them."[22] And how they hated that he was leaving them.

A. Busch, a Brewery and Almost a Pennant, 1956–1957

With Comiskey Park in the rear-view mirror, Frank Lane had headed down historic Route 66 toward his new assignment as the general manager of the St. Louis Cardinals. August A. "Gussie" Busch Jr., owner of the Cardinals and of Anheuser-Busch Inc., had hired him mere weeks after the close of the 1955 season on the recommendation of *The Sporting News* editor J.G. Taylor Spink, one baseball's most influential voices.

The winter would be quiet. Lane made one minor deal, purchasing from the Boston Red Sox ancient right-handed reliever Ellis Kinder, who admitted to having been born in 1914. Lane had hoped to do more at the winter meetings, so he left them with a bit of disappointment. "I've talked with every club in our league," he said, "and absolutely nothing has come of all the talks." Once Lane got to the Cardinals' spring base in St. Petersburg, and saw all the young talent blending in with Hall-of-Famers-to-be Stan Musial and Red Schoendienst, he began thinking that great things might await the 1956 Cardinal. But general managers cannot afford to be too optimistic and Lane had to remind himself that he was looking at a team that in '55 had finished 68–86 and below even the inevitably hapless Cubs.

"I've got to fight it," he told Robert Creamer, then working for *Sports Illustrated*. "I'm just as vulnerable to the high spirits around a training camp as anybody else. But, as general manager of this club, I've got to be realistic and look at the hard facts. Some people have said that last season the Cardinals were the greatest seventh-place ballclub in history. Well, maybe I'd rather have the lousiest first-place ballclub in history."[1] His hand-selected manager, Fred Hutchinson, echoed Lane's reaction to others' praise of the 1955 Cardinals. "A team finishes in seventh place because it isn't any better than that," Hutchinson declared.[2]

Such realistic speech was startling to Cardinals fans, who were accustomed to celebrating almost all Cardinals as heroes who could do no wrong. Apparently they had not bothered to check the standings, especially the last two years. (St. Louis had finished sixth in 1954 at 72–82; whether or not that club was hailed as the greatest sixth-place team in history is not known.) And yet, Lane was confident that he and Hutchinson, brought in from Seattle of the Pacific Coast League, would be able to make progress in their first season. "We've got a great manager in Fred Hutchinson — I got another great manager out of Seattle in Paul Richards. I told Mr. Busch when I nominated Hutchinson, 'Mr. Busch, you can be sure that any manager I pick will be the best man for Frank Lane.' That's the way I look at Fred Hutchinson. But, as I say, a general manager can't let himself be carried away.... But what I sense in this camp, to a degree that I've rarely seen in all my years in baseball, is an attitude — a great attitude. That's the big thing if you're playing ball, preaching a sermon or selling shoes. It's the attitude that counts. But I've got to be realistic, as I said.... I don't want to say we're going to beat out Brooklyn and Milwaukee."[3]

Lane had made a habit of finishing third in the American League with the White Sox. Perhaps because of that, along with the presence of the Dodgers and Braves in the NL, he made this optimistic prediction: "The Cardinals will finish third." They actually finished fourth, at 76–78, but it was quite a ride, just as Lane had promised it would be. "I didn't come to St. Louis to raise red roses or tell after-dinner stories or take the tenor lead in 'Hearts and Flowers,'" he told a young sportswriter named Roger Kahn. "When I moved in as general manager of the Cardinals last October, I was determined to build the kind of team I like. I suppose you've guessed the reason.

Even misplays in spring exhibition games would bring pain to Frank Lane. Here he reacts during a St. Louis Cardinals game at St. Petersburg, Florida. Lane took over the Cardinals in 1956, after they had finished seventh (in an eight-team league) in 1955. The Cardinals moved up to fourth in '56 and second in '57 before he moved on to Cleveland (courtesy Lane family).

It's no state secret. I came here to win a pennant, and that's exactly what I intend to do, *any* way I can."[4]

Busch had given him full authority on all player moves, as had been the case in Chicago. He had also given Lane a new Jaguar as a signing bonus. Soon enough, Frank was pulled over for going 120 m.p.h. on a Florida highway. "I'll say this about driving at that speed," he said to Kahn. "You come up on the other cars awful quick."[5]

Lane knew changes on the roster had to be made, but, unlike his approach to highway driving, he was going to take his time. The Cardinals convened at spring camp at St. Petersburg's Al Lang Field, a couple of tape-measure shots from Lane's home. Young talent seemed to abound, especially in the outfield, where Wally Moon, the NL's 1954 Rookie of the Year, shagged flies alongside center fielder Bill Virdon, the 1955 Rookie of the Year, and a new outfielder seen as a candidate for 1956 Rookie of the Year: Jackie Brandt, just out of the Army and looking terrific. Also just out of the Army was left-hander Wilmer David Mizell, who years later would become a U.S. congressman. His home was in Leakesville, Miss., only 10 miles or so from the Alabama border town of Vinegar Bend, where he was born. In the crucial world of nicknames and marketing, he certainly was not going to be called "Leakesville" Mizell. "Vinegar Bend" Mizell, however, was a different matter indeed. He had won 10 games as a rookie in 1952 and 13 more in '53 before getting the call from Uncle Sam. In the Army in '55, he had gone 22–0. "The year before," he said, "I wasn't so good: fourteen and two was the best I could do."[6] There was still more young talent in second-year third baseman Kenny Boyer and, next to him, a rookie shortstop named Don Blasingame. "The Blazer" had played second base at Triple-A Omaha in '55 after having struggled at the shortstop position the previous two seasons. Lane and Hutchinson hoped he would be adequate at shortstop. After all, at second base they already had nine-time All-Star Schoendienst.

One of Lane's first moves was to replace the traditional "birds-on-the-bat" insignia on the Cardinals' uniforms with a script "Cardinals" across the front. Fans were outraged, but Lane had a reason: "I explained that we took the bird insignia off to make the uniforms lighter. Those insignias were all backed up by canvas. I wanted a light uniform because of the hot summers in St. Louis."[7] Tradition, cried the fans. What about Cardinals tradition? "To me," Lane said years later, "tradition meant the men who wore the uniform, not the uniform. Of course, I was wrong. When I was with the White Sox, we received lots of letters from fans who wanted us to go back to the old white stockings. They were convinced that Fielder Jones' stockings had been more important than Fielder Jones."[8]

The controversy over the new uniforms notwithstanding, the Cards opened quickly, going 22–13 in the first 35 games, thanks mostly to their offense. They scored 10 or more runs eight times in those first 35 contests. They also had games in which the pitchers were tagged for 10, 13 and 14 runs. The record might have been worse had it not been for Kinder, Lane's first St. Louis acquisition. He saved six of the club's first 14 wins, pitching a total of 10 innings and allowing but six hits and zero runs. But then Kinder lost his touch, and so did the Cards—down, closer and closer, to the .500 mark. It was time for Lane, silent until now, to go to work.

This would have been business as usual to Chicago writers, but the St. Louis newsmen were about to find out why Paul Richards and their Windy City counterparts had long since dubbed Lane "Frantic Frank." Between May 1 and May 17, Lane announced six deals involving 17 players, with most of the new arrivals being pitchers. Truth be told, only two of the transactions were major ones. On May 11, Lane sent lefty Harvey Haddix, reliever Stu Miller and a minor leaguer to the Phillies for right-handers Murry Dickson and Herm Wehmeier. When critics joked about the 39-year-old Dickson joining the ranks of fellow oldsters Max Surkont and Ellis Kinder, Lane had a ready response: "It doesn't bother me that Murry is 39 or that Surkont and Kinder are, shall we say, in the upper-age group. Hell, I'd sign Methuselah if he could win for us."[9] Unable to land Methuselah, Lane settled for a starting rotation of Mizell, Dickson, Wehmeier, Tom Poholsky and Willard Schmidt.

"The Haddix trade," Lane said later, "left a lot of St. Louis fans seriously and honestly puzzled. 'Haddix is our ace,' they seemed to figure, sentimentally. 'Why did we give him up?' The unsentimental truth is that Haddix *was* an ace. But take away the sentiment and take a look at Harvey as he was when I let him go. All last year he'd been off form. All spring training he'd been just as bad. In the first month of the season, he was no better. Our hitters got him 30 runs in four starts, yet we lost three of those games."[10] Indeed, Haddix's ERA after those four starts was 5.32. (though he then went 12–8, 3.48, with Philadelphia the rest of 1956.)

On May 17, Lane, disappointed in the play of Bill Virdon, who was hitting just .211, sent him to Pittsburgh for another center fielder, good-field no-hit Bobby DelGreco, and much-traveled lefty Dick Littlefield. Lane had flown to Pittsburgh to watch DelGreco play against the Phillies on May 13, and the right-handed-hitting speedster had put on a good show: two excellent catches to go with two home runs off Haddix. But when the deal was announced, Cardinal fans flooded the newspapers with calls, complaining about Virdon's sudden departure. Again, Lane had his explanation ready: "If players don't produce and you stand with them too long, you'll soon find yourself off your feet and on your knees and then off your knees and on your back."[11] He told another reporter: "Bill wasn't even hitting the ball hard.

Although he hit .281 last year, he hit only .215 in September and just .222 in spring training."[12]

Naturally, Virdon went on a tear with his new club, , hitting .334 the rest of the way to finish at .319. (Littlefield, meanwhile, was soon on the move again, and DelGreco did little, save for making one spectacular catch after another to help snuff out Milwaukee's pennant hopes on the season's final weekend.) But after 1956, Virdon, never hit higher than .269 the rest of his career, except for his final season, 1965, when he batted .279. In addition, he never hit double figures in home runs again, nor was his lifetime .318 on-base percentage ideal for his role as the Pirates' leadoff man. Defensively, Virdon won only one Gold Glove, in 1962, but of course his competition during those years—Willie Mays and Curt Flood—was formidable.

Meanwhile, on the field, the Cards' fast start was soon just a fleeting memory. St. Louis dropped a Memorial Day doubleheader to the Reds at Busch Stadium plus another twin bill at home a few days later, this to Brooklyn by scores of 8–6 and 6–4, Don Newcombe and Carl Erskine getting the wins. By then, Lane supposedly had begun negotiating with the Phillies on a trade that was never consummated but led, in the end, to his departure from St. Louis. Lane, though denying so later in life, had offered Stan Musial to Philadelphia for perennial 20-game-winner Robin Roberts. As outlandish as that seems, keep in mind that, as late as May 25, when the Cubs came to town for a three-game series, Musial, who was to turn 36 at season's end, was batting just .272 and had hit only two home runs all month.

The way the story goes, Julius "Biggie" Garagnani, Musial's St. Louis-born business partner, got wind of rumored trade talks and called J.G. Taylor Spink at *The Sporting News* to see if there was anything to it. Indeed there was, Spink discovered. "Biggie" put in a call to the brewery to speak to Gussie Busch. The boss couldn't be found immediately, so Musial's pal talked to either John Wilson or Dick Meyer, top brewery officials both, and said, "If it's true, I got news for you: The kid won't report. He'll quit." The word got to Busch, who summoned Lane and read him the riot act. Subsequently, Lane issued this statement: "August A. Busch Jr. and myself are in complete accord that Musial will not be traded."[13]

And he wasn't. Musial started hitting and wound up with 27 homers, 109 RBIs and a .310 batting average. Roberts, incidentally, had a sub-par year, finishing 19–18 with a 4.45 ERA. Still, looking back to May and June of 1956, one can almost make a case for a Musial-Roberts trade. As much as trading Stan Musial would be, to St. Louis fans, sacrilege of the highest order, Lane knew—as did everyone else in the league—that the Cardinals badly needed an ace starter and had needed one for years. He couldn't have gotten one much better than Roberts. The right-hander from Springfield, Illinois, had won 20-plus games six years running, had twice led the NL in strikeouts, had posted ERAs of 3.02, 3.03, 2.59. 2.75, 2.97 and 3.28 the last six seasons and had topped the league in complete games the past four. Not only that, he was six years younger than Stan and, like Musial, was also on the path to Cooperstown. (One other note: Lane knew he could partially make up for Musial's departure by summoning Joe Cunningham from Triple-A Rochester. The lefty-swinging first baseman/outfielder had spent the previous season in the minors after having hit .284 as a rookie with the Cards in 1954. He was to spend all of '56 in the minors, batting .320, and then would hit .318, .312 and .345 for St. Louis in '57 through '59.)

Stymied by Busch in his grand plan to improve the pitching staff, Lane now decided something had to be done about the problem in the middle infield, where young shortstop Blasingame was proving with each passing day that there were good reasons why the Cardinals' minor-league people had switched him to second. It was decided, then, that Schoendienst would be dealt for a shortstop. If Lane couldn't trade Musial, he would trade his roommate. On June 14, Lane sent Schoendienst, Brandt, Littlefield, catcher Bill Sarni and infielder Bobby Stephenson to New York for a foursome of Giants: first baseman/outfielder Whitey Lockman, catcher Ray Katt, lefty reliever Don Liddle — the man who threw the pitch to Vic Wertz in the '54 World Series that helped make Willie Mays a legend — and two-time All-Star and three-time pennant-winner Alvin Dark, the shortstop whose presence was to allow Blasingame to return to second base.

The trade eventually worked out well for the Cardinals as Schoendienst's best day's were behind him and Brandt never became the star Redbird fans were expecting. Nevertheless this move won no popularity contests for Lane in St. Louis. Schoendienst was in his 12th year with the Redbirds and was hitting .314 at the time of the deal to Dark's .252. Not only that, Red was part of the community. His roommate, who with the rest of the club got the news as they boarded a train at St. Louis' Union Station, was livid. "It was the saddest day of my career," Musial told author George Vecsey decades afterward. "I slammed the door of my train berth shut and didn't open it for a long time."[14] In the meantime, the newspapers were being inundated with fans' angry calls, and Busch, within days, informed Lane that, from that moment forward, all deals would have to be cleared by him or by Dick Meyer at the brewery. Lane was somewhat surprised by the reaction. "The way they carried on there," he recalled in a 1968 interview, "you'd have thought I had *killed* Schoendienst."[15]

As it happened, Schoendienst ended the '56 season having batted .302 to Dark's .275, but both fielded well and became the vocal and spiritual leaders of their respective infields. Those developments didn't help their teams that much, however: the Cards wound up fourth, the Giants sixth. For Lane, the rest of the season was eerily quiet, as he made only two deals. At the All-Star break, he sold Ellis Kinder to "old friend" Chuck Comiskey and the White Sox, whose manager, former St. Louis hero Marty Marion, seemed intent on collecting ex-Cardinals. The Chicago roster then included ex-Redbird pitchers Gerry Staley, Howie Pollet and Paul LaPalme plus pinch-hitter supreme Ron Northey. Lane's only other second-half deal was the waiver pick-up of first baseman Rocky Nelson, the minor-league hitting terror, from the Dodgers' organization in late July. Lane seemed to enjoy trading for players he'd had before: with Chicago, he had purchased Nelson from the Pirates in September 1951 and then, not three months later, sent him to Brooklyn's Montreal farm for third baseman Hector Rodriguez.

On the field, the Cardinals were up and down, with winning streaks of six, five and six games being offset by skids of seven and five along with a stretch of eight defeats in nine tries. But they played some exciting ball at times, enough to keep the Busch Stadium turnstiles clicking. Attendance leaped from 849,130 in 1955 to a final 1956 total of 1,029,773. Perhaps the most exciting series of the season was the final one, when the Milwaukee Braves arrived in St. Louis with a one-game lead (with three games to go) on the world champion Brooklyn Dodgers. The Dodgers and Pirates were rained out in New York, and in St. Louis, the Braves looked in trouble from the get-go when Ken Boyer's bases-loaded double in the first inning knocked starting pitcher Bob Buhl and put the hosts ahead, 3–0. Wes Covington's pinch double and Billy Bruton's sacrifice fly tied things at 3–3 in the fifth, sending starter Tom Poholsky to the clubhouse and bringing Lindy McDaniel to the mound. In the sixth, Bobby DelGreco came through with an RBI single and eventually came home from third on Blasingame's bases-loaded roller when catcher Del Crandall couldn't come up with first baseman Joe Adcock's throw. Bruton doubled and Henry Aaron singled him in to make it 5–4 St. Louis in the eighth, but relievers Jackie Collum and Larry Jackson shut the door thereafter. Milwaukee's lead was down to a half-game.

That lead was gone by the time the Braves and Cardinals began Saturday night's contest before 25,587 at Busch Stadium. The Dodgers had swept a doubleheader 6–2 and 3–1, from the Pirates at Ebbets Field behind the pitching of Sal Maglie and Clem Labine and home runs by Sandy Amoros, Carl Furillo and Gil Hodges in the opener and by Roy Campanella in the second game. Thus Milwaukee now trailed by a half-game, making this matchup a must-win for the Braves. Herm Wehmeier was Fred Hutchinson's choice as starting pitcher; 20-game-winner Warren Spahn opposed him. Billy Bruton homered on the game's first pitch to put Spahn and the Braves ahead 1–0, but back-to-back doubles with two out by Don Blasingame

and Alvin Dark tied the score 1–1 in the sixth. At this point, the spotlight
began to shine on the man whose acquisition in May had resulted in major
criticism of Frank Lane's methods. The Cards' DelGreco, who had recorded
just one putout through the first seven innings, suddenly stole the show.
For the next five innings, he ranged far and wide in center field to make
seven catches, several bordering on the magnificent. Two of them came in
the ninth. First he sprinted to the deepest spot of the ballpark to rob Bruton

*Frank Lane, then general manager of the St. Louis Cardinals, presents slugger
Del Ennis with a Cardinals jersey and cap during a press conference on November 20, 1956, at old Busch Stadium. Lane had landed Ennis from the Phillies the
day before for fellow outfielder Rip Pepulski. Note the 1956 jersey, which was
missing the traditional "birds-on-the-bat" insignia for the first time since the
1920s. Lane had made the change with the players' comfort in mind. But Cardinals fans complained loudly, and the old uniforms returned the next season.
Ennis hit .286 with 24 homers and 105 runs batted in for St. Louis in 1957 (courtesy AP Images).*

for the first out. With Joe Adcock on first base with two out, Jack Dittmer drilled a shot to right-center, a sure double and possibly a triple. DelGreco, getting a terrific jump, snared the ball as he crashed into the wall but held on for the final out. Finally, with one out in the home 12th, Stan Musial doubled to right off Spahn, who had allowed just three hits and a walk through the first 11 innings. Boyer was given an intentional walk to get to Rip Repulski, hitless in four tries. This time, Repulski lashed a liner off third baseman Eddie Mathews' leg, the ball scooting toward the rolled-up tarpaulin in foul territory just beyond third base. As Mathews gave futile chase, Musial scored and the Cardinals had all but wrecked Milwaukee's World Series dreams. The Braves finally won on Sunday, but so did Brooklyn. The Dodgers were NL champs again.

It was an exciting finish to Frank Lane's first season in St. Louis, a season that had been a financial success and something of an artistic one as well. His spirits boosted by the Cardinals' performance against Milwaukee on the final weekend, Lane went into the winter seeking to upgrade the team's outfield power and, of course, the starting pitching. On November 19, he dealt Repulski — who had finished the year with only 11 homers and a disappointing total of 55 RBIs — and infielder Bobby Morgan to the Phillies for veteran slugger Del Ennis, who had averaged 26 homers and 113 RBIs over the last five years.

Ennis' right-handed bat, Lane figured, would give number three hitter Musial terrific protection and would make things easier for Wally Moon and Boyer. "The Cardinals' crying need," Lane said, "has been for power, and Ennis should supply it. He ranks as one of the outstanding power hitters in baseball."[16]

At 31, Ennis had batted .260 in '56 with 26 homers and 95 runs driven in. He saw no reason why he wouldn't do as well or better in Busch Stadium. "I'm not worried about the left-field fence being a little longer here (351 feet from home plate) than in Philadelphia (334 feet)," he said at a St. Louis press conference. "The fact is, this park is longer only down the line — not in left-center, straightaway center or right-center. I've found I've hit better by trying to go through the box. So I think the park here will help me, not hurt me. The ball carries well in St. Louis, and I've always hit good here."[17]

Some three weeks after announcing the Ennis deal, Lane handed pitchers Tom Poholsky, Jackie Collum and Wally Lemmers (a minor-leaguer) plus catcher Ray Katt to the Cubs. To St. Louis came Sam "Toothpick" Jones, who had led the NL in strikeouts (and walks, for that matter) in each of the previous two years while winning 23 games for dreadful Cub teams. Along with Jones came three decidedly lesser lights: lefty reliever Jim Davis, back-up catcher Hobie Landrith and veteran utility man Eddie Miksis. Of Miksis, it was once written that he "was the sort of guy who, if you were introduced to him at a party and he told you he was a big-league ballplayer, you'd think he was kidding. In a way, he would have been."[18]

Difficult though it might be to believe, Lane made zero deals in the new year's first two months—an offer from the Phillies involving center fielder Richie Ashburn went nowhere — and he made only one during spring training. The Giants, to their extreme chagrin, had just watched the Army call up their outstanding young first baseman, Bill White, who had hit 22 home runs as a rookie in '56. Lane, with first basemen coming out of his ears (among them Musial, Moon, Cunningham, Whitey Lockman and, if really necessary, Miksis), came to the New York club's aid. Off to the Giants went Lockman, a Giant up until the previous June. In return, the Cards got Hoyt Wilhelm, the knuckleball king who, going on 34, seemed to be losing some of his magic. Brilliant in 1952 and '54, Wilhelm had seen his ERA rise to 3.93 in 1955 and 3.83 in '56. Wilhelm, as shall be seen, would not become one of Lane's favorites.

When the season began in April, Lane noticed what was going on in Chicago, where the Cubs had played three center fielders in the first five games. So Lane traded Bobby DelGreco to the Cubs along with lefty Ed Mayer for Jim King, a decent extra outfielder with some left-handed pop. Not that the Cardinals needed a whole lot more offense. In the season opener at Cincinnati April 16, they lit up Reds pitching for 17 hits in a 13–4 romp. Blasingame scored twice and had two hits; Dark had three hits and scored four times; Musial went 4-for-4; Ennis and Moon each had two hits and drove in three runs, and Hal Smith had a couple hits and scored twice. In addition, a new center fielder, Bobby Gene Smith, up from Double-A Omaha where he had batted .299 with 21 homers and 109 RBIs in '56, broke in with two hits and a pair of runs batted in.

Of the starters, only Boyer had gone hitless, and Ken's slow start continued for several weeks. Indeed, after 17 games, he was batting all of .203. He wasn't alone. Ennis, on June 1, was at .224 and had clubbed only three home runs. Despite those numbers, Lane was confident his off-season deals for Ennis and Sam Jones had vastly improved the ballclub. But his boss, Gussie Busch, wasn't quite that sure. He gave Lane authority to use a check for $500,000 to buy Ernie Banks from the Cubs, then owned by chewing-gum king P.K. Wrigley. To Busch's surprise but certainly not to his, Lane failed to sway Wrigley. He reported back to his boss: "Mr. Busch, Mr. Wrigley said to tell you he needs a half-million dollars about as much as you do." Then came an order from Busch to see if the New York Giants, who were headed to a new home in San Francisco the next year, would take $1 million for Willie Mays.

Lane shrugged his shoulders and dialed up owner Horace Stoneham's right-hand man in New York, Chub Feeney. The conversation, though friendly, was short. Lane went in to see his boss again. "Mr. Busch, Chub said that if they traded Mays and then moved out to San Francisco, the people out there would throw them into the Bay."[19] Said Lane, much later: "Gussie Busch is one of the grandest guys anyone would want for a boss. But I couldn't convince him that a ballclub can't be run like a brewery."[20]

In the meantime, on the field, Ennis eventually got going and Boyer too began hitting. The rookie Smith, however, did not. So on May 23, Fred Hutchinson installed another rookie, Eddie Kasko, an aspiring shortstop, at third base and shifted Boyer out to center, while Smith moved to the bench. The moves worked, although Boyer, a bit uncomfortable at his new position, never got his batting average higher than the .279 he was hitting on July 30. But all that truly mattered was that the Cardinals were in a pennant race, a five-team event, one club more than the four-team race Lane had sweated through two years before in the American League. The Cards were in first place at the All-Star break, which made St. Louis' role as All-Star Game host that much more special. St. Louisans now wondered if their city might not also play host to the 1957 World Series. They also wondered how Frank Lane could have allowed the June 15 trading deadline to pass without making headlines. There likely were two answers: Lane truly believed there was nothing available that would strengthen the club, and he hated the idea of having a baseball novice such as Busch or Meyer reserving final approval on his deals.

In any event, the race became white-hot toward the end of July. Through games of Sunday, July 28, just 2½ games separated the five contenders: Milwaukee led the second-place Cardinals by a half-game, the Dodgers were 1½ games back and the Reds and Phillies stood 2½ behind. That afternoon, the Cards had swept a pair from Pittsburgh at Busch Stadium in especially impressive fashion. In the opener, the amazing rookie right-hander, Von McDaniel, 18-year-old younger brother of rotation starter Lindy — himself a bonus baby signed in September 1955 — had been masterful again. Signed by Lane on May 23 for a $50,000 bonus out of high school in Hollis, Oklahoma, he had broken in on June 13 with a four-inning, one-hit scoreless relief outing at Philadelphia. Three days later, at Ebbets Field, he turned in the exact same numbers against the two-time defending NL champion Dodgers and got credit for the win. Manager Hutchinson decided he'd give the kid a start on Friday night, June 21, against the Dodgers at home. In front of 27,972 admiring fans, and with millions listening to Harry Caray's broadcast over the Cardinals' radio network, Von took a no-hitter into the sixth inning of a scoreless tie. Junior Gilliam led off with a looping liner just out of the reach of a leaping Don

Blasingame at second to break up the no-hit bid. The crowd rose for an ovation, then it was back to work.

Next, Musial misplayed Pee Wee Reese's sacrifice bunt for an error, and Duke Snider stunned everyone with another bunt, which he beat out to load the bases. But this was Von McDaniel's summer. He got Elmer Valo, the long-time Lane favorite, to bounce into a pitcher-to-home-to-first double play, then retired Gino Cimoli on another comebacker and walked to the dugout to thunderous applause. The Cards pushed across a run in the home sixth and got another in the eighth when, after a standing ovation for first batter McDaniel, Blasingame tripled and came in on Alvin Dark's single. Leading now 2–0, Von took the mound and, when Dark fielded Gil Hodges' two-out grounder and fired to first, the bonus kid had pitched a two-hit shutout and boasted a scoreless-innings streak of 17.

And yet his performance against the Pirates on July 28 was even better. In the second inning he allowed a two-out double to Gene Baker. And that was it. McDaniel walked no one (he had walked three Dodgers on June 21), struck out four, retired the final 22 hitters in succession and finished with a one-hit, 4–0 victory. Then, in the second game, St, Louis trailed 8–5 in the last of the ninth but sent the game into extra innings on Kasko's two-out game-tying double. After Hoyt Wilhelm survived two passed balls and escaped jams in the 10th and 11th, Cunningham belted a "walk-off" homer in the 11th for a 9–8 triumph.

The Sunday sweep started the Cardinals on an eight-game winning streak that put them on top. They stayed there until the Braves overtook them on August 6, the night the lowly Cubs came to town to begin a three-game series. The Cards lost all three, then were blasted 13–2, 9–0 and 5–1 by the visiting Braves, who pounded first Lindy McDaniel, then brother Von and finally Sam Jones into submission. The skid did not end there. The Cardinals went to Chicago for three games and scored a total of four runs and lost to the same trio of right-handers who'd beaten them a week earlier: Bob Rush, Moe Drabowsky and rookie Dick Drott. The tailspin was at nine now, and the Milwaukee lead had ballooned to 8½ games. During the losing streak, the club's longest since 1929, the Cards' team batting average was an unsightly .207. Later that month there was a stretch during which St. Louis scored only 15 runs in seven games. Part of the problem was that Stan Musial had been sidelined since August 22 with a chipped left shoulder blade (and a torn muscle in the shoulder), and would not start another game until September 15. "I sure wish this hadn't happened to prove my point," Frank Lane said, "but I've been saying all along that 'Stosh' has been carrying us, that we might have trouble staying out of the second division without him, and now we're finding out how really valuable he is."[21]

Later in August, the Cardinals exacted some revenge during a final trip to Wrigley Field, where they swept three one-run games in a series that began on August 30. But when the Redbirds dropped two to the Reds on Labor Day while the Braves were making merry at the Cubs' expense, 23–10 and 4–0, St. Louis' deficit was 8½ games, and the race, most everyone figured, was over. Someone forgot to tell that to Lane, Fred Hutchinson and the Cardinal players, however. The next night, Del Ennis belted his 18th homer and drove in three runs in a 14–4 rout of Cincinnati. Then the Braves came to town, bent on lowering the magic number for clinching by four. Instead, the Cards won the opener, 5–4, in 12 innings on Wednesday night as Don Blasingame doubled, stole third and scored when Bob "Hurricane" Hazle dropped Ennis' fly to right. And, on Thursday night, former Yankee outfielder Irv Noren had three hits, Ennis went 3-for-4 with his 19th homer and Sam Jones fired a four-hitter as St. Louis blitzed Lew Burdette, 10–1. The deficit was 6½ games.

Next on the guest list were the Reds, who dropped two of three, the lone St. Louis defeat coming in the opener on September 6 when 36-year-old lefty Bill Kennedy — a reliever for Frank Lane's 1952 White Sox club who had spent the entire season in the Pacific Coast League — came in and shut out the St. Louisans on three hits over the final four innings. In Sunday's finale, the Reds and Joe Nuxhall led 3–0 in the eighth before a rally that included Stan Musial's first appearance since August 22 — he delivered a pinch single in that inning — and ended with Alvin Dark's bases-loaded single in the ninth. St. Louis now trailed by 5½ games, with the Phillies due in for games on Tuesday and Wednesday night. Lindy McDaniel scored the winning run in the 14th on Kenny Boyer's single off Robin Roberts for a 4–3 win in the series opener, and Ennis hit his 22nd and 23rd home runs and Wally Moon his 21st the next night, as the Cardinals rolled, 14–6. That result, coupled with Pittsburgh's 2–1 triumph that afternoon at Milwaukee, trimmed the Braves' edge to 4½ games.

The Braves beat Brooklyn, 2–1, on Thursday, September 12, an idle date for St. Louis, and Milwakee led by five. The Dodgers' Don Drysdale then defeated Milwaukee, 5–1, on Friday night to provide an opening, but the Cards could not take advantage. The visiting New York Giants scored three in the eighth and three in the ninth; Willie Mays and Whitey Lockman each had three hits and former Cardinal third baseman Ray Jablonski drove in three runs in New York's 7–3 victory. For the Cardinals, five games back with 14 to go, a pennant surely had to seem only a dream. But now things would get interesting again. On Saturday, after the Dodgers' Carl Erskine fired a four-hit, 5–2 beauty to beat the Braves before 40,775, a much smaller turnout (11,726) at Busch Stadium saw Don Blasingame drive in three runs with a single and home run to help "Vinegar Bend" Mizell top Johnny Antonelli and the Giants, 6–1. Then, on Sunday the 15th, after the Braves fell to Philly 3–2 at County Stadium on a 10th-inning RBI single by weak-hitting utility infielder Ted Kazanski, 24,577 believers—including Frank Lane, seated atop the roof behind home plate—showed up to see Stan Musial in the starting lineup for the first time in 24 days and, far more important, to see if the Cardinals could make the race even closer.

They enjoyed quite the afternoon. In the first game of the day's doubleheader, Musial was 1-for-4 with an RBI; Ken Boyer drove in two with his 19th homer; 42-year-old third-string catcher Walker Cooper collected three hits, including a home run; Eddie Kasko chipped in with a clutch two-run double, and the Cards pounded Pittsburgh 9–6. In the second game, with one out in the home first, Wally Moon singled and went to third on Musial's double. Joe Cunningham walked to fill the bases for Del Ennis, who popped one up along the first-base line. The Bucs' first baseman, Frank Thomas, made the catch but was running away from the plate and couldn't make an effective throw, as Moon raced home from third to score on one of the shortest sacrifice flies in Redbird history. The crowd, and the ballclub, was energized. Cunningham stole second, and Boyer walked, loading the bases again, and second-string catcher Hobie Landrith lined a base hit to right to score two runs, and the rout was on. Handed a five-run first-inning lead, Sam Jones was not going to let this one get away. He went 6 one-third innings, struck out seven and walked only one batter en route to his 12th win of '57. When Dick Groat grounded to first for the final out of this 11–3 triumph, St. Louis, 8½ games out just two weeks before, was now only 2½ behind the "runaway" Braves.

The next day, Lane decided that the printing of World Series tickets was no longer something he could put off. He ordered that process to begin and also assigned two scouts to cover and study thoroughly the Yankees for the next two weeks. "I feel the pennant race is going down to the last three games: our final series with the Cubs here and Milwaukee's with Cincinnati," Lane said. "Every game is a big one now, but at least we've got a chance. And, I believe, a pretty good one."[22] Manager Hutchinson agreed. "At least we're close enough that, by winning the Brooklyn series [September 17–18 at home], we'll have a chance to beat Milwaukee ourselves over there next week," he said.[23]

There would be no miracle ending. Perhaps the moment when the Cardinals were forced to accept that came on Wednesday, September 18. The night before, after trailing visiting Brooklyn, 5–3, St. Louis got a bases-loaded pinch triple from newcomer Irv Noren that capped a seven-run rally in a 12–5 triumph. But the following evening, young Don Drysdale notched his 16th win, shutting down the Cards, 6–1, while Milwaukee was beating

New York, 8–2, behind Lew Burdette. The crushing loss left St. Louis four games back with only nine remaining. The pennant was going to go to Milwaukee, though that did not become official until September 23, when Henry Aaron's 11th-inning home run off St. Louis rookie Billy Muffett gave the Braves a 4–2 victory — and the pennant. "I guess it's justifiable retribution," Lane said afterward. "We [helped take] the pennant away from them [on the final weekend] last year, and they beat us to win it this year."[24] That the clinching home run was the first homer in 44 big-league innings allowed by Muffett, called up on July 30, mattered little. What mattered was that the Cardinals' improbable pennant bid — improbable to all but Frank Lane, anyway — was over.

Shortly, Frank Lane's stay in St. Louis would be over, even though his contract ran through 1958. He had brought in reinforcements down the stretch, landing Noren from Kansas City and two former Lane employees, lefties Bob Kuzava and Morrie Martin, from Pittsburgh and Baltimore, respectively. Noren was especially valuable, hitting .367 (11-for-30) and driving in 10 runs after his August 31st purchase. But even the Cardinals' final 87–67 record, their improvement from two games under .500 to 20 over, the increase of nearly 154,000 in home attendance to 1,183,575 in 1957 and the welcoming into the organization of several amateur free agents, among them a terrific Creighton University athlete named Bob Gibson, were not enough to save Lane's job. Winning *The Sporting News*' Major League Executive of the Year award didn't do it, either.

Gussie Busch had stood up at a St. Louis sports dinner the previous winter and said, "If we don't win this year, I know we will win next year [1958]. If we don't, Frank Lane will be out on his ass." Lane wasn't certain if Busch had been kidding or not. To test the limits of the boss' loyalty to him, Lane suggested the two discuss a contract extension. When Busch responded with a telegram stating simply, "Kiss my ass," Frantic Frank had a fairly good idea as to just where he stood.[25] He started looking around, and by late November, he had a new address: Cleveland, Ohio.

At season's end, however, Lane had praised his players to the utmost. "Milwaukee won more games than we did," he said, "but the Redbirds are my champions. They never gave up. They went down fighting, right to the end." In particular, he had major compliments for Stan Musial, the man whom Lane had considered trading 15 months earlier. "My admiration for 'Stosh' is indescribable, the way that old champion performed when hurt. I still think he's the MVP."[26]

In St. Louis, meanwhile, Busch had promoted Bing Devine to Lane's old job. Apparently, Gussie did have second thoughts about losing Lane, because at a dinner party he hosted that fall at his Grant's Farm estate, he repeatedly sought reassurance from Cardinals broadcaster Harry Caray. "What do you think about Lane?" Busch kept asking. "Do you think we're better off?" Caray didn't want to say anything to anger his boss, but he finally had had enough. "I think Frank Lane would have been great, just perfect, if there weren't so many stumbling blocks thrown into his path," Caray said. "Hell, are you kidding? Who the hell do you have who can carry Frank Lane's briefcase?"[27]

Quite obviously, not every baseball man in St. Louis was delighted to see Frank Lane depart.

6

A Troubling Debut as the
Wigwam's Bigwig, 1958

On the night of November 12, 1957, Frank Lane stepped off the airplane that had brought him to Cleveland from St. Louis and did a bit of a double take. There waiting for him was a crowd of newsmen and photographers, welcoming him to a city whose baseball team and baseball fandom needed the infusion of excitement that he had shown he could supply. Reporter after reporter questioned him until the newspaper types dispersed to their offices to file their stories and develop their film for the next day's editions. When those papers came out, there was Lane all over Page One, smiling and waving and, most of all, sounding anxious to get started on his new job. After all, he had flown to Cleveland rather than take a train simply because he wanted to get started sooner. "I'm not a patient man," Lane told *Cleveland Plain Dealer* sports editor Gordon Cobbledick, among others. "I want to find out what trades have to be made and then make 'em."[1]

The Indians, American League champions in 1948 and '54 and solid contenders in all other seasons since '48, had fallen on tough times. The pitching staff stalwarts — Early Wynn, Bob Lemon and Mike Garcia — were getting old. Heroes of '54 like Bobby Avila, Al Rosen and Larry Doby were gone or going. The future of the brilliant young lefty, Herb Score, was in doubt as the result of a Gil McDougald line drive that had struck him in the eye the previous May. Al Lopez, the Indians' highly successful manager from 1951 through 1956, had departed Cleveland after the '56 season to manage the Chicago White Sox. Attendance had been dropping precipitously since 1955, when the Tribe finished three games out and drew 1,221,780. Another runner-up club drew just 865,467 in 1956, which alarmed Lopez enough to hand in his resignation. Attendance fell to 722,256 in 1957, when the Indians finished 76–77 and dropped to sixth place. General manager Hank Greenberg, fired earlier that November, took the fall for the loss of 500,000 paid admissions over just two years. Now a new man would get a chance to get the Tribe on the move again.

Reaction poured in from all over. American League President Will Harridge said: "I certainly want to congratulate the Indians on their selection, and I'm delighted to welcome Frank back into the American League's official family. He is a capable and energetic executive, and I'm sure he'll do a great job with the Indians. I was sorry to see him leave Chicago and move to the National League a few years ago. I always felt that Frank was an American Leaguer at heart. Now I'm sure of it." Longtime pal Bill Veeck, the former Indians president, added: "Frank Lane will infuse new life into the entire Cleveland organization. I think his appointment is a good thing for Cleveland baseball, and that's most important. I'm extremely fond of Frank. He'll give the fans an interesting and exciting team." Said Red Sox general manager Joe Cronin: "Frank was very successful with the White Sox before moving to the Cardinals, and we're glad to have him back in our league." Then came a call from Tigers GM John McHale, who seemed to be reading from a prepared statement: "The Indians' selection of Frank Lane will put new life in the American League." Lane replied, "Forget the congratulations. Just tell me: do I get Harvey Kuenn?"[2]

Checking in from Cuba, where he was managing a winter-league team, was new Cleveland manager Bobby Bragan. Bragan had been hired by Greenberg shortly before the latter's dismissal and, despite his carefully chosen words of welcome, was wary of working with Lane from the get-go. "I just heard the news and I'm delighted," he told reporters. "The Indians couldn't have hired a more colorful man. I'm sure Frank and I will get along fine. I've admired him for a long time." Lane responded by playfully tweaking the new manager. "I'm looking forward to giving my tonsils a rest next year," he said. "With Bragan on the job, I'll be lucky to get a word in edgewise."[3]

There was also a call from home in St. Petersburg, Florida, where wife Selma had been getting reports in the newspapers and on radio. "What's this I read in the paper? Where do we live now?" she wanted to know. Lane turned to a reporter: "She's used to moving. She had never been north of the Florida state line until she married me 26 years ago. But now she's been with me in Cincinnati, Kansas City, New York, Chicago, St. Louis and more way stations than I can remember." Mrs. Lane no doubt brightened when she learned what William R. Daley, the club's board chairman, had in mind for contract terms. Lane signed a three-year deal at $50,000 per season; he also would collect a nickel-a-head bonus for every paid admission above 800,000. Daley also stated that, unlike the situation in St. Louis with Gussie Busch, Lane "will have a free hand to operate as he sees fit."[4]

Lane went to work almost immediately, what with the winter meetings, set for Colorado Springs, just a couple of weeks away. Among his first moves was to name Hoot Evers assistant farm director and Bob Kennedy assistant scouting director. Lane had the utmost respect for the two recently retired former big-leaguers. Years later, he said: "When I got to Cleveland, Hoot Evers was scouting for them in Florida. Bob Kennedy was working for the playgrounds in Cleveland. I brought Hoot Evers and Bob Kennedy into my office in Cleveland, and within one year we were fighting for the pennant. I always took pride in the quality of the people I chose to work with me. That was part of the job, too."[5]

He also made it known that Herb Score and Roger Maris were the team's only untouchables. Said Lane: "We will not talk about Herb Score or Roger Maris. If you're interested in anybody else, let me hear your propositions." Suddenly, he began getting calls from his counterparts, everyone asking

Frank Lane talking trade in January 1958, during his first off-season as Cleveland Indians general manager (courtesy AP Images).

about Wynn, Avila, Ray Narleski, Don Mossi, Rocky Colavito, Al Smith, Cal McLish, Bud Daley, Chico Carrasquel and others. "I'm going to demand a recount on the pennant race," Lane said. "If we've got as many good ballplayers as these other guys seem to think, we must've finished higher than sixth."[6]

Among the first deals discussed at the meetings in Colorado Springs involved the Tribe, the White Sox and Washington. This proposal had Al Smith going to Chicago for Larry Doby, with Lane passing along Doby and unnamed others to the Senators for Roy Sievers, who was coming off a season in which he had hit .301 and led the AL in homers (42) and RBIs (114). Senators boss Calvin Griffith nixed the idea, however. Instead, the Sox and Orioles got together on a six-player transaction on December 3 that put Doby, Jack Harshman and minor-league pitcher Russ Heman in Baltimore uniforms and sent third baseman Billy Goodman, outfielder Tito Francona and pitcher Ray Moore to Chicago. Al Lopez, the White Sox manager, recalled getting ready to go to dinner with Sox vice presidents Chuck Comiskey and John Rigney when suddenly Lane walked into their suite. "Congratulations," said Frank, "I heard you made a deal. But those are just mediocre ballplayers. If you really want to make a deal, let's make a deal for a name ballplayer." Said Lopez, decades afterwards: "Frank was always like that."[7]

The name ballplayer Frank wanted was Minnie Minoso, who was coming off a .310, 103-RBI season and was still as dynamic at age 35 as he was when Lane first traded for him in 1951. Lane said he'd give up Lopez favorite Early Wynn in return. The Sox said they needed more, given Wynn's age (38) and the 14–17 record he had compiled in 1957. When Lane put Al Smith in the deal, Lopez, Comiskey and Rigney went to an adjoining room to discuss things. "Geez," said Lopez, "it's a hell of a deal for us, if he'll make it." Lane was more than ready to make it. So the White Sox had added two building blocks for the 1959 pennant winners, and the Indians had added some excitement to the lineup. Indeed, Detroit manager Jack Tighe said: "Nobody ever paid a nickel to watch Al Smith play ball. They'll pay to watch Minoso."[8] The next target was Washington's Pete Runnels, an infielder known more for his bat than his glove. Lane thought that Runnels, a left-handed "ping" hitter, might come cheap because he had batted just .230 in '57 after having hit .310 the season before. He offered Griffith lefty Hank Aguirre and two essentially Triple-A players—first baseman Joe Altobelli and infielder Larry Raines—for Runnels and catcher Lou Berberet. Had Lane made a better offer, the Indians and not the Boston Red Sox might have reaped the benefits of Runnels' two AL batting championships (1960 and '62).

Lane, hoping to pull another major deal before departing Colorado, made his first known bid for Tigers star Harvey Kuenn. For the future batting champ, Lane offered outfielder Gene Woodling, first baseman Vic Wertz, catcher Jim Hegan and Aguirre. (There was no mention of Rocky Colavito being part of the package). While the Tigers weighed the pros and cons of that proposal, Lane set out after Yankees GM George Weiss. Desperate for infield help, Lane was willing to send standout right-hander Ray Narleski and aging infielder Bobby Avila to New York for third baseman Andy Carey, second baseman Bobby Richardson and one of two pitchers— Don Larsen or Johnny Kucks. Weiss, as always, fled when he saw Lane coming. Yankees manager Casey Stengel listened to Lane's proposal but did not seem interested. Detroit's McHale turned down the Kuenn bid the same day. That night, McHale also said no to what would have been the biggest trade in the game's history. Years later, Lane provided C.C. Johnson Spink, then editor and publisher of *The Sporting News*, with the details:

> I had been trying to make a deal with John for two or three days. About 2 o'clock one morning, we had been going on for several hours without getting anywhere. Finally I told McHale, "I'll trade you the first 15 players on my club for the first 15 on your club. You make a list of the 15 you want and I'll make a list of the 15 I want." Jack Tighe, the manager of the Tigers, was there, and I

said he could be the witness. McHale took a piece of paper out of his pocket as if we were going to write down names. But then he hemmed and hawed and backed off. I was sober. I don't drink. I would have made the deal. After all, the Indians finished in sixth place (76–77) in '57 and we didn't have a lot to lose.

Detroit had finished fourth at 78–76, so the Tigers didn't have a lot to lose, either. It is unclear whether these talks took place before or after Lane's acquisition of Minoso. If Minoso was already on the Cleveland roster, it is to be assumed that Minnie and either Al Kaline or Harvey Kuenn would not have been included in the 30-player blockbuster. But think of those who could have been. From the Indians: pitchers Don Mossi, Ray Narleski, Herb Score, Cal McLish, Bud Daley and Hoyt Wilhelm; outfielders Rocky Colavito, Roger Maris and Gene Woodling; and infielders Vic Wertz, Bobby Avila and Chico Carrasquel. And that's only 12. Then from the Tigers: pitchers Jim Bunning, Frank Lary, Paul Foytack and Billy Hoeft; outfielders Charlie "Paw Paw" Maxwell, Johnny Groth, Gus Zernial and either Kaline or Kuenn; and infielders Frank Bolling, Billy Martin, Ray Boone and Gail Harris. And that's only 12.[9]

Even without the mega-deal, Lane and the Indians — especially Lane — were at the center of attention for the baseball working press, a fact not lost on Bragan, himself no shrinking violet in the conversation league but now relegated to second fiddle behind his always loquacious GM. "This is great," Bragan said. "I've never had it so good. I don't have to say a thing."[10] There were high marks from Lane's new bosses as well. "He really showed me something during the league meeting," one Tribe board member said. "There isn't a selfish bone in his body. He has the interest of all baseball at heart and not only his own club."[11] That was unlike the position staked out by Lane's Yankee counterpart, Weiss, who continually fought proposals that might lessen the overwhelming strength of the Yankees' farm system and improve the overall strength of the AL. In one exchange during the league meeting on December 7, Lane took Weiss to task: "George, you think only of what is good for the Yankees. You don't realize that what is good for all is good for the Yankees, too. We're in competition, but as members of a league we are also in partnership. One cannot survive without the help of the other."[12]

Meanwhile, Lane received unsigned contracts back from Colavito and Maris, as well as from Hoyt Wilhelm, whom Lane and the Cardinals had released the previous September 21 and who had been used only two times during that exciting final month of the National League race. The Indians had claimed him on waivers, and now Lane and Wilhelm were reunited, for better or for worse. Eventually, the three players were signed, although Maris' and Colavito's negotiations caused acrimony. The Colavito-Lane contract fights would become legend and annually would succeed in getting Rocky on the trading block — though it wasn't till 1960 that Lane, in a move he would regret, sent his slugging right fielder packing. But this was still 1958, and the mood in the new general manager's office was upbeat. Spring training was just around the corner, and Lane, Evers, Kennedy and others of the home office staff prepared for the trip to Tucson.

Once Lane and Bobby Bragan started to get better acquainted under the Arizona sun, it became obvious that the two were not destined to have a good working relationship. Said Bragan in his 1992 autobiography: "Frank Lane was a constant presence. He didn't offer advice, or even constructive criticism. All Lane wanted to do was blow his own horn and denigrate everything and everybody else."[13] Bragan had been something of a showman in his recent tenure as Pittsburgh manager. No doubt he felt a touch of jealousy as he watched scores of writers and photographers following Lane around the Tribe's spring facility. Indeed, one writer asked Lane about the likelihood of a troubled marriage between the two. After all, Bragan had been hired by Hank Greenberg, not by Lane.

"People are always asking Bobby what he's going to do if I start criticizing him publicly," Frank responded. "Well, I resent them asking that question. I don't think it's right. I'll criticize Bobby if I think he's wrong. A general manager is responsible for his manager. If he makes a mistake and I don't like it, I'm going to sound off. After all, he's my man. If he goes wrong, I go wrong.... As a general manager, I'm doing everything I can to help the manager, because I'm selfish. I want him to win for my own sake."[14]

As the exhibition schedule swung into high gear, so did Lane. Seemingly just to move bodies around, he purchased right-hander Chuck Churn, a future Dodger, on waivers from the Red Sox, acquired infielder Milt Bolling from the Senators and then, a couple weeks later, sent Bolling and former Cubs reliever Vito Valentinetti to the Tigers for pitcher Pete Wojey and $20,000. Lane then made a major move, a trade with old friend Paul Richards on April 1 that was front-page news in the *Plain Dealer*: Larry Doby was reacquired from Baltimore, along with lefty Don Ferrarese, for Gene Woodling, Dick Williams and left-hander Bud Daley. Woodling, a native of Akron, Ohio, was incensed. He had hit .321 with 19 homers and 78 RBIs in '57 with the Tribe, he'd been named the Indians' Man of the Year by the local baseball writers, he was playing at home, his family was with him — and now he was being sent to the East Coast. Years later, he was still upset: "Frank Lane? How do guys like that get in baseball?"[15]

Once the regular season got underway, Lane's new team produced little of the excitement he had hoped for. The Indians opened at home and drew a crowd of 35,307, which meant there were close to 40,000 empty seats at

Municipal Stadium (1958 seating capacity 73,811). Kansas City's Ned Garver shut out the Tribe on seven hits while the A's collected four walks, four hits and three runs in three innings against Herb Score, who was making his first regular-season appearance since that infamous night of May 7, 1957. Lane's acquisitions from the White Sox — Minnie Minoso and Fred Hatfield, a throw-in from the Wynn deal — both went 0-for-4, Minnie chipping in with an error. Larry Doby celebrated his return to the wigwam with two singles and a walk, but there was no question this was not the way Lane had hoped to get his show started. Things were worse the next day. Only 2,270 turned out; Score's roommate, Rocky Colavito, squirmed on the bench while he watched Roger Maris play right field for the second straight day; starting pitcher Ray Narleski was knocked out in a five-run first inning, and Kansas City won again, 9–4. Finally, the team's third game, the Tribe emerged victorious. Colavito was in the starting lineup, but at first base instead of right field, and his two-out double tied the game at 1–1 in the opening inning. Cleveland trailed 2–1 in the ninth and appeared on the verge of wasting a fine performance by young Jim "Mudcat" Grant when, with two on and two out, 40-year-old Mickey Vernon batted for Grant and doubled home the tying and winning runs.

For most of the season's first half, the Indians seemed married to the .500 mark, never getting more than a couple of games above or below breakeven. There was a flash of excitement on April 23, when Score struck out 13 and three-hit the White Sox, 2–0. Shortly thereafter, however, the lefty injured his elbow and was all but useless from then on, getting into just eight more games, two of them starts, during the remainder of the 1958 season. The team plodded on, winning two, losing two, winning one, losing one, while Frank Lane grew impatient. By late May, he was ready to move. He hadn't made any deals of importance since April 1. (He had caused some raised eyebrows by trading Hatfield to Cincinnati for pitcher Bob Kelly on April 23, only to buy the future Florida State baseball coach back on May 18.) The deal he supposedly was finalizing out in the right-field bleachers with Washington front-office boss Calvin Griffith on Saturday, May 24, was one that would do more than raise eyebrows. The six-player trade, if it went through, would send Colavito and pitchers Cal McLish and Mike Garcia to the Senators for slugging outfielder Jim Lemon, third baseman Eddie Yost (almost yearly the league's leader in bases on balls but hitting .206 at the time) and pitcher Pedro Ramos.[16]

It is far more understandable that Lane talked of trading Colavito in May 1958 than when he discussed doing so in '59 or '60. At this point, Colavito, coming off a 25-homer year, was not yet the Cleveland folk hero he would become after hitting 41 and 42 home runs in '58 and '59. Moreover, Colavito had started only 24 of Cleveland's first 36 games and was currently in the throes of an 8-for-54 (.148) slump. Going into this game, he had hit just two home runs and none since April 22. In any event, the deal supposedly was scheduled to be announced after the game, which the Tribe seemed to have in the bag, leading 3–0 entering the eighth. When the first four Washington hitters reached against starter Don Mossi, Bobby Bragan finally reacted and called upon Garcia to halt the rally. "The Bear" just made it worse. First Rocky Bridges singled off first baseman Preston Ward's glove to make it 3–2 and leave the bases filled. Lemon followed with a bullet to left for two runs, and the Senators led, 4–3. Yost also lined a hit to left, two more runs came across and it was 6–3. When Garcia walked Ken Aspromonte, Bragan mercifully removed him and the score stayed as it was. Meanwhile, Colavito had popped out twice and struck out. When the game ended, Griffith, still out in the right-field bleachers, told Lane, "No deal."

Lane two weeks later was in the Fenway Park right-field bleachers, enjoying the sunshine but not the ballgame — until, that is, the Indians scored four in the 10th to beat Boston, 7–5. Sitting with Frank was the *Plain Dealer*'s Harry Jones, who was enjoying Lane's commentary. It started with Minnie Minoso popping out to first, the second straight popup of the first inning. Said Lane: "If we ever meet a team that has trouble catching pop flies, we'll beat hell out of them." Next inning, Billy Harrell sent a softly hit blooper that barely made it to shortstop Billy Klaus on a fly. "I don't see how the ball can stand it," said the GM. Later, Roger Maris swung weakly and missed for strike three. Lane: "Looked like he was stirring soup." And in the 10th, when the Tribe took the lead, Dick Brown, on second base, gingerly approached third and held there on Bobby Avila's groundball single to right. "If you had been on base as seldom as he has," Lane told Jones, "you wouldn't be able to find third base, either."[17]

Another player who spent little time on the basepaths that year was J.W. Porter, a 1951 White Sox bonus baby from Oklahoma. Shortly before pitchers and catchers were to report to Tucson for spring training, Lane had traded catcher Jim Hegan and lefty Hank Aguirre to Detroit for another left-hander, Hal Woodeshick, along with Porter, still just 25. The young player hadn't had much of an opportunity thus far in the '58 season: one hit in five at-bats, all as a pinch-hitter, entering the May 27th Tuesday night game at Municipal Stadium. The Indians trailed the Baltimore Orioles 6–4 in the last of the ninth when Bill Harrell led off by drawing a walk from Orioles right-hander Billy Loes. Roger Maris was sent up to swing for the pitcher, Don Mossi, but Orioles manager Paul Richards countered by bringing in lefty Billy O'Dell. Bobby Bragan responded by calling down to the bullpen for Porter, a right-handed hitter, to face O'Dell. Lane, in the press box, asked, "Who's Bragan bringing in now?" Baltimore writer Lou Hatter responded, "Porter." Lane assured all those around him that "Porter is an automatic strikeout." O'Dell got ahead 0-and-2 and then fired a fastball right down the middle. Porter watched it go by. Plate umpire Frank Umont, however, simply missed the pitch. Porter, with new life, swung at O'Dell's next pitch and sent it over the fence in left-center to tie a contest the Tribe would win in the 10th. Lane jumped out of his seat, yelling, "That's my boy! I signed Porter to his first contract!" Hatter was amused: "But Frank, you said Porter would strike out." Said Lane: "He did. But the damn ump wouldn't call it."[18]

The homer did not guarantee Porter a permanent job in Cleveland. Late in the season, Porter was sitting in the lobby of the team hotel, adding some material to a diary he had been keeping. Lane walked up and asked, "What are you writing?" Porter replied, "I'm writing a book." Lane's reaction was priceless: "Well, put this in your book: You just got traded." The deal wasn't officially announced until after the season, but J.W. Porter indeed was on the move again, this time to Washington for infielder Ossie Alvarez.[19]

As the June 15th trading deadline drew closer, Lane was on the phone constantly, trying to drum up some major activity. One proposal, involving the A's, reportedly was on the table. In this one, Colavito was to go to Kansas City for six players: Vic Power, Hector Lopez, Woodie Held, Bill Tuttle, pitcher Duke Maas and rookie outfielder Dave Melton. The A's finally said no, although the weeks of talks between Lane and A's GM Parke Carroll at least provided momentum for two deals that actually were completed by the two clubs. Kansas City was also asking about Maris, who wasn't playing much for Bragan. The Tribe manager believed Maris was wall-shy on the field and surly off of it.

After sifting thru all sorts of offers and counter-offers, Lane first traded his once-prized acquisition, Chico Carrasquel — heavier and slower than he was during the "Go-Go" days in Chicago — to Kansas City for another short-stop, Billy Hunter. Then, on June 15, he turned to K.C. again and sent Maris, Preston Ward and left-hander Dick Tomanek to K.C. for Power and Held. Finally, with Bragan and scout Red Kress listening in on the phone line as witnesses, Lane asked Carroll to wait at least a little while before the Athletics did what they generally did with all their good-looking young players: trade them to the Yankees. "I'm not kidding myself," Lane told Carroll. "I know that if this guy [Maris] turns out to be any good, he'll wind up with the Yankees. But you've got to give me your word that you won't make the deal before midnight tonight."[20] Carroll granted Lane's request, and it would be fully 18 months before Maris was traded to New York.

Meanwhile, the pursuit of Lopez, a Panamanian with a terrific bat but troubled glove, was to continue until his trade to the Yankees on May 20,

1959. At the Indians' '59 season-opener in Kansas City, Lopez homered but was roundly booed for having committed two errors at second base that led to two runs, the margin of victory in the Tribe's triumph. Said Lane: "Now's the time to go get Hector Lopez. They may give him to me for nothing."[21]

The 1958 Tribe certainly could have used Lopez. The club was 29–30 at the trading deadline, but, after Lane's deals, they dropped six of eight, and that sealed the fate of Bobby Bragan. The last two losses were at home to Boston. In the first one, Power went 4-for-4 with a homer and three RBIs, and the Indians led 3–1 in the seventh. But then Hoyt Wilhelm, whom Lane had sold to Cleveland when he was running the Cardinals in '57 because he had grown weary of all the strange things that happen when a knuckleballer is on the mound, threw a flutterball that eluded catcher Dick Brown, enabling a run to score. It was still 3–2 in the ninth, when Wilhelm allowed a walk and single and then hit Frank Malzone with a knuckler to load the bases. For Lane, this was a flashback to 1957. As he seethed, Jackie Jensen lifted a sacrifice fly to Colavito in right, tying the score. With the go-ahead run at third, Wilhelm fanned Dick Gernert for the second out, but Power, a Gold Glove first baseman, booted Lou Berberet's grounder and the Red Sox were up, 4–3. That was the final score.

The next afternoon, McLish and Boston's Ike Delock battled pitch-for-pitch through eight innings of a 1–1 thriller. Ted Williams led off the top of the ninth with a home run, and the Tribe came to bat in the home ninth trailing 2–1. The Indians did not exactly rally. Colavito struck out, as did Doby, in a pinch-hitting role. When Woodie Held popped to right to end it, Lane decided Bragan's time had come. He summoned the skipper to his office and told him, "Well, Bobby, I don't know how we'd ever get along without you, but starting tomorrow, we're gonna try."[22]

In from Sacramento came former Indians second baseman Joe Gordon, and though the Indians finished just 77–76 and in fourth place, they were 46–40 under Gordon's leadership. Most important of all, he was Lane's guy, unlike Bragan. As a result, Lane was certain the entire Cleveland baseball situation would be better, far better, the next season. The Indians continued to run hot and cold in the second half, taking 11 of 13 from July 27 through August 10 and then turning right around and losing 11 of 13. The surge of victories was highlighted by a seven-game winning streak during which Tribe pitchers gave up only 14 runs. For starters, McLish, age 33, and "Mudcat" Grant, age 23, whipped the Yankees by identical scores of 7–2 before 39,170 at the lakefront on July 27 as Colavito hit a two-run homer in the opener and a grand slam off 1958 Cy Young award winner Bob Turley in the second game. Baltimore fell twice, 21-year-old Gary Bell topping 19-year-old Milt Pappas 9–4 in the series opener, and then came 7–1, 3–1 and 4–1 decisions registered in that order by McLish, Hal Woodeshick and Grant over the Ted Willams–Jackie Jensen Red Sox.

At the beginning of September, though, the Indians were still six under .500 (62–68), attendance was down from even the weak 1957 levels (the Tribe had drawn 722,256 in '57; the '58 total would be 663,805) and people were wondering if Frank Lane's rebuilding magic was a thing of the past. The Tribe, however, began the month by sweeping a Labor Day twin bill in Chicago (Minoso launched a three-run homer off Billy Pierce in the first inning of the first game to get the ball rolling) and went 15–8 for the month.

Before the season was over, Lane, for the second straight year, had rid himself of Hoyt Wilhelm, putting him on waivers in late August, when Baltimore picked him up. "Dr. Wilhelm and His Dancing Medicine Show," in the words of Chicago broadcaster Bob Elson, went on to have some sensational years for the Orioles and especially the White Sox, for whom he was nearly unhittable. He also was helped by a Paul Richards innovation, an extra-large and much more flexible catcher's glove, made solely to handle knuckleballs. But Lane didn't have that benefit in 1957 and '58, when he continually complained about "damn knuckleball pitchers." The problem with the pitch was that no one, not even Wilhelm, knew where it was going. "The best way to catch a knuckleball," Bob Uecker used to say, "is to wait until the ball stops rolling and then pick it up."[23] *Los Angeles Times* columnist Jim Murray put it this way: "Part of the trouble with a knuckleball is that it approaches the plate like a kid on his way to a bath."[24]

While there is no doubt that Frank Lane's decisions on Wilhelm were sadly misguided, his choice of Gordon over Bragan was the correct move. Gordon's presence, coincidentally or not, had a positive effect on both Minoso and Colavito. Minnie had gotten off to a rather uninspiring start in '58, a fact he later partially blamed on the big winter trade with the White Sox. "I felt like the whole world was over for me," Minoso said. "Like my city—you know it's my city [Chicago] because I still live here—had put me out.... I never believed it, that I was traded. But it was true."[25] Minoso was batting only .268 by Memorial Day, his worst start since 1955 in Chicago. Eventually he snapped out of his malaise and hit safely in 20 of 22 games from August 2 through August 24, going 33-for-86 (.384) to finally reach the .300 mark for the season. At year's end, he had a career-high 24 home runs plus 80 RBIs, a .302 batting average and .388 on-base percentage.

Colavito was another big gun who responded well to the managerial change. Seemingly more relaxed under Gordon, Rocky hit 31 of his 41 home runs after July 4. He finished with a .303 batting mark and a .405 on-base percentage and topped the league with a .620 slugging average. He drove in 113 runs and, though he fanned 89 times—not bad at all for a slugger—he

Before they begin their traditionally acerbic contract negotiations during the winter of 1959–60, Cleveland Indians GM Frank Lane and his star outfielder, American League home run champion Rocky Colavito, share a rare light moment. Lane, looking ready for the opening punch, delivered the big blow several weeks later when he traded Colavito to Detroit for the league's batting champion, Harvey Kuenn (courtesy Corbis-Bettmann).

also drew 84 walks. Even when his power output was down earlier in the season, he hit safely in 22 of 23 games (May 27 through June 17), during which he was 34-for-88 (.386) with eight homers and 20 runs driven in.

But Colavito, no matter which club or general manager he was playing for during his career, was always involved in a fight over salary. His first encounter with Lane was the off-season Frank arrived in Cleveland. Colavito in 1957 had belted 25 homers and driven in 84 runs but had batted just .252; in 30-some fewer games as a '56 rookie, he had recorded 21 home runs, 65 RBIs and a .276 batting average. Still he demanded a $3,000 increase, while Lane held fast at a raise of $1,500. The two went back and forth for weeks, neither budging. Finally, Lane, according to Rocky, told him to take the $1,500 right then and that Frank would give him the other $1,500 if he played well during the '58 season. Colavito agreed. So, in September, with "the Rock" rolling toward his best year, he reminded Lane about the money he still had coming. "Lane acted like he didn't have any idea of what I was talking about. He said he never promised me the other $1,500. I called him a no-good liar.

He lied to me and he knew it, and I lost all respect for him at that moment."[26] Contract disputes between the two men became an annual ritual. Bob Kennedy, a Lane aide at the time, remembered that "Frank would be hollering and swearing on the phone ... hollering like blue blazes, and you could hear him out in the office. And I know that all Rocky was saying on the other end was, 'No.' He wouldn't argue with Frank. He'd just say no, and I think that made Frank 10 times madder."[27]

Colavito's April 1960 trade to Detroit, by the way, did not end his squabbles over money. Tigers general manager Jim Campbell recalled one dispute that ended up being the first time one of his Detroit players had held out and missed the start of spring training. At last, Rocky came into Campbell's office in Lakeland, Florida, "and I had the contract right in my desk, because I wasn't going to budge off it. He said, 'Where is it? Where is it?' I said, 'You want the contract?' He said, 'You're not going to change it, are you?' 'Nope,' I said. He said, 'Give it to me.' He took it and signed it. He threw it down on the desk and started out the door." As Rocky was going out, Campbell remembered that Colavito told him, "You're at the top of the totem pole." And then, Campbell said, "He went out and he slammed the door. I thought the building would come down. But it wasn't done shaking when the door flies open again. And Rocky said, 'I want to add something to what I told you. Frank Lane is still No. 1, but you're No. 2.' I used to tell that to Frank, and he'd laugh like hell."[28]

7

Fighting Some Old
Friends for the Flag, 1959

Rocky Colavito was still a member of the Cleveland Indians in the winter of 1958–59, and trading him was not, for the time being, in Frank Lane's plans. Frank instead was determined to upgrade his team's scrappiness and intensity when the winter meetings convened in the national's capital. He had targeted Billy Martin for second base and Jimmy Piersall for center field. The first order of business was Martin. After several meetings with Tigers GM John McHale, Lane traded pitchers Ray Narleski and Don Mossi and infielder Ossie Alvarez to Detroit for Martin and pitcher Al Cicotte, another former Yankee.

"Martin was the man I wanted when I came to Cleveland a year ago," said Lane. "In fact, I tried to get him even before I hung up my hat. I don't want to overpublicize him because he's not a Mickey Mantle. He's simply a good, day-in, day-out player who can take charge of an infield." Before the Tribe and Tigers agreed on the deal, Lane had called manager Joe Gordon in Sacramento to seek his opinion. Said Lane: "I called Joe the other day and told him about the deal. He said, 'It's a good deal for us. Don't let the Tigers back out of it.'"[1]

The Red Sox were hotly pursuing Martin, as were Washington and Kansas City. "That's why I had to go high," Lane told reporters. "We needed him more than anyone else did, and so I thought we should pay more. He's better than anyone we had at second base last year." In '58, Martin, a second baseman by trade, had played out of position (at shortstop and third base) and had batted .255 for Detroit. He was like Ferris Fain, also a former Lane employee, in that he was not afraid to throw a punch or two. "The Indians have needed a leader. I don't mean simply a 'holler guy.' What we have needed is a hustling, scrappy player who will keep the others on their toes. That's the sort of player Martin is."[2]

Next on Lane's shopping list was Jimmy Piersall, Boston's Gold Glove center fielder. Almost 20 years after Lane landed him, he recalled the circumstances under which the trade went down: "Once you get it in print, then

92

you're OK. Like when I got Piersall from the Red Sox. Not that they didn't want to give him up, but they wouldn't have given him up for what I was offering." Lane offered Vic Wertz, who had broken his leg in spring training and batted only 43 times in 1958, plus skinny outfielder Gary Geiger, a fielding whiz who hit just .231 in 91 games for the Tribe as a rookie in '58. Red Sox owner Tom Yawkey spotted Lane in the lobby of the Statler Hilton, talking to *Cleveland Plain Dealer* sports editor Gordon Cobbledick and *Plain Dealer* beat writer Harry Jones. Yawkey hollered: "You wanna make a deal? We'll make a deal. Come up to my suite." "Yawkey," Lane said, "had always been after me to come and be his general manager, but most of the time he [spent enjoying adult beverages]." When they got to the suite there was no concern on Yawkey's part that Boston GM Joe Cronin was nowhere to be seen. "Tom," said Lane, "what about Cronin?" That served to annoy the Boston boss. "Bleep Cronin!" he said. "Where is my general manager, anyway? I've got a 7-or 8-million-dollar tab against this club, and all I do is keep advancing Cronin money. He assured me the other day he was gonna get Billy Martin, and I pick up the paper and you got him. Someone else we wanted, and you got him too. I told him, 'That goddamn Lane doesn't have two quarters to rub together, and all I get from you is conversation while Lane gets the ballplayers.'"

So if Yawkey was going to play GM, Lane figured he might as well talk deal, Cronin or no Cronin. Lane and Yawkey sat down, and the Boston owner asked, "OK, who do you want?" Lane picked up the conversation from there.

"'I want Piersall, your center fielder.' 'Who you gonna give me?' 'I'll give you Vic Wertz, who's a hell of a hitter, and Gary Geiger, a goddamn good little defensive center fielder who'll hit .250, .260 for you.' He comes over, sticks out his hand and says, 'It's a deal.' "'But I don't want to go over Cronin's head.'

"'You're not going over *my* head.'

"'Well, if you want to renege...'

"'Renege, nothing! It's a deal.'

"So I put in a call to our PR guy, Nate Wallack, and I couldn't locate the son of a bitch. I wanted him to break it, get it into print. I was anxious to make the goddamn deal. I always liked Piersall. Exciting son of a bitch. A little wacky, but a real good ballplayer.

"Now, in the meantime, Cronin and [Red Sox manager] Pinky Higgins come in, and Yawkey says, 'Pinky, I just made a deal. If it's a good deal, you made it. If it's a bad deal, I made it.' And Cronin says, 'But Tom, we'd agreed we wouldn't make any deals after 6 o'clock.' Because that's apparently when Tom usually would start drinking.

"So Yawkey gets mad at Cronin: 'Are you implying that I don't know what the hell I'm doing?' So then Higgins says, 'Well, Tom, tell me: What was the deal you made?'

"And just then the phone rings, and it was Nate Wallack. I said, 'Yes, Nate, you release it. We just traded Vic Wertz and Gary Geiger for Jimmy Piersall.' Cronin was madder than a son of a bitch. But it wasn't my fault he wasn't there when the deal was being discussed. I was on the job and Cronin wasn't."[3]

Lane even worked on the off-season banquet circuit. In January 1959, he showed up, without a ticket, at the annual Chicago Baseball Writers' Association dinner at the Palmer House. Cubs GM John Holland made room for Frank at his table, and they wound up working out a four-man deal: Earl Averill, Jr., and former White Sox/Cardinals lefty Morrie Martin to the Cubs for outfielder Jim Bolger (Cincinnati native Lane always had a soft spot for Cincinnati kids) and pitcher Johnny Briggs. Averill had hit .347 for San Diego in '58 and was named MVP of the Pacific Coast League.

Then came a deal with Detroit, one that most Tribe fans later called the best Lane ever made in Cleveland. To Detroit went the rapidly fading Larry Doby, 34, who had always hit well in Briggs Stadium. To Cleveland came young left-handed-hitting outfielder Tito Francona, highly regarded as a Baltimore rookie in 1956 but a disappointment the last two seasons with the Orioles, White Sox and Tigers. "That turned out sensationally," said Lane, years later, "but that was a shot in the dark. I would've traded Doby for a dozen bats."[4] Francona started the season tearing it up in a pinch-hitting role, getting three hits in his first four tries, including a two-out, three-run walk-off homer on May 1 to stun the Yankees 4–2 in the 10th before a Friday night turnout of 36,682. He did not start a game until June 2, and then he promptly went on a 17-for-41 (.415) roll to win a regular job. Playing first base and center field, he finished the season with 20 home runs and 79 RBIs and a remarkable .363 batting average. That mark was 10 points higher than that of batting champion Harvey Kuenn, but Francona did not have enough plate appearances to qualify.

Lane, meanwhile, had a game of musical chairs going on at third base during the season's first couple of months. Such old National League favorites as "Handsome Ransom" Jackson, the former Cub, plus former Phillies Granny Hamner and Willie Jones patrolled the position for various stretches, as did veteran Tribesman George Strickland and youngster Gene Leek. In May, Lane landed Jim Baxes, a 31-year-old rookie, from the Dodgers' Spokane farm club. Though Baxes could hit for some power (28 homers at Spokane in '58), his defense left a bit to be desired. Yet the lack of a polished regular third baseman didn't prevent the 1959 Indians from staying at the top of the American League. They opened the season winning six straight, lost one and then won four more in a row. Just like that, Cleveland was off to a 10–1 start.

Among those 10 wins were three at Detroit on April 21–23 over the

Tigers, expected to be top contenders in '59. The scores were 14–1, 10–1 and 10–4. In the opener, the top third of the batting order did the damage: Jimmy Piersall was 3-for-5, Vic Power went 3-for-6 with four RBIs and a home run, and Minnie Minoso was 5-for-6 with two homers and six runs driven across. In the middle game, Piersall led the way with a single, home run and four RBIs and, in the finale, Billy Martin blasted a three-run homer off Jim Bunning to get the Indians rolling. Chicago, which also had started well, arrived for a four-game weekend series and, after dropping the Friday night game, won the next three to cool off the Tribe. Because of inclement weather, the Indians did not play again until Friday, the night Francona delivered his game-winning homer against the Yankees. On Saturday, Herb Score struck out 13 Yankees and beat them 5–2 as Power, Martin and Rocky Colavito all homered. The next weekend, though, included four more meetings with the White Sox, who after dropping the first game won the next three, Billy Pierce and Early Wynn getting the wins at the Mother's Day doubleheader on Sunday, May 10. Wynn's record against Cleveland since Lane traded him to Chicago was now 6–0. That had to be disturbing to Lane and Joe Gordon, given the realization that: (a) there were six more series with the White Sox remaining, (b) they would surely face Wynn several more times, and (c) the Indians, thus far, were just 2–6 in competition with Chicago.

The Indians responded by winning seven of the next nine, including a May 22nd gem by Gary Bell, who fired a four-hitter to blank Detroit, 1–0, Minoso driving in the lone run with a two-out double in the seventh. The triumph improved the Tribe's record to 22–11 and left the Indians in first place by a half-game over Chicago. The Yankees? The perennial champs were in last place, 9½ back, at 12–20. But then the Indians' inconsistency of 1958 returned, and Cleveland dropped seven straight and 11 of 13. Toward the end of the skid, a rough weekend (June 5–7) against the visiting Yankees came just when the Indians were starting to get the turnstiles turning. On Friday night, the Yankees—having traded once again with Kansas City to add Hector Lopez and pitcher Ralph Terry, much to Frank Lane's chagrin—routed Bell 11–2 before 51,935. Bob Turley outdueled Don Ferrarese 2–1 on Saturday and McLish dropped his third straight decision in a 4–3 second game defeat on Sunday. Score recorded the only Tribe victory of the weekend, winning 7–5 on Tito Francona's three-run homer in the seventh inning of the Sunday opener in front of 59,823. Cleveland had fallen to third in the standings behind Chicago and Baltimore.

The trade deadline was now a week away. Frank Lane had already made a number of minor moves since the season began. He had traded for catcher Ed FitzGerald, sent veteran first baseman Mickey Vernon to the Braves for young right-hander Humberto Robinson, turned around and sent Robinson to the Phillies for Granny Hamner, shipped Randy Jackson back to the Cubs for pitcher Bob "Riverboat" Smith and, just the previous Saturday, had dealt outfielder Jim Bolger to the Phils for Willie Jones. Soon he was to add an old personal favorite, outfielder/pinch-hitter deluxe Elmer Valo, from the Pacific Coast League. He liked the club as it stood, but Lane believed if there was one more move to make, better to make it than hesitate and lose an opportunity. So talks with the White Sox and other teams now resumed.

Among Cleveland fans, the talk the week before the June 15 deadline was more about what had transpired on the field than what the trade-makers were discussing off of it. In particular, fans were talking about Rocky Colavito's big evening in Baltimore on June 10. In the first inning, facing Jerry Walker, Colavito drew a walk and scored on Minnie Minoso's three-run homer. In the third, he homered to drive in Vic Power and increase the Tribe lead to 6–3. The blast also served to knock out Walker, who was replaced by Arnie Portocarrero. In the fifth, with one out, Colavito hit second homer of the night, this off Portocarrero, making the score 7–3. In the sixth, with a run in, two out and Francona aboard, Colavito clouted another one, and now the Tribe led, 10–3. The lead was down to 10–7 when Rocky came to bat in the ninth against Ernie Johnson, the ex–Milwaukee Braves reliever. Colavito swung at an inside fastball and away it went, a 400-foot-plus shot, this one landing in the bleachers in left to clinch an 11–8 victory, the first of seven consecutive Indian wins. The Baltimore crowd arose to pay homage to a slugger who had just become the eighth player in major-league history to hit four home runs in a single game and only the third to hit four straight. Most remarkable is that Colavito performed his feat in Memorial Stadium, which, with its high walls and distant power alleys, annually ranked among the most difficult parks in which to hit home runs. "I think the only park harder to hit it out of," said Lane, "was Yosemite."[5]

Meanwhile, on the trade-rumor front, White Sox president Bill Veeck, through Sox VP Hank Greenberg, reportedly had offered 25-year-old right-hander Bob Shaw, third baseman Bubba Phillips and rookie catcher Johnny Romano to Cleveland for Minoso, McLish and Baxes. McLish had not won since May 12. As of June 12, Lane had not turned down the offer but had feigned a lack of interest. "Sure, Bill and Hank can have Minnie, but not for nothing. This isn't Christmas."[6] Lane did not accompany the Tribe to Washington, choosing instead to stay in Baltimore, where the Sox were playing that weekend (June 12–14). As it happened, it seemed like every time Minoso stepped into the batter's box that weekend, the price for him went up a little more. Minnie clobbered a grand slam and ended up with nine RBIs in the June 14th doubleheader at Washington. The next afternoon, he homered with two men on in the fourth inning at Boston to snap a 1–1 tie; the Tribe went on to win 5–1 and moved into first place. That night, the deadline came and went, with no action taken by Cleveland, Chicago or New York. Lane said he never seriously considered trading Minnie to the White Sox. "I'm glad he's still on our side." Did the nine–RBI afternoon have anything to do with Lane's rejecting the Chicago offer? "That had nothing to do with it. I had made up my mind long before the doubleheader in Washington that we wouldn't trade him without getting plenty in return." He also said the Yankees had made a last-second bid for Woodie Held, an offer that was flatly rejected. "I'm satisfied with the club we have," said Lane, who then added a statement that was at odds with his reputation: "I wasn't going to make a deal just to make a deal."[7]

As the season progressed, the Indians and White Sox discovered they could conduct a pulsating American League pennant race just fine without the inclusion of the Yankees. The New Yorkers, though, served as valuable opponents. Without slugging first baseman Bill Skowron, lost for the season in July because of a broken wrist, the Yankees still provided tough competition for two teams that, in the past, had not always played their best baseball against the perennial champs. Chicago exuded increased confidence as July arrived, due in no small part to having just won three of four from New York at Comiskey Park and improving to 6–5 versus the Yankees. The Indians, too, carried a winning record (6–5) against New York as the race moved into July. Each team's matchups with New York would provide almost as many thrills as the Cleveland-Chicago meetings. Several were to be played in July, a month in which Cleveland was 19–12 (an excellent .613 clip) and yet went from two games ahead of the White Sox at month's beginning to one game back at month's end, all because the Chicagoans went 20–7 (a remarkable .741).

The Indians dropped three in a row July 14–16 at Yankee Stadium, enabling the White Sox to take a one-game lead. In the series opener, a crowd of 32,210 watched Whitey Ford outduel Herb Score, 1–0. Rain forced postponement of Wednesday's game, forcing a doubleheader on Thursday. Some 38,674 fans turned out that afternoon, along with *Sports Illustrated* writer Walter Bingham, who spent the first game sitting next to Frank Lane in the box seats adjacent to the Cleveland dugout. Bingham got himself plenty of Lane nuggets as the game moved along. Jim Baxes, a third baseman by trade but playing second because Joe Gordon had soured on Billy Martin, came in for special treatment from the GM. On one occasion, Baxes lollipopped a relay throw on what should have been a double play. "Did you see that? A sure double play and he screwed it up. That was a Spokane play." Later, Tony Kubek hit a chopper over pitcher Cal McLish's head. Baxes came in for it and fielded the ball but could manage only a soft throw that Kubek beat out. Lane: "It's not his fault. He tries. He's just not a second baseman. He's too big. Billy

Martin makes that play." In the fifth, with the bases filled, Kubek grounded to Baxes' left. Jim whirled and fired the ball in the general direction of short-stop Woodie Held. The ball sailed into left field and the tying and go-ahead runs crossed the plate. Lane, shouting, after the third out: "That's a crime! We gave them seven outs that inning." The Tribe failed to score in the sixth and seventh, and New York still led, 4–3. Lane's concession speech was brief: "It's over. We lose."

But there was more baseball to be played, of course. A new Cleveland pitcher was making his way in from the faraway bullpen. Lane could only hazard a guess as to the reliever's identity. "Looks like [Bob "Riverboat"] Smith," he said. Then came the public-address announcement that lefty Don Ferrarese, who had made only one appearance since mid–June, was taking over the pitching duties. "Ferrarese?" Lane said. "He hasn't pitched in so long, I forgot we had him." Ferrarese did the job, but his successor, Gary Bell, did not. He got through the eighth but, with the Indians up 5–4 in the ninth, the young right-hander prepared to face Yogi Berra, Hector Lopez and Hank Bauer. Said Lane: "Here comes Berra. Here it comes now. One swing. Watch." Sure enough, Berra hit Bell's first pitch, a fastball, deep into the right-field stands to tie the game. Lane was silent for a couple minutes, then said, "See? I told you. Now it's over. Stupid, just stupid. Bell cost us the game. We're through. We're just getting exercise until they win it."[8] That came about in the 11th inning when, with two out, Mickey Mantle, with Bobby Richardson aboard, launched a Bell delivery well over the right-field fence for a 7–5 New York triumph. Lane was silent. But he stuck around for the second game, which the Yankees won, 4–0, getting home runs from grand old men Bauer and Enos Slaughter and four-hit pitching from Bobby Shantz.

The story was different a week later in Cleveland. McLish (now 12–3) threw a three-hitter and beat Shantz 5–1 in the series opener before 46,912 on July 21. In the sixth, Power singled, Minoso doubled him home and then scored ahead of Francona's homer to snap a 0–0 tie. Some 42,747 turned out the next night, when Hector Lopez collected a homer and two singles as New York pounded Herb Score and won, 8–5. In Thursday night's finale, in front of 50,766, the Yankees led 4–0 in the last of the sixth when the Tribe scored seven runs, four on Minoso's two-out grand slam off Eli Grba, and went on to win, 8–5. Cleveland was a half-game behind Chicago, with third-place Baltimore six back and fourth-place New York seven behind.

The Yankees returned to Cleveland on August 25, with the Tribe having won six straight and having received a boost from Lane's lone post-deadline acquisition, left-hander Jack Harshman. The former White Sox pitcher, 12–15 and 2.89 in '58 with Baltimore, had struggled with the Orioles and Red Sox in 1959, but once he went to work for Lane, his old boss, he regained his effectiveness (3–0, 1.69 in his first five games after Lane picked him up on July 30). But Lane's hottest hurler was the wondrously named Calvin Coolidge Julius Caesar Tuskahoma McLish, who improved to 16–6 when the Tribe blitzed the New Yorkers, 6–3, with 36,143 on hand. The game was all but decided in the first inning, when Vic Power led off with his 10th home run, Minoso and Francona walked and Colavito crushed a three-run homer, his 36th of the season. In the fifth, Francona's sacrifice fly and Colavito's 37th homer made the score 6–1. The next evening, 31,800 showed up and the Indians sent them home happy as Colavito unloaded on the usually unhittable smokeballer Ryne Duren, hitting home run number 38 to unknot a 4–4 eighth-inning tie and giving Cleveland its eighth straight triumph, a 5–4 victory. (Rocky ended the season with 42, tying Washington's Harmon Killebrew for the AL home run title.)

Now came the season's biggest series, a four-game weekend matchup at the gigantic stadium on the lakefront that began on August 28. The Indians, by winning eight in a row, had sliced the Chicago lead from 4½ to 1½ games. Emotions were mixed: "I didn't want to be beaten, but if I was gonna be beaten, I'd rather be beaten by the guys I'd left in Chicago: Billy Pierce, Nellie Fox, Sherm Lollar, Jim Rivera ..."[9] Crowds were huge: 70,398 on Friday night, 50,290 (including Ladies' Day guests) on Saturday and 66,586 for Sunday's doubleheader. The stakes were just as high: If Gordon's men could take three of four, the American League would have a new leader come Monday.

The White Sox had other ideas. After Harshman and Bob Shaw battled through six innings tied 3–3 Friday night, the Sox won 7–3 when Lollar lofted a flyball to deep left with two on in the seventh. Minoso went back to the wire fence, jumped and had the ball bounce out of his glove and over the fence for a home run. Almost 20 years later, Lane smiled at the recollection. "Minnie couldn't wait for the ball to come down. He jumped up to catch the ball and knocked it over the fence. And I can still see Minnie, on his hands and knees, trying to reach through the wire fence, trying to get at the baseball. And as badly as I felt about it, I couldn't keep from laughing."[10]

Dick Donovan, like Lollar a Lane acquisition from the Chicago days, took control of the situation on Saturday when he subbed for scheduled starter Ken McBride, a rookie from Cleveland who had developed a case of tonsillitis. "Tricky Dick," who was to win 20 games for the 1962 Indians, went out and blanked the Tribe, 2–0. Now Chicago led by 3½ games. Clearly Cleveland could use a Sunday sweep. But Early Wynn, traded to Chicago in Lane's first deal as Tribe GM, hit a home run in the opening game and won 6–3, improving his 1958–59 record against the Indians to 8–1. Finally, 22-year-old right-hander Barry Latman, a Lane era signee back in 1955 out of the University of Southern California and a future Cleveland Indian, downed the Tribe 9–4 in the finale. The Chicago lead was 5½ games, and even though the Indians rebounded the following weekend in Chicago to win two of three, the issue was all but decided.

Lane truly believed the Indians should have been on top. And he wasn't alone. Said Jimmy Piersall, decades later: "Gordon did everything he possibly could to make us lose that championship that year."[11] Lane was about to deal with Joe Gordon, but not before the Indians and White Sox met for the season's final time on September 22, before 54,293 at Cleveland. Chicago, ahead of the Tribe by 3½ games with five to play, led 4–2 in the ninth when the Indians suddenly came alive against Shaw, who had relieved starter Early Wynn. With one out came an infield hit by Jim Baxes, who was batting because Gordon's lefty-swinging pinch-hitters, Elmer Valo and Chuck Tanner, had already been used. Next, Harshman, who had pitched the eighth and ninth innings, batted for himself and singled to right. Piersall, already with two hits on the night, lashed a hot grounder off the glove of second baseman Nellie Fox that went for an infield hit. The bases were filled, the place was rocking and Al Lopez, Chicago manager, was calling in Gerry Staley, the sinkerball specialist, to face Vic Power, batting a solid .291. Power swung at the first pitch and grounded the ball sharply to shortstop Luis Aparicio, who stepped on second and relayed to first baseman Ted Kluszewski for a game-ending, pennant-clinching double play.

Immediately after the game, Lane called a press conference and announced that Gordon, had been fired and that pitching coach Mel Harder would manage the remaining four games. It seemed rather harsh punishment for a manager whose team drew 1,497,976 fans at home, an increase of better than 830,000 over the 1958 total. "I've got to apologize to Bobby Bragan," Lane had said earlier in the season. "When I fired him last year, I told him he was the worst manager in baseball. Now I've got to tell him he's only the second-worst."[12]

Rumors now swirled that Lane was in discussions with Leo Durocher on a 1960 contract, but the next afternoon, when Lane called a press conference to name his new manager, Leo was nowhere to be seen. Instead, Lane announced. "I have decided that the best man to succeed Joe Gordon is Joe Gordon."[13] A few years later, Lane told the *Chicago Tribune*'s Ed Prell that Durocher missed a chance for a contract that would have paid Leo more than $100,000 per year. "When Durocher was indecisive, I decided to keep Gordon," Lane said. "Leo finally called back, and I told him of my decision. I'll say this: Leo proved he was a big leaguer when he told me: 'Gordon's a good man. I blew the job.'"[14] Lane also stated that Gordon would get a two-year contract with a raise of $10,000 per season.[15] That was not good news for Jimmy Piersall or Billy Martin, whose playing time had shrunk considerably with Gordon at the helm. However, "after the last game, on our stools by our lockers, Lane had put a new contract, with a raise," Piersall recalled. "Because, he told us, Billy and I never quit, despite what was going on between us and Gordon. It was just fascinating."[16]

The 1960 season promised to be fascinating. Indeed it turned out to be just that — but not in a positive sense. Minnie Minoso, Cal McLish and Billy Martin, among others, would be gone before the calendar turned to 1960. And then, by Opening Day, gone too would be Herb Score and, incredibly, Rocco Domenico Colavito.

8

No More Rocky,
No More Frank, 1960

December soon arrived and, with it, baseball's winter meetings. The Minnie Minoso trade talks, broken off in mid–June, now resumed in Florida. Manager Joe Gordon, the Indians' point man on trades until Frank Lane arrived in Miami Beach, proposed a deal to White Sox manager Al Lopez and vice president Hank Greenberg: Minoso, Herb Score and catcher Dick Brown for lefty Billy Pierce, catcher Sherm Lollar and third baseman Bubba Phillips. Greenberg asked for catcher Russ Nixon instead of Brown; Gordon in turn requested that either of two veteran reserves, Earl Torgeson or Jim Rivera, be included in the trade. When Lane arrived, he offered Minoso and three second-line players for Phillips and catcher John Romano, who as a rookie had hit .294 for Chicago and led the league in pinch-hitting (8-for-13, .615 average). Gordon's reaction: "I like Romano and Phillips, but not at the expense of Minoso."[1] Gordon clearly wanted Lollar in the deal.

Veeck finally flew in to Miami Beach on December 5, and the opinion among the media was that a White Sox deal with Cleveland was just hours away. First, though, Lane expressed disappointment that the Phillies had traded shortstop Chico Fernandez, one-time Dodger prospect, to Detroit in a five-player deal that afternoon. Frank thought he had made a decent offer for the Cuban gloveman, whose presence would have enabled Woodie Held to switch from short to third base. "Now that Fernandez is no longer available," Lane said, "it looks as if we'll have to get a third baseman. There aren't many shortstops around."[2]

Then he and Veeck went off for four hours of talks that yielded nothing, save for the basic premise that any deal finalized would have Minoso going to Chicago for Phillips and, in most likelihood, Romano. This being Frank Lane and Bill Veeck, however, all present knew that this could not possibly be just a three-player trade. When the two old friends announced the trade the next evening, it included seven players in all. Chicago sent Phillips, Romano and first baseman Norm Cash to the Tribe for Minoso, Brown and left-handed pitchers Don Ferrarese and Jake Striker, a rookie. Like Romano,

Cash, the White Sox's Opening Day first baseman in '59 as a rookie, had been signed by Lane during the latter's Chicago years. Though Cash had failed to keep the starting job, he was only 25 and still highly regarded. Lane was delighted with the deal, except for the loss of Minoso.

"I hated to let them have Minoso," Lane told reporters. "You know how fond I've been of him. He calls me Papa Number 2, and to me there isn't a player in baseball who plays harder than Minnie. But we need a third baseman in the worst way, and Phillips can plug that hole for us. He's a good, hustling ballplayer and I've been trying to get him since last June. What held up the deal was Romano. The White Sox didn't want to let him go because he has a chance to be a real good catcher. But we insisted on Romano being in the deal, and when they started mentioning other names, we also wanted Cash, who can play both first base and the outfield and is a real good prospect."[3]

With Minoso gone, Tito Francona was to become the full-time left fielder, with Piersall in center field (when Gordon wasn't angry with him) and Colavito in right. At the corners, Vic Power was set at first base and Phillips likewise at third. Held was the shortstop, with Romano and Nixon sharing duties behind the plate. The problem was second base: Gordon simply did not want Billy Martin around, despite Lane's admiration for him. ("Gordon hated my guts," Piersall said, years later, "but he hated Billy more.")[4] Another '59 Tribe second baseman, Jim Baxes, had proved he could hit the occasional long ball; he also had proved that he was not a major-league second baseman. Facing That being the case, Lane set out to acquire a top-level performer to fill the position. He ran into Cincinnati Reds general manager Gabe Paul, to whom he offered both Martin and 19-game winner Cal McLish for NL All-Star second baseman Johnny Temple. During the past season, Temple had batted .311 with eight home runs and 60 RBIs, an excellent total for a leadoff man. Paul said he'd think it over. A few hours later, he told Lane he wanted Indians rookie Dick Stigman, a good-looking left-hander, in the deal too. But Lane was thinking of using Stigman as part of a deal that would also send McLish and infielder Ray Webster to Washington for pitchers Pedro Ramos and Russ Kemmerer. In the meantime, Lane had offered Martin and another player to his former assistant at St. Louis, the Cardinals' Bing Devine, in a bid for second baseman Don Blasingame. Devine said no. Nothing seemed to be working according to plan.

The next day, after turning down a Boston bid of catcher Sammy White and outfielder Marty Keough for newcomer Romano, Lane was startled to hear that Veeck had pulled off a surprise deal that was the talk of the meetings. Chicago, filling its need for a third baseman, had landed Gene Freese, 25, from the Phillies in exchange for top prospect Johnny Callison, 20, who had opened the '59 season as Al Lopez's starting left fielder but ended up spending most of the season at Triple-A Indianapolis. Whereas Callison had batted .173 during his stay with the White Sox, Freese, after not clinching a starting job until June, had hit .268 in 1959 with 23 home runs and 70 runs driven in. Four of his homers had been grand slams. His defense was questionable, but the strength of the Chicago defense was up the middle (Sherm Lollar behind the plate, Luis Aparicio and Nellie Fox in the middle infield and Jim Landis in center). A lesser fielder at one of the infield or outfield corners was a shortcoming that could be overcome. Lane seemed genuinely stunned by the trade. "The White Sox made a great deal," he said. "I never thought they could get Freese. In fact, [Phillies GM] John Quinn told me he wouldn't trade him. I figured they'd get a third baseman to replace Phillips, but I never dreamed they'd get someone like Freese."[5]

Next came more bad news for the Indians: Roger Maris, the fast-developing left-handed power hitter Lane had dealt to Kansas City on June 15, 1958, was heading to the Yankees in an eight-player transaction. This one was less of a surprise. Lane, after all, had made the A's promise back in June 1958 that they would not turn Maris over to the Yankees before the trade deadline, which had been just hours away. A year and a half later, the inevitable had happened.

Now the new interleague trading deadline of December 15 was closing in. Most club representatives had departed the meetings, including Gabe Paul, but Lane was not going to leave without a final attempt to land Johnny Temple. He did it, too, just beating the midnight deadline by sending the Reds Cal McLish, Billy Martin and 25-year-old minor-league first baseman Gordy Coleman, who had put up remarkable numbers at Double-A Mobile that season: a .355 batting average, 35 home runs and 125 RBIs. Lane revealed that he had made at least a dozen calls to Paul during the evening. Joked Lane: "The cost of the phone bill alone makes this a major trade."[6] Then he turned serious. "But when a team finishes second, as we did last season, it has to think in terms of the pennant. We were reluctant to give up McLish, but we're hoping some of our young pitchers can pick up the slack. Johnny Temples don't come along every day." The deal was also welcomed by Joe Gordon, who had used 12 different players in the leadoff spot in '59, and praised by White Sox president Bill Veeck: "Lane made a good deal. Temple is a solid player and a real competitor. Of course you can't give up a pitcher like McLish without hurting your team. I think the Indians strengthened themselves with Temple in the infield. I'm sure he'll help them quite a bit."[7]

McLish was not happy with the trade but was glad to have escaped Lane, who once responded thusly to a question as to whether or not McLish was part Native American. Said Lane: "I think he's part Irish, part Scotch and part Canadian Club."[8] "I should've known I was going to be to be traded somewhere," said the 34-year-old right-hander, who was 35–16 for Lane and the Tribe in 1958 and '59. "I never could please him. And I don't understand why. I hate to leave the American League, because I know the hitters so well. Cincinnati is a good club, but it's going to be tough to start all over again."[9] Martin was thrilled with the deal, because now he was free of Joe Gordon, who played Martin sparingly and considered him an undermining influence in the clubhouse. "I won't knock Joe the way he knocked me," said Billy. "All I can say is it'll be a pleasure to play for a real competitor over there (in manager Fred Hutchinson)." Said Gordon: "I'm not going to get into any verbal fisticuffs with Billy. At times he played good ball for us. He was hurt quite a bit. He's probably a better player than he looked last season."[10]

Lane then made one of his occasionally mistaken forecasts. He told reporters that the Temple deal had been finalized once the Reds agreed to take Coleman, the minor-league first baseman, instead of pitcher Bobby Locke. Intoned Lane: "I doubt that Coleman will ever be a big-league hitter. Our reports were that he wouldn't be ready next season and may never be able to hit breaking stuff."[11] Coleman got into only 66 big-league games in 1960 but in '61, when the Reds won the NL pennant, Coleman helped out in a big way by hitting .287 with 26 home runs and 87 RBIs.

When the spring-training camps opened in February, much attention again was focused on the American League's big three: the White Sox, the Indians and the Yankees, Everyone figured the New York attack would be stronger with the presence of Roger Maris, and the experts raved about the White Sox's powerful new lineup that now included Minnie Minoso and Gene Freese — plus World Series hero Ted Kluszewski and, in addition, slugger Roy Sievers, acquired from Washington on April 4. The prognosticators were not as certain about the Indians, whose lineup had lost some pop and dash with Minoso gone and whose starting rotation appeared far less formidable without McLish. Lane envisioned a solid catching staff of Romano and Nixon, a fine infield of Phillips, Held, Temple and Power, plus an excellent outfield of Francona, Piersall and Colavito. Yes, Colavito was still an Indian. But another rancorous contract negotiation with Lane once again had left both men upset with the other. This time, Rocky held out into March. And this time, Lane promised himself he would not go through another spring squabble with his star slugger. A majority of his phone calls that March were directed toward Lakeland, Florida, spring home of the Detroit Tigers, and their president, Bill DeWitt. The topic of discussion: the Tigers' top hitmaker, American League batting champion Harvey Kuenn.

Remembered Bob Kennedy, who along with Hoot Evers had become Lane's top confidants: "Frank came up to us and said he wanted to trade Colavito for Harvey Kuenn. And we said, 'Frank, you're gonna get killed if you do this.' But he wanted Kuenn as a leader. He was always on base. He was a steady .300 hitter, no matter who pitched. Frank thought he would be better for our club."[12] Lane and DeWitt talked for weeks, got nowhere and, in mid–March, announced jointly that there was nothing to the trade rumors. Then, on April 12, Lane called DeWitt to get reacquainted and also to make a seemingly minor deal: DeWitt gave infielder Steve Demeter to Lane in exchange for Norm Cash. This deal did not represent Lane's finest hour: Demeter went 0-for-5 in his "career" with Cleveland, while Cash hit 373 home runs for Detroit — and won the batting title in 1961 with a .361 average. More important at that time, though, was that Lane and DeWitt were again talking Colavito-Kuenn. In the end, the ball was in Lane's court. He went to dinner with Kennedy and Evers on the night of April 16 in Memphis, where the Indians were to play their final exhibition game the next day, Easter Sunday, against the White Sox.

"Hoot and I were still pretty much against the trade," Kennedy said. "Frank was giving us all the pros and cons.... He finally said, 'You guys sleep on it and let me know tomorrow.' So we didn't do much sleeping. We talked half the night."[13] Both men were well aware of Kuenn's abilities, but they also knew Kuenn could never replace Colavito in Cleveland as a rock-star type of attraction or as a power hitter, and that Lane had already traded away substantial power in the Minnie Minoso deal with Chicago. Also to consider was the age factor: Colavito was 26, Kuenn 29. "Finally," Kennedy recalled, "we just said, 'Well, Frank's going to do it anyway, so it won't make any difference.' So Hoot and I went to the ballpark. We gave him our reasons for not doing it but said, 'If you think it's that important to you, and if you really want to do it, just go ahead and do it.'"[14]

Lane did it, announcing the deal during that day's game, not too long after Rocky had hit his eighth homer of the spring. Back in Cleveland, fans were enraged, flooding newspapers and radio and TV stations with angry calls. Some people took to hanging Lane in effigy. There was at least one sighting of a coffin marked "FRANK LANE" being carried through the streets by Colavito backers. At the opener on Tuesday, April 19 — against Detroit, of course — hundreds in the crowd of 52,756 brought signs that made their feelings known. Even Bob Hope, then a minor investor in the Indians, was moved to comment: "I'm afraid to go to Cleveland. Frank Lane might trade me."[15]

"We knew there was going to be an explosion, no doubt about it," Bob Kennedy said later, "but Frank didn't care."[16] Lane tried to explain his reasoning. "I say we swapped a hamburger for a steak," he said. "Colavito will hit a home run every 14 at-bats. It's the other 13 at-bats that are frustrating. It's a home run or nothing with him ... and there was plenty of nothing." Lane noted that Colavito had struck out 86 times in 1959 to 36 for Kuenn.

"And [Kuenn] made 47 more base hits [than Rocky]. That means we elimi-nated 50 strikeouts and picked up that many more hits."[17] Joe Gordon liked the trade, but his players didn't share his enthusiasm for it. Said Jimmy Pier-sall, decades afterwards: "That wasn't a good trade. Kuenn did a good job for us, but Rocky was a local hero. But see, the year before that, Rocky had hit about 25 groundballs to third with a runner on third base and either none or one out. That kind of upset Lane. He didn't like that."[18] Jim "Mudcat" Grant repeated the question: "You want to know why Lane traded Rocky? That's easy. Lane was an idiot."[19]

Lane's new-look Indians dropped the opener to the Tigers, 4–2 in 15 innings. The marathon took 4 hours and 54 minutes, making it the longest opener in AL history. Colavito, who actually heard a few boos as the game moved along, had a day to forget, striking out four times en route to an 0-for-6 afternoon. Meanwhile, Kuenn went 2-for-7 but pulled a leg muscle late in the contest, a mishap that kept him out of the starting lineup for a week. All told he would miss 28 games that season, most of them in the closing weeks after he suffered a fractured ankle. When healthy, he batted .308, a far cry from the .353 he had posted in 1959. As for Colavito, he also experienced a bit of an "off" year: 35 homers, 87 RBIs, and a .249 batting average. It was rather obvious he missed Cleveland and Cleveland missed him.

Herb Score, too, missed his old roommate. But he was leaving, too. The annual "Meet the Tribe" luncheon had taken place on Monday, April 18, the day before the American League opener. Indians vice president Nate Dolin approached Herb and told him the White Sox, in particular manager Al Lopez, were interested in him. Would he want to be traded to Chicago? You'd better believe it. So Dolin, who owned 40 percent of the ballclub, strongly hinted that it would be in Lane's best interests to send Score to Chicago. Lane heeded the request, and soon Score was on his way to Comiskey Park in exchange for second-year right-hander Barry Latman, 8–5 as a rookie in '59.

Even with the injuries to Kuenn and to Johnny Temple — and some dis-tracting on-field behavior from Jimmy Piersall — the Tribe definitely played like a contender in the first half of the 1960 season. The highlight came on May 30, when the Indians, before 45,731 at Comiskey Park in Chicago, swept a Memorial Day doubleheader from the defending AL champs and moved into second place at 21–14, a game behind surprise leader Baltimore. Frank Lane enjoyed the entire afternoon as old friend Bill Veeck stewed. Lane's club won the opener, 4–1, behind the brilliant pitching of young Jim Perry and then went on the offensive in the second game, winning 9–4 as ex–Sox Johnny Romano and Tito Francona each collected three hits and Latman outpitched Bob Shaw. During the third inning of the opener, Piersall, leading off second base, began to complain about the calls of plate umpire Larry Napp. At first he was merely hollering, but then he began waving his arms. When rookie second-base umpire Cal Drummond attempted to calm him down, Jimmy began berating Drummond, who soon gave Piersall the heave-ho. The umpires and Joe Gordon finally succeeded in getting Jimmy off the field, but the show had only just begun. From the first-base dugout, Piersall tossed bats, balls, gloves and water bottles onto the field as the huge crowd roared. Then he emerged from the dugout and made his way along the big screen behind home plate toward the Sox dugout, through which visiting team's players had to walk in those days because both clubhouses were on the third-base side. He waved to the fans, stepped into the home dugout and began chucking more equipment onto the field. Again the crowd of 45,000-plus reacted loudly, the cheers edging out the boos. Piersall played the entire second game and became visibly upset when Veeck's new exploding scoreboard erupted to salute Earl Torgeson's pinch homer in the seventh and then went off again — by mistake — when Minnie Minoso's double off the wall just missed going out. Finally, after catching Ted Kluszewski's long flyball for the final out, he showed his contempt by firing the baseball right at the board.

"It's damn nerve-wracking," Piersall complained. "All those lights flashing and all those bombs bursting all over the place. I thought it was funny the first time it went off. But once was enough." At the close of Jimmy's wild afternoon, Lane spoke to him. "I told him, 'You're letting me down. We're paying you to play ball, not to umpire or be the groundskeeper or to amuse the customers.'"[20] Lane's words were not exactly heeded: Piersall was sidelined from June 26 through July 4 for psychiatric treatment after his fourth ejection in a month.

Meanwhile, as his team put together a five-game winning streak in early June, Lane got back on the phone and started patching holes here and there. Already his May 15 acquisition of infielder Ken Aspromonte (from Washington for ex–Cub outfielder Pete Whisenant) was paying dividends; Ken filled in at third for the slumping Bubba Phillips and at second for the banged-up Johnny Temple and hit like he never had before, finishing the season at .288. On June 2, Lane sold Bobby Tiefenauer, another of those accursed knuckleballers, to St. Louis. On the same day, he traded outfielder Johnny Powers (whom he'd only had since May 12) to Pittsburgh for catcher Hank Foiles. Then, two days before the deadline, he traded catcher Russ Nixon and outfielder Carroll Hardy to Boston for lefty Ted Bowsfield and outfielder Marty Keough.

It was then that the Indians went on a brief tear, winning 12 of 15 from June 21 through July 4 to reach Cleveland's high-water mark for 1960 — a 42–28 record that left the Tribe in second place, 1½ games back of first-place New York. The Indians had played the Yankees tough during the New Yorkers' recent four-game visit to the shores of Lake Erie June 25–27; crowds of

39,675 (Friday), 40,033 (Saturday) and 57,621 (Sunday) turned out to see the two contenders split the series. So baseball interest in Cleveland was still high, Colavito or no Colavito. Rocky was hitting .253 with 14 homers for the Tigers; Harvey Kuenn was batting .320 for the Tribe. Maybe this was going to work out, after all.

And then, everything came undone. In six straight Indians–White Sox matchups (two at home and a four-game weekend series in Chicago), the '59 champs flexed their new-found muscles and defeated the Tribe five times. In the first contest, on July 6, Gene Freese tied the game with a homer in the eighth, and Roy Sievers' two-run shot in the ninth won it, 7–5. On the next night, Freese blasted a three-run homer off Jim Perry and Al Smith was 4-for-4 to help Billy Pierce to a 9–3 triumph. At Chicago on Friday night, 48,321 saw Frank Baumann go the distance and win, 4–1. Sievers' two-run double and Freese's RBI triple highlighted the White Sox's five-run first inning Saturday in an 8–4 Chicago romp. Perry beat Early Wynn 6–2 in the opener on Sunday as Vic Power collected a single, double and triple, and the Tribe led 4–1 in the sixth inning of the nightcap. But Jim Landis homered, Minnie Minoso delivered a two-out RBI single and Sievers (12-for-24 in the six games with eight RBIs) followed with a three-run homer and the Sox won, 6–4. This left the Tribe with a 43–33 record at the All-Star break, two games back of New York, one up on surging Chicago and two ahead of Baltimore. The race was tightening and would remain tight until the final two weeks, but it would not include the Indians.

One reason was the loss of shortstop Woodie Held for 6½ weeks. Held suffered a broken finger during the July 18th game with the Yankees and did not return until September 1. At the time, Held already had hit 15 home runs and knocked in 50 runs in the season's first 81 games. The mishap was a huge blow to a team already missing right-handed power threats Colavito and Minoso from the '59 club. The Indians dropped 10 of the remaining 13 games in July and were 48–45 and out of contention by month's end. Interest fell off, as did action at the gate. Minus the attraction of the beloved Colavito, Cleveland home attendance totaled 950,985, causing Lane's bonus (a whopping $34,899 in '59) to dip to just $7,549.

Before the Tribe dropped below .500 on August 21, Lane and Detroit's DeWitt got together on one of the strangest trades ever consummated. Instead of firing their managers, Lane and DeWitt swapped them. Joe Gordon, with his Indians at 49–46 and in fourth place, went to Detroit for Jimmy Dykes, whose Tigers were 44–52. Said DeWitt: "I was discussing possible player deals with Lane and I said, 'Frank, we're getting nowhere on this, so let's trade managers.' I meant it to be facetious." That it certainly was. Even Lane admitted: "I thought he was kidding. But he pressed the point."[21] And Lane, as usual, was getting antsy: this was August 3, and he hadn't made a deal in four days. That deal was the sale of right-hander Johnny Briggs to Kansas City. The day before that move, he had purchased former Dodger pitching great Don Newcombe from Cincinnati. And three days before that, he had dealt catcher Hank Foiles to Detroit for infielder Rocky Bridges and catcher Red Wilson, who had reached the majors to stay in 1953 with Lane's White Sox.

And so the deal that began as a joke became history, to be followed a couple days later by a swap of the two managers' top aides: Coach Luke Appling went to Cleveland and Jo-Jo White to Detroit. Truth be told, the trade of managers was not that earth-shaking to most of the players, but it did matter to Jimmy Piersall. The mercurial center fielder was no fan of Gordon, and vice versa. Said Piersall: "When Lane traded Gordon for Jimmy Dykes, I wanted to send him orchids."[22]

Lane likely would have welcomed orchids or any gift at this point in this most disappointing of seasons. (One of the Tribe's few positives of 1960 was the signing, on June 16, of 6-foot-6-inch lefty Sam McDowell out of a Pittsburgh high school.) The change in managers, as expected by most observers, did not help. Dykes could write out a lineup card but he couldn't play shortstop. The loss of Held, the failure of Johnny Temple and Bubba Phillips to play up to expectations, and the fact that only Jim Perry was able to win in double figures summed up rather well the demise of the 1960 Cleveland Indians. That, and the absence of Rocky Colavito. So the season ended with the Tribe finishing a distant fourth, 21 games behind the champion New York Yankees and posting a won-lost record of 76–78, a half-game worse than the '57 Indians' 76–77 mark. Several players had completed individually successful seasons: Piersall, despite his troubled first half, ended up with 18 homers and batted .282; Vic Power had 10 homers, 84 RBIs and hit .288; Tito Francona totaled 17, 79 and .292; Harvey Kuenn, battling injuries, batted .308; Held's numbers read 21, 67, .253, even with his missing six weeks; and John Romano, in his first full season, hit .272 with 16 homers and 52 RBIs. But the pitching was missing in action and the team's home run total, not surprisingly, plummeted from 167 in 1959 to 127 in '60.

Lane didn't know it but he had come to the end of his final season in Cleveland. He went right on planning for 1961, with his aim being to improve the pitching and, interestingly, to add some power to the outfield — this one year after he had traded away Rocky Colavito and Minnie Minoso, who smashed 55 homers between them in 1960. As he left for St. Louis and the winter meetings, his top target for the pitching staff was Philadelphia's Dick Farrell, but he eventually lowered his sights and went after the Giants' Johnny Antonelli, a two-time 20-game winner but just 6–7 and 3.78 in 41 games in '60. On December 3, 1960, the Indians landed Antonelli and left-handed-hitting outfielder Willie Kirkland, who in his third year with the Giants had hit .253 but had slugged 21 home runs. And the man Lane gave up to get those two? Harvey Kuenn. Among Lane's tenets as a trademaker was this: "When you make a mistake, admit it. Don't keep your mistake on your ball-club." There was also this to consider: Lane and Kuenn had become friends. There exists the belief that Lane knew the Cleveland franchise was in for some down years and he wanted to make sure Kuenn had the opportunity to play for a contender. Said Bob Kennedy in 1996: "Knowing Frank, he would do that. He was a lot better man than a lot of people thought."[23]

The Giants won the National League pennant in 1962, as Kuenn hit .304. Lane, meanwhile, had left Cleveland a bit prematurely. He had gone before the Indians' board of directors at the end of December 1960 and asked for a contract extension. Even those closest to him on the board told him there was no chance and invited Frank to look elsewhere. They granted the two new AL expansion franchises, Los Angeles and Washington, permission to interview him for their GM positions. Then came a call from new Kansas City A's owner, Charles O. Finley, who presented Lane an overwhelming offer. On January 3, 1961, Lane handed in his resignation to the Tribe board. He was Kansas City bound.

A tale that had started with Frank Lane stepping off an airplane that November evening in 1957, cast in the role of franchise savior, was ending with even people who liked him saying that Cleveland would be better off without him. "I leave with regrets," he said, "because I've always wanted to win a pennant, and I think the Indians have a hell of a chance to do it this year."[24] It wasn't until 1995 that the Cleveland Indians would run away with the AL Central title, roll through the playoffs and, finally, win the American League pennant. Frank Lane was only 34 years off.

9

Kansas City, Here He Comes, 1961

One might say that the Charlie Finley-Frank Lane union of 1961 was baseball's answer to the Nazi-Soviet Non-Aggression Pact of 1939 between Stalin and Hitler. Most people knew it could not and would not last, that it was just a matter of time before one would attack the other. Admittedly, the Finley-Lane alliance is not the perfect analogy, because Finley, at the time he gained control of the Kansas City Athletics, was new to the baseball world and people didn't know what kind of person he was. They soon found out. Bob Elson, many years later, after he had spent the last season (1971) of his 40-year broadcasting career doing the A's games in Oakland for Finley, put it this way: "He put together a championship team, all by himself, but he missed the human equation: People don't mean anything to him. And that's a sad state of affairs."[1]

The Lane-Finley partnership was initiated at a January 3, 1961, press conference in Kansas City, where the Athletics' new owner, a Chicago insurance man who had become a millionaire by devising the concept of group insurance for physicians, introduced Lane as the team's new general manager. Finley announced that Lane would be getting paid $100,000 because he wanted to demonstrate that he was willing to spend the most to get the best. "I can't think of anyone who could do a better job of pumping life into a ballclub than Frank Lane," Finley said. "Even at $100,000 a year, Lane is an exceptional bargain. We won't be cheap. I believe in hiring the best men, regardless of their price."[2]

It turned out that while Lane was getting $100,000, he was not getting it in one year. Rather, he would be receiving it spread out over four years—through December 31, 1964, to be the A's GM, and then he was to get another $100,000 for the next four years to serve as a consultant. He also received a $13,500 Mercedes-Benz 300 SL as part of his new deal. (More on that Mercedes later.) Lane, by the way, took the job even though the A's had hired Joe Gordon as manager before Finley bought the club in mid–December.

There would be the usual skirmishes between Lane and Gordon as time

112

went along, but the ones between Lane and Finley were far more entertaining, and it was no surprise that the pair ended up in court in January 1965 in a row over back salary owed to Lane by Finley. The first skirmish came just before the introductory press conference. Finley told Lane he was not to wheel and deal without Finley's approval. "Lane jumped up," Finley testified in court four years later, "walked toward the door of my office, and said, 'If you're looking for an office boy, you've got the wrong guy.' Then he came back and said he had never dealt without consulting the owner."[3] The consultation, though, generally occurred after Frank had made the deal. Lane was used to operating free of interference from ownership, save for that short period in St. Louis with Gussie Busch, so when he pulled off an eight-man deal on January 24, a theft in which he picked the pockets of a former employee, Baltimore's Paul Richards, he was surprised to get an angry reaction from Finley when he phoned him at 1 A.M. with details of the trade. "I hit the ceiling," Finley recalled, "I said, 'Frank, I thought we had an agreement.' He said Paul Richards had insisted the deal be made now or never. Lane assured me it would never happen again, and it didn't."[4]

Incidentally, Lane's first trade as Kansas City GM sent outfielders Russ Snyder and Whitey Herzog — a far better manager than a player, as it developed — plus another player to be named later to Richards' Orioles for onetime bonus-baby infielder Wayne Causey, lefty Jim Archer, outfielder Al Pilarcik and two of Lane's earlier Chicago acquisitions: first baseman Bob Boyd and catcher Clint Courtney. When the time came for Lane to send Richards that player to be named later, he sent him Courtney. Other deals followed. One was the purchase, for $50,000, of Dodgers backup catcher Joe Pignatano. This move made perfect sense: the Athletics' catchers in 1960 — Pete Daley, Harry Chiti and Danny Kravitz — almost needed the pitcher to relay their throws to second base to catch would-be base stealers. A whopping 76 percent of stolen-base attempts against the A's in 1960 had been successful. "What we have in Pignatano," Lane said, "is someone who should provide Kansas City with the novelty of a catcher who can throw somebody out."[5]

Lane, almost immediately upon getting the Kansas City job, talked openly about attempting to acquire Jimmy Piersall from Cleveland. "I'd like to get Piersall. He'd stir up the fans in Kansas City. He's just what we need. We have to bring people into the ballpark, and who can create more excitement than Piersall?" Said Jimmy: "He has to keep the fans coming. He apparently thinks I might help. I appreciate that. But if I were to be traded and had a choice of where, I'd take Boston."[6] Joe Gordon, having no interest in having to deal further with Piersall's antics, read Lane's comments with increasing concern. Reported Lane: "Gordon doesn't want him back. He said the other day, 'Please, Frank, not Piersall!' He knows the position we're in, though. But it doesn't look like the Indians will trade him." Lane, remembering the reaction in Cleveland to the Rocky Colavito deal, then added: "They're afraid of the bobby-soxers."[7] Lane later said that if he were to make a deal with the Tribe, he likely would target some of the Indians' top prospects, chief among them pitchers Sam McDowell and Frank Funk and outfielder Ty Cline.[8]

One player who eventually did get traded, lefty starter Bud Daley, was giving Lane a hard time on the contract circuit. But at a luncheon in St. Joseph, Missouri, Daley — who had won 16 games for the Athletics in both 1959 and '60 — seemed closer to signing after endless back-and-forth talks on the phone with Lane. "I'd sign right now," he said, "if they'd pay me the sum of Frank Lane's phone bills."[9] Daley soon signed, leaving his right-handed staff counterpart, Ray Herbert, still outside the fold. At a late January press conference, center fielder Bill Tuttle signed his contract and then modeled the club's new road uniform, which for the first time had "Kansas City" emblazoned across the front. Lane, who when he took over as GM had called both Daley and Herbert outstanding pitchers, took time during the confab to point out that Herbert had returned his contract unsigned. "He wrote that he thought our offer was good for a 'good' pitcher," Lane related. "But he said he has read that he is an 'outstanding' pitcher and feels he should receive an outstanding salary."[10] A few days later, Herbert provided some background on his salary talks. "In the second or third letter he sent me," Herbert said, "Lane told me I could do one of three things with the contract: Sign it, hang it up on the wall or tear it up. So I tore it up and sent all the pieces back to him. That's when he got mad."[11]

Lane was not yet angry with Joe Gordon, however. In fact, it appeared that the two men were going to have a much better relationship than they'd had in Cleveland. They had a grand time entertaining the Optimist Club of Kansas City shortly after Lane's hiring, only this time Gordon got most of the laughs. "I'd rather not talk about the roster now," Gordon said in response to a query as to what the team might look like by Opening Day. "With Lane around, you never know who's on your club." He also described his reaction to the news that his new GM in Kansas City was to be his old GM from Cleveland. "I almost fell out of my chair. I had just gotten home from a fishing trip, and the Associated Press called to ask me what I thought of Kansas City's latest deal. All I could think of was that the A's probably had landed a good ballplayer in a deal. Then the guy told me it was Frank Lane. Shocked? You're darn right I was. Don't think Frank and I don't get along, though. Frank and I have lots of fun kidding around."[12]

The pair's favorite target would turn out to be Finley, of course. "Finley has admitted, and Lane repeatedly seconds it, that he does now know much about baseball," wrote Rex Lardner of *Sports Illustrated*.[13] Soon, though, Finley would be challenging Lane's every trade proposal and Gordon's every pitching change. Said Lane, who was closing in on 30 years in the game: "Charlie thinks he has learned more [about baseball] in 29 minutes than I have in 29 years."[14] Lane also was critical of his boss' "theft" of some of Bill Veeck's ballpark innovations. Finley, as Veeck had done in Chicago's Comiskey Park a year earlier, constructed a picnic area, this one along the left-field line, to provide a place for fans to sit and enjoy the game from field level while dining on typical picnic fare. Finley, like Veeck, had painted the outside walls of the stadium. Like Veeck with his Sox-O-Gram, Finley added a similar message board to his scoreboard and termed it the "Fan-O-Gram." Like Veeck a year before in Chicago, he had installed a device (dubbed "Little Blowhard") under home plate that, when needed, would blow dirt off the plate and save the umpire from the demanding task of using a whisk broom to tidy things up. And like Veeck, who in Chicago had installed a ball basket that, upon the plate umpire's summons, would pop out of the ground behind the home plate area with a fresh supply of baseballs, Finley had come up with the same thing — only his ball basket was "held" by "Harvey the Rabbit," a caricature with a striking resemblance to a cartoon icon who went by the name of "Bugs." Lane, wrote Lardner, didn't share Finley's enthusiasm for Harvey and some of the other spectacles at the stadium. "He's trying to out-Veeck Veeck," Lane told Lardner, "but Veeck has the horses. What makes a fan come to a ballpark is a team that scores one more run than the other guys. If the team doesn't do well, I don't think the fans are going to give a damn for Bugs Bunny."[15]

Attempting to help the team do well, or to at least improve substantially over the 1960 Kansas City team that had finished in last place with a 58–96 record, Lane went to work on the phone. The day after the eight-man deal with the Orioles, he had dealt pitchers John Briggs and John Tsitouris to Cincinnati for veteran lefty Joe Nuxhall. He also had traveled to Chicago that weekend to meet with the White Sox's Veeck for talks that bore no fruit. "I talked to Bill ... but we didn't get anywhere," Lane reported. "You know Bill: He'll give you a biscuit for a barrel of flour."[16] Veeck, knowing that Nellie Fox was on his way down, offered reliever Turk Lown as well as Fox's backup, Sammy Esposito, in a bid for A's second baseman Jerry Lumpe. With that, Lane laughed and then fled. But just before training camp broke in West Palm Beach, Lane was able to make a rather profitable deal. He sent right-handed pitcher Howie Reed and cash to the Dodgers for right-hander Ed Rakow, who had a 12–6 record and 3.26 ERA at Triple-A Spokane in 1960. Rakow worked mostly in relief in '61, then would win 14 games in 1962. Just before Opening Day, Lane was taken to the cleaners by Baltimore's Richards, who received both reliever Dick Hall and utility man deluxe Dick Williams in exchange for pitcher Jerry Walker and outfielder Chuck Essegian. Exactly three weeks after he got him, Lane sold Essegian to Cleveland. Also, in a move with implications for the future, Lane signed a Cuban infielder named Dagoberto Campaneris, 19, as an amateur free agent on April 25.

There were no trades, for the time being anyway, with the New York Yankees, not after a February stadium press conference during which Lane doused an old school bus with gasoline in Sam's Parking Lot beyond the left-field fence and then torched it while Finley declared that the shuttle between Kansas City and Yankee Stadium existed no more. For years, because of the close business and personal ties between Arnold Johnson, original owner of the Kansas City club, and Del Webb, co-owner of the Yankees, the A's had helped keep the Yankees on top of the American League by making it a practice to send their best players to New York for players the Yankees either no longer needed or for young players not quite ready for pennant-race pressure in New York. Then, when those youngsters were deemed ready by New York, the Yankees would summon them to the Big Apple via another trade. Intoned Finley: "A new era will start in Kansas City, and that I can promise — no more deals with the Yankees." He also declared that he wouldn't trade the A's batboy for Mickey Mantle.[17]

In May, Finley said that henceforth he alone would give final approval on all trades and that under no circumstances would there be any trades with the Yankees in 1961. But Lane, finding it more and more difficult to operate under Finley's constant scrutiny, had a dogged response that could not have gone over well with his boss. "I'll trade with New York," he said, "if I think we can get a player who will help us. It [the Yankees-K.C. shuttle] was always a one-way street before. I want to make it go both ways."[18]

In the standings, the A's were on a one-way street to 100 losses after what had been a relatively successful start. The home opener had attracted 25,727 to a 5–3 loss to Cleveland despite an excellent outing by Herbert. A road trip of epic proportions (23 games, seven cities) began on May 26 and went surprisingly well. The tour was highlighted by a 9–3 romp over powerful, red-hot Detroit before 51,791 on Memorial Day at Tiger Stadium as Jerry Walker went 6 and one-third innings and allowed just two hits and drove in two himself, while Bob Boyd went 3-for-5 and Norm Siebern (3-for-4) smashed a two-run homer and a three-run shot. Triumphs like that were not exactly typical, of course. Still, when the A's and Joe Nuxhall — who had two hits and two RBIs to help his cause — defeated the Red Sox, 10–6, on June 5 at Fenway Park, Kansas City carried a 22–22 record.

It was during this trip that Lane really swung into action. On June 1, he traded Tuttle to the Twins for third baseman Reno Bertoia and pitcher Paul Giel, the former University of Minnesota All-American quarterback and the school's future athletic director. A week later, Marv Throneberry went to Baltimore for outfielder Gene Stephens. Next evening, in New York, Lane signed one of his favorites, "Jungle Jim" Rivera, the hustling, head-first-sliding former outfield star of the White Sox. He had been released by Chicago on June 6, after sitting around and basically doing nothing for the season's first seven weeks (he did get into one game, as a pinch-runner). The year before, he had gotten into just 48 games and collected five hits in 17 official at-bats (.294). So with 1961 shaping up as a '60 rerun, Rivera welcomed the chance to return to play for the person under whom he had developed as a player.

Lane got in a playful jab the night he signed Rivera as a free agent. "I have great respect for Jim. He is still an exciting ballplayer at age 38. He has a good arm, he can field and, *occasionally*, he gets a hit."[19] Lane always had been a Rivera fan. Once, he was telling a story about a White Sox-Yankee trade proposal that would have sent Billy Pierce to New York. "I wanted Hank Bauer, Joe Collins and Jerry Coleman," Lane said. "They could've had Billy and somebody else." "Rivera?" the interviewer asked. "No, oh no," Lane shot back. "That's my pride and joy." And he meant it.[20]

Kansas City's biggest move came the next day, June 10, when Lane, Finley and White Sox vice president Hank Greenberg completed an eight-player deal. The White Sox, in last place in what was now a 10-team American League, had to do something to shake things up. They acquired from Kansas City pitchers Ray Herbert and Don Larsen, third baseman Andy Carey and reserve outfielder Al Pilarcik. To the A's went starter Bob Shaw, like Herbert a tough cookie at contract time; reliever Gerry Staley, like Shaw a 1959 Chicago hero; and a pair of left-handed-hitting outfielders: Wes Covington, the former Milwaukee Brave, and Stan Johnson, who was at the Sox's San Diego farm at the moment but as a September call-up the previous season had pinch-hit for Minnie Minoso one night in Cleveland and drove the first pitch he saw out of the ballpark. Lane, years later and with great mirth, revealed that Finley had completely confused Johnson with another young Chicago outfielder, Floyd Robinson, also a lefty swinger but one who was on his way to a .310 season — and a solid career — with the White Sox. "Charlie thought he was getting Floyd Robinson," Lane said, laughing. "He thought we were stealing them blind. I don't think Johnson ever played for him."[21] Actually, Johnson did get into three games with Kansas City, beginning on June 11, and was 0-for-3. Also sent packing on June 10 was another former White Sox, Bob Boyd, sold by Lane to Milwaukee.

Then came the trade that broke the camel's back, not to mention Finley's. With the trade deadline just days away, and with Lane running up the usual huge phone bills, Finley, wary of what Lane might do, repeated his vow about trades with New York. "I gave the fans in Kansas City my word that we would not trade with the Yankees, and my word is my bond."[22] That was on June 9. Five days later, Lane dealt Bud Daley to New York for pitcher Art Ditmar — arguably the Yanks' best pitcher in 1960 — and infielder/outfielder Deron Johnson, a strapping 22-year-old who in a few years would develop into one of the National League's top power hitters (a league-leading 130 RBIs in 1965 with the Reds). Said Lane later: "When Finley pulled that bush-league trick of burning the charter bus to Yankee Stadium and announcing he wouldn't even trade the A's batboy for Mickey Mantle, I was determined to make a deal [with New York] if I could. I told Finley at the start not to make those stupid promises that he would never deal with the Yankees. I deal with any club and always have. And if he hadn't interfered, I would have made a better deal with the Yanks than the one we finally made."[23]

None of the three players in this deal made much of an impact in 1961. Daley, 4–8, 4.95, with the A's, was 8–9, 3.96, with a 109–63 Yankee club; Ditmar, 2–3 with New York before the trade, never won another game in the majors (0–5 in '61 and 0–2 in '62); Johnson hit only .216 in '61 but had eight homers and 42 RBIs in just half a season and wound up having a 16-year career — and returned to Finley and the A's in 1973, when they were in Oakland, to contribute 19 homers and 81 RBIs to the franchise's second straight world championship club. Incidentally, the Daley-to-New York trade might never have taken place were it not for a brilliant performance the evening before (June 13) by 24-year-old White Sox left-hander Juan Pizarro, making just his second start for Chicago after coming over from the National League on December 15, 1960, in a blockbuster also involving Milwaukee and Cincinnati. Lane, enthralled with the fireballing lefty's potential, was close to a deal that would have netted, basically, Pizarro for Daley. But Pizarro chose that night to allow just four hits and strike out 10 Angels en route to a 10–2 victory, Pizarro's first in a Sox uniform. The Sox's Al Lopez and Hank Greenberg, finally realizing what they had in young Pizarro, told Lane and Finley they had decided they were going to keep him. That's when Lane made the trade with New York.

Meanwhile, Lew Krausse, Jr., just out of high school, was signed to a $125,000 bonus on June 8, and Finley decided he would go straight to the big leagues. He informed Lane and Gordon that the youngster would debut on June 16 against the Los Angles Angels, one of the AL's two new expansion teams. The event drew 25,869 to Municipal Stadium, and the kid from Chester, Pennsylvania, did not disappoint, allowing just three hits and blanking the Angels, 4–0. It wasn't the first time Finley had insisted on doing something his way. Earlier, Lane and Gordon had decided to farm out pitcher Ken Johnson, but Finley demanded that Johnson be given another opportunity. He made another start against Baltimore and failed to survive the opening inning. Said Lane: "If we're going to extend spring training into July, we'll drop so many games behind it won't be funny."[24] Another time, on cutdown day in May, Lane decided that rookie right-hander Norm Bass, brother of L.A. Rams defensive back Dick Bass, should be sent out for more work in the minors. Again, Finley protested and asked that Bass be given another shot. Sure enough, Bass, though losing the game, pitched well against the White Sox, well enough to be given another start, which he won. "Well," reasoned Lane, "if this club can't experiment, then who the hell can?"[25]

He had a point, for by now the A's definitely were heading in the wrong direction. After reaching 22–22 on June 5, they dropped 11 of the next 15, giving Finley, who had been wanting to cashier Gordon for weeks, a good reason to pull the plug on the "Joe" half of "The Frank and Joe Show." Lane disagreed: "I told him, 'Charlie, you can't do that. The team is coming off a real good road trip."[26] Indeed, the 10–13 trip was the best by the A's since they first arrived in Kansas City in 1955. But that didn't stop Finley. On June 19, he declared Gordon's turn at the helm was over. The new manager was to be right fielder Hank Bauer, still playing half the time at age 38 but ready to take the step long predicted for him by so many who had watched him during his career. Bauer had played for the Triple-A Kansas City Blues in the Yankees' farm system in the late 1940s. In fact, it had been Lane, then in charge of the western half of the Yankees' farm system, who had signed Bauer to his first professional contract. Lane had driven from Kansas City to Bauer's home in East St. Louis, Illinois, and watched as Bauer, a Marine during World War II, affixed his signature to a contract with Quincy (Ill.) of the Three-I League. "He signed me for $175 a month," said Bauer, "and then he gave me a $150 bonus. But he put in a clause that said I had to last 30 days to collect the bonus."[27] He lasted the 30 days and then some. Bauer played in his final game on July 21, 1961, starting in right field against the Tigers in Kansas City, and giving 2-for-3, his RBI single driving in the eventual winning run in a 3–2 victory for Jim Archer.

That game, though an A's triumph, was not quite as fulfilling for Bauer as his first night on the new job, which had been June 19, just hours after the press conference called to announce his ascendancy to the field manager's position. The opponents that night at Municipal Stadium were the New York Yankees, for whom Bauer had put in 11 full seasons before being "demoted" to K.C. in the Roger Maris deal of December 1959. On this night, Maris broke a 2–2 tie in the ninth by slugging his 25th home run of the season, and the A's came to bat, trailing 3–2 but with 16,715 fans providing vocal encouragement. The support didn't help Gene Stephens, who grounded out, but ex–Yankee Norm Siebern launched Yankee rookie Roland Sheldon's next pitch 421 feet, high off the center-field fence. The ball ricocheted past Mickey Mantle allowing Siebern to circle the bases for a game-tying inside-the-park home run. Now Bauer sent up newcomer Wes Covington, a left-handed long-ball hitter, to bat for right-handed Leo Posada. Yankee manager Ralph Houk, a former Bauer teammate, countered by bringing in his ace reliever, Luis Arroyo, a lefty whose trademark screwball actually made him tougher against right-handed hitters than left-handed ones. Covington, in just 20 at-bats over five games against New York earlier in the season as a member of the White Sox, had collected six hits—three of them home runs—and driven in eight runs. He too picked on the first pitch, driving Arroyo's offering over the 379-foot marker in right-center to win Bauer's managerial debut, 4–3. "They tell me this was a coincidence," Bauer said, smiling, "but I'd get a hell of a lot more satisfaction out of it if we would beat them four in a row."[28]

It was not to be. The Yankees won the final three games of the series, and, after the A's split four with visiting Boston, they dropped 14 of the next 16 games and, despite Bauer's efforts, effectively gave up the ghost. The hitting and defense went south — though rookie shortstop Dick Howser was enjoying a marvelous season — and, outside of Bob Shaw and Jim Archer, the pitchers were consistently ineffective, save for occasional bursts of excellence by Norm Bass and Jerry Walker. As for the youngster Krausse, perhaps Finley would have been better off not rushing him to the major leagues. He finished the season 2–5, 4.85 in 12 games, eight of them starts, and he had to wait almost exactly three months from his first win until he notched his second one on September 17 in Washington. In that outing, he went the distance and allowed five hits and just one walk in a 3–2 victory. Krausse was optioned to the minors in 1962 and didn't return to a regular role with the A's until 1966, when, still just 23, he was 14–9 with a 2.99 ERA, the best season of his career.

By season's end, though, the two men who had been overruled by Finley's decision to use Krausse immediately were no longer around. Gordon was back home in Sacramento, with plenty of time to do what he loved most — going on fishing trips. (He would return to Kansas City to manage the expansion Royals in 1969.) Lane was also taking it easy: He was down in Mexico, sunning himself in Acapulco. The end for Frank in Kansas City came on August 22, when Finley finally decided it was time to part ways with the man he had praised as the greatest general manager in baseball. That the Athletics had just dropped three in a row at home to the White Sox, Finley's favorite team as a youth in Gary, Indiana, did not help the situation. He had been trying to get Lane to step down for weeks, since the day Lane had blurted out, during one of their office discussions, "You so-and-so! Why don't you fire me?" Finley had replied, "Why don't you quit?"[29] When it became obvious that Lane wasn't about to quit, Finley called a press conference at his insurance company headquarters in Chicago to announce that Lane was no longer general manager. His replacement was Pat Friday, a business associate of Finley's who had no previous baseball experience. When rumors arose that Finley had his eyes on White Sox front-office figure Ed Short (who was about to be named Sox GM), Finley replied, "Pat Friday is our general manager. Lane to the contrary, I think we 'insurance men' will do a reasonably good job running the ballclub."[30] Lane, reached in Mexico, agreed with Finley's prediction. "They'll be all right," Frank said, "as long as Charlie and Pat keep up their subscription to *The Sporting News*."[31]

Lane seemingly had been on vacation since early July, anyway. The team's poor play, the constant interference from Finley, the fact that his team was nowhere close to being in the pennant race — all served to make the job a difficult one. How he must have longed for the exciting "Go-Go" days and the huge crowds in Chicago, the pennant race in St. Louis in 1957 and the near-miss in Cleveland in '59. Yet there was always the chance to make a trade via waivers, even with the regular deadline long since passed. He checked on July 2 with the Phillies, buried in last place in the National League, and saw that old friend Bobby DelGreco was still on the roster, having hit .259 thus far in only 41 games. Lane called Phils GM John Quinn and suggested a swap of DelGreco for Wes Covington, who had cooled off (7-for-44, .159) since that game-winning blast against the Yankees. Quinn jumped at the offer. Del-Greco played two full seasons with the A's in '62 and '63, while Covington turned in marks of .303, .283, .303 and .280 in Philadelphia. Then, on July 31, in his final deal as A's GM, Lane put together a four-player proposal that the second-place Detroit Tigers, 1½ games behind the Yankees, were more than happy to accept. To Detroit went reliever Gerry Staley and the onetime Tigers bonus baby Reno Bertoia; to last-place Kansas City went pitcher Bill Fischer and infielder Ozzie Virgil, Sr.

And that was it. Finley agreed to pay off Lane's salary with checks at regular intervals, but Lane was prohibited from taking another job in baseball. At least he no longer would have to worry about the Kansas City A's. And with the A's, there was much about which to worry. Norm Siebern led the club with 18 homers; the next-highest total was eight, by Deron Johnson and Wayne Causey. So A's power was just a rumor. The pitching was awful, once one got past Jim Archer (9–15, 3.20) and Bob Shaw (12–14, 4.14). Thus the A's had difficulty scoring runs as well as preventing them, an excellent explanation for their 61–100 finish, which tied them for last place with the new Washington club — and left them nine games behind the other expansion team, eighth-place Los Angeles. The only real bright spot was the infield. Third baseman Causey hit .276 and fielded decently, second baseman Lumpe (.293) continued his improvement and first baseman Siebern (.296, 98 RBIs) was developing into the star the Yankees always thought he would become.

Meanwhile rookie Dick Howser was a revelation at shortstop, hitting .280, posting a .377 on-base percentage and stealing 37 bases in 46 tries.

But now Frank Lane was done with the Athletics, and they with him. He was not done, however, with Charles O. Finley. The fun started with the new $13,500 Mercedes-Benz 300 SL that Finley had promised him as part of his new contract Lane had signed back in January 1961 to become general manager of the A's. After Finley fired him, Lane kept the keys to the car but couldn't drive it—because Finley had kept the title. So the Mercedes sat, undriven, in a Florida garage for almost four years. To the rescue came Pirates GM Joe Brown, who had heard about the situation. Brown offered to end the deadlock once and for all. In true Frank Lane fashion, Brown got the men to agree to a "three-team" deal: Brown bought the car keys from Lane and the title from Finley, allowing him to drive off in a brand-new, albeit four-year-old, Mercedes-Benz.[32] That was just one of the stories that emerged during the January 1965 court case in Chicago that had resulted from Lane's having sued Finley for breach of contract. The case, like the relationship between the two men, provided many comedic moments.

It turned out that Finley had held back on certain portions of the contract Lane signed in '61. Lane had told newsmen on August 27, after a final meeting with Finley in Kansas City, that his contract, which ran through December 31, 1968, would be fulfilled by Finley in all details. "I will draw a paycheck every two weeks," Lane said.[33] He was supposed to have received $25,000 per year through 1968—through 1964 as the A's general manager and then for the next four years as a consultant to Finley. However, somewhere along the line, the checks stopped coming. So Lane and his attorney, Charles Stein, filed a $144,166.60 suit on October 8, 1963, against Finley in federal district court in Chicago, seeking that amount as pay still owed Lane. The suit contended that Lane had received no salary from the Athletics once Lane took a job as general manager of Chicago's second-year National Basketball Association team—the Zephyrs—on May 7, 1962. Even after April 30, 1963, when Lane left the team—which moved to Maryland to become the Baltimore Bullets (now the Washington Wizards)—he still failed to receive payments from the Kansas City club, the suit claimed. Lane and his lawyer contended that only a similar job or restoration of Lane by the A's to his former position and at the same salary would warrant dismissing the suit.[34]

After several delays, a jury trial in the Chicago courtroom of Judge James B. Parsons finally began during the first week of January 1965, and the testimony from Finley, Lane and others—including Bill Veeck, a witness for Lane—provided much entertainment for the jury and courtroom spectators. Even the judge participated in the humor. As Finley recounted his business success story on the first day of testimony, he mentioned that he had purchased the A's for $4 million despite his belief that owning a ballclub was a risky investment. Stein, Lane's lawyer, told the court, "I think baseball's generally a good investment. I wish I had a ballclub." At which point Judge Parsons sighed: "I wish I had $4 million."[35]

Finley took the court back to his life as a youngster in Gary, describing how he had worked hard to get ahead and how he had suffered from tuberculosis and spent 27 months in a sanitarium. When he had recovered, Finley testified, he realized that "health and happiness was everything; money was secondary." That's when Lane was heard to crack, "Then why doesn't he pay me off?"[36] Later that same day, the rather amusing notion of Frank Lane as color commentator became the subject of testimony. One reason Finley believed he shouldn't have to pay Lane was because the latter, in 1963, had turned down the job of color analyst on the Athletics' TV and radio broadcasts—even though Finley knew full well that Lane's rather blue language was hardly fit for family consumption. Finley also told the court that Lane had turned down another Finley job offer—that of "assistant to the president." According to Lane, Finley told him the hours of this alleged job would be from 9 to 5, five days a week. He would not have the title of general manager, he would not travel and would not make any trades. Lane's response: "I told him that at my age I did not expect to start over as an office boy."[37] As for the radio-TV gig, Lane admitted he was often as loud as the loudest fans in the ballpark and that his cursing, almost always aimed at his own players, would embarrass the most foul-mouthed longshoreman. "I got too close once to [White Sox radio voice] Bob Elson's open mike and was chased away," he said. Veeck concurred with Lane's opinion. "Under no circumstances would I hire him for radio or TV," he said. "He gets carried away. I don't think he could produce a calm, factual report of a game. Let's put it this way: if I were hiring broadcasters, Frank Lane would be the last man I'd want near a mike."[38]

During a break in the trial one morning, courtroom spectators got a look at how major baseball deals are sometimes completed. He hadn't realized it at the time, but Finley, who made the proposal, was responsible for one of the greatest deals in White Sox history. In the corridor outside the courtroom were Sox GM Ed Short and the club's farm director, Glen C. Miller, who had driven over from their Comiskey Park offices to take in a portion of the testimony. Finley spotted the pair, waved them over and said, "Tell you what: You can have Rocky Colavito for Jim Landis, Mike Hershberger and Dave Nicholson."[39] Short, for whatever reason, dismissed the offer out of hand. Colavito was only 31, had missed only two games during the previous season, played an acceptable right field, still had a terrific arm and had hit .274 (.366 on-base percentage) with 34 home runs and 102 RBIs, Landis, soon to turn

31 himself, had batted .208 with one home run in 1964, while Hershberger had hit .230 with two homers and Nicholson .204 with 13. Finley then said he would accept $500,000 for "The Rock." Again Short said no. Then Lane took center stage in front of reporters, court personnel and enthralled onlookers. "As a neutral observer," he said, "I agree with Charlie that, from his side, it's a fair offer. Rocky isn't going to win a pennant for Kansas City, and a second-division club has to get extra value in players when trading a star. Giving up three outfielders is risky, though. Maybe two, plus a Triple-A prospect at another position." Pat Friday, Finley's GM, stepped in. "We'd take a guy like Fred Talbot instead of Nicholson," said Friday, referring to the 23-year-old right-hander who had registered a 4–5 record and 3.70 ERA with Chicago in '64.[40]

There were no further trade discussions that day, as court was called to order and the trial resumed. Two weeks later, however, the A's did indeed trade Colavito to the White Sox for Landis, Hershberger and Talbot, and the deal did not end there. Chicago's Short immediately forwarded Colavito to his beloved Cleveland—along with backup catcher Camilo Carreon—for slugging John Romano (the catcher traded to the Tribe after the '59 season) and two excellent prospects: center fielder Tommie Agee and left-handed pitcher Tommy John. Lane had to be beaming over the work of Short, his former publicity man in Chicago. Here was a Frank Lane staple, a three-team trade. It had involved the same clubs as Lane's Minnie Minoso deal in 1951, and the White Sox again were getting the best of it. Short had learned well from his former boss.

Soon another development would be pleasing to Lane. On January 8, after Stein and Lane met for two hours in the judge's chambers with Finley and his attorneys, the two sides reached a settlement that heavily favored Lane. He settled for $13,000 on the claim of $44,166—the unpaid back wages through 1964—and then received the full $100,000 due him from January 1, 1965, through 1968. Frank was free from Finley and thus free again to pursue another job in baseball, from which he had been away since August 1961. To his disappointment, offers had been slow in coming during the winter of 1961–62; but then one had come that caught his fancy—even though it had nothing to do with baseball.

Time out for the
NBA, 1962–1963

On a bright and warm April 1962 morning, Frank Lane was sunning himself in Acapulco, miles away from Charlie Finley, and minding his own business when a telegram arrived from Dave Trager, a Chicago businessman who was the owner of the Chicago Packers. Frank did a double take. The Chicago Packers? Then he remembered. Chicago had been granted a National Basketball Association expansion team in 1961, whether Chicago wanted one or not. In his mind, Lane — who for more than two decades had officiated Big Ten and other college basketball games— reviewed as best he could the brief history of pro basketball in Chicago and the even briefer history of the Packers.

Pro basketball had failed to gain a foothold on the Chicago sports scene, despite the presence of a fairly successful team, the Stags, who played in Chicago Stadium for four seasons (1946–47 through 1949–50) and posted records of 39–22, 28–20, 38–22 and 40–28. Yet while the team was an artistic success it was hardly a financial one, which is why it folded, with few tears shed by Chicago sports fans. Eleven years later, it had appeared that few Chicagoans were excited about the NBA's second coming to their city: Only 103,126 people found their way down to the Packers' stockyards-area home arena, the International Amphitheatre, for the club's 28 home games, an average of 3,683 per contest. The Packers finished with an 18–62 record, including a home-court mark of 9–19. The only player worth paying to see was the 6-foot-11-inch rookie center from Indiana University, Walt Bellamy, who averaged 31.6 points and 19 rebounds per game on his way to the NBA Rookie of the Year award. "It was misery," said Bob "Slick" Leonard, another Indiana alumnus who eventually became Chicago's coach. "You'd walk down the street with your Chicago Packers player's bag and you would turn the 'Chicago Packers' to the inside so nobody would see it. It was that bad."[1]

Trager couldn't afford another awful year. Thus, in his telegram, he suggested that Frank come up to Chicago to discuss the possibility of becoming the team's general manager and pumping new life into this motley crew. Lane wondered if he really wanted to go to work for the NBA's equivalent of the Kansas City Athletics. But in Acapulco, he was out of circulation, an afterthought, no longer a fixture in the headlines. He finally decided to accept Trager's invitation to at least talk over the job offer. The team couldn't possibly be worse than the inaugural season's edition, and in the previous month's NBA draft, Trager & Co. had selected some potential point-producers in Utah's Billy "The Hill" McGill, Purdue's Terry Dischinger and Iowa's Don Nelson with their first three picks.

On the flight to Chicago, Lane began thinking that the pros outweighed the cons. When he arrived, he sought out old friends, like *Tribune* sports columnist Dave Condon, to get their input. Condon gave him the then-common attitude toward pro basketball in Chicago: It wasn't going to work, there was almost zero interest, etc. But Lane had already made up his mind. "OK, it's a challenge. I never ran from a challenge. OK, it gets me back in action and in the headlines. That I could go for, too ... [but] I'm really serious about Trager's offer because of one big thing: This town is filled with my kind of people. It's the greatest town in the world. Coming back to Chicago would be coming home."[2]

Lane met with Trager and was offered a contract, a one-year deal that paid him "more than Walt Bellamy was making," Trager noted. Bellamy had signed for $27,500, so Lane's salary likely was in the $30,000 neighborhood.[3] He signed on May 7, 1962, and the first telegram of welcome came from an old St. Louis friend, Ben Kerner, who had been owner of the Hawks for several years, dating back to Frank's Cardinals days. Kerner suggested that Lane trade Bellamy, his lone star, to St. Louis. Kerner most certainly remembered 1956, when Lane traded away Red Schoendienst and was working on that Stan Musial-for-Robin Roberts blockbuster when Gussie Busch ordered a halt in negotiations. "I sent the telegram as a gag," Kerner admitted. "Knowing Frank Lane, he'll try to start with a splurge, but everybody in the league is going to ask for Bellamy." Lane was not about to trade Bellamy, but it was safe to assume that the Chicago roster for 1962–63 would have a different look from that of 1961–62. "I'm happy Lane's here," Kerner said. "He'll help the Packers, and he'll add some life to the league."[4]

Some sports fans—even in Chicago, where he was known best—wondered how Frank Lane, a baseball man, would do in the new environment of basketball. Many were surprised to learn that Lane had played semipro basketball in his younger days and then had been a longtime referee. Not surprisingly, he handled the latter position in a manner that left no doubt as to who was in charge on the floor. "We only used one official for basketball then, and I'll never forget the time I drew Lane as referee," remembered Stu Holcomb, later head football coach at Purdue and Miami (Ohio), athletic director at Northwestern and vice president of the White Sox but then — in the 1930s — a neophyte coach at Findlay (Ohio) College. "Frank never wore the long-sleeved official's shirt [that were in vogue back then]. He liked those real tight shirts with short sleeves so the fans could see his muscles. And Frank was a showboat. Every time he'd call a foul, he'd whack the guy on the back. They weren't friendly pats, either. He'd hit the kids about as softly as Cassius Clay does. My kids got awfully upset." So Holcomb had a short chat with Lane at halftime. "Mr. Lane, I'm just a young and new coach here at a little college, but if you whack one more of my players, I'm going to flatten you." Lane heeded the warning of Holcomb, a former Ohio State football player, and there were no more whacks that night. But on one other occasion, there was more than a whack. Notre Dame's basketball team was playing at Pitt, and Lane was officiating. At one point during this heated contest, a Pittsburgh fan came out onto the floor to challenge Notre Dame center Ed "Moose" Krause. Krause, also a football standout, was able to take care of himself, but Lane refused to allow the intruder to get close. He stepped in front of Krause and, with one punch, knocked out the fan.[5]

Now, decades later, Lane was showing that he was still a man of action. Within weeks, he had announced the signings of the club's first- and third-round draft picks, Utah's McGill and Iowa's Nelson; the firing of coach Jim Pollard and the hiring of his replacement, Jack McMahon; the change of the team's nickname from Packers to Zephyrs; and the news that the team would be returning to the International Amphitheatre for the 1963–64 season. (The Coliseum's seating capacity was about 7,200 compared to the Amphitheatre's 11,300, plus the completion of the new Dan Ryan Expressway meant the trip from downtown Chicago to the arena at 42nd and Halsted Streets now took just 11 minutes.) Lane even marked baseball's June 15th trading deadline by making a basketball deal — with Ben Kerner and the St. Louis Hawks. To St. Louis went 6–4 guard Ralph Davis, who had played collegiately at Cincinnati. To Chicago came native South Sider, DuSable High School grad and Bradley alum Shellie McMillon, a 6–5 forward, and Al Ferrari, a 6–4 guard out of Michigan State. There were other deals as well. Dave Piontek went to Cincinnati (he had starred at Xavier in that city) for Larry Staverman, a refugee from the American Basketball League and a graduate of little Thomas More College in Kentucky, in an exchange of backup forwards. Lane later sent a future second-round draft pick to St. Louis for former Northwestern guard Nick Mantis. In January, he signed Maury King, a guard from Kansas, as a free agent and traded 6–7 forward Woody Sauldsberry — onetime Harlem Globetrotter and the NBA's Rookie of the Year in 1958 — back to St. Louis, from whence he had come the season before. In return, Chicago received 6–7 forward Barney Cable, a Bradley alum.

In October, Lane completed a three-step, three-team deal, a transaction of which he was particularly proud. The Zephyrs owned the rights, via the 1961 NBA expansion draft that stocked the Chicago franchise, to Gene Conley, the 6–8 center-forward who also doubled as a major-league pitcher. Conley had announced he would not play for an expansion team, so the league placed him on the inactive list. Even Lane, his fellow baseball man, could not convince Conley to come to Chicago, so on September 10, he traded Conley to the New York Knicks—for whom Conley did agree to play—for 6–10 center Phil Jordon and forward Chris Luyk. The Knicks then wanted Luyk back, for whatever reason, so Lane let them have him for $1,000. Next, on October 7, Lane traded Jordon to St. Louis for the Hawks' 1962 third-round draft pick, 6–8 forward Charlie Hardnett of Grambling State, plus $3,500. "So far, $4,500 plus Hardnett," Lane said. "But there is more profit: in trading Jordon for Hardnett, I traded off a $15,000 salary for one of $9,000."[6] Furthermore, Hardnett won a starting job opposite Dischinger on the front line and averaged 10.6 points and 7.7 rebounds per game that season. Lane had also kept busy by making visits to the sports departments of the four major Chicago newspapers—the *Tribune*, *Daily News*, *Sun-Times* and *American*—and had spent several lunch hours with the papers' sports editors and columnists in order to get the word out that Chicago's pro basketball team was going to make people sit up and take notice in the 1962–63 season. He had met with mixed success. "No one knew there was an NBA team in Chicago," recalled Nelson, who after a long playing career became a highly successful coach and executive in the league. "We were in the back pages of the sports section every day. It didn't matter who we were playing. We never got any headlines—only a box score and a very small write-up."[7]

Nelson was exaggerating a bit, but the Zephyrs were not front-page material too often. One time they did make the front of the sports section was on September 10, when Lane signed 6–7 forward Terry Dischinger, the Big Ten scoring champion from Purdue, on the day the Zephyrs began preseason workouts in Brown's Lake, Wisconsin. Yet even the signing of Dischinger came with a little bad news: He would be able to play only on weekends until he completed work on his degree in chemical engineering, which wouldn't be until February. The Zephyrs managed to make the third page of the *Tribune* sports section when they pumped in 70 first-half points and then held on to beat the Cincinnati Royals, 113–109, on October 20 in their home opener before 6,780 curiosity-seekers. Walt Bellamy led the way with 23 points, guard Sihugo Green added 21 and Dischinger 17. (The Royals' Oscar Robertson led everyone with 29.)

Sports department bosses might well have given the Zephyrs lead-page coverage in their December 20 sections had the team managed a victory the night before in Detroit. Instead, the Zephyrs, bidding for their fourth straight triumph, dropped a 115–113 decision despite a fourth-quarter surge, led by Bellamy, that put Chicago ahead, 105–104. Bellamy finished with 30 points and two of the rookies—Nelson (14 points) and McGill (10)—contributed. The absence of Dischinger might well have been the difference in the game, a highlight of which came in the second quarter, when Lane, sitting courtside at the scorer's desk, delivered a steady, mostly negative verbal critique of the officials' performance. The officials halted play, called a technical foul on Lane and banished him from the scorer's desk.[8] Frank hadn't learned his lesson, apparently. Two months earlier, during the fourth quarter of a 118–107 victory over the Los Angeles Lakers on October 24 at the Coliseum, Lane had lit into ref Richie Powers from his seat at the scorer's table. Powers called two technicals on Lane, one for heckling him and the second for Lane's failure to leave the table when ordered to do so. He was later tagged with a $250 fine by NBA president Maurice Podoloff. "We have big-league players in the NBA, but not all the officials are big league," Lane stormed. "That was a bush-league stunt by Powers."[9]

By the end of the calendar year — on December 28, to be exact — Lane had convinced Trager that it was time to dump Jack McMahon as head coach. The team had fallen on difficult times, as evidenced by its 12–26 record. The new coach was to be guard Bob Leonard, who at age 30 became the NBA's youngest. Leonard in fact had applied for the job during the off-season before Lane and Trager decided on McMahon, who had coached the Kansas City Steers to the ABL regular-season title in '61–62. Thus, the Zephyrs were paying three head coaches, one to coach and two not to. But Trager and Lane were in complete agreement that McMahon had to go. Trager especially was disappointed in the team's second coach. "We feel the Zephyrs have the personnel to compete on equal terms with the other teams in the league," he said, "but our record [doesn't support that belief.]"[10] They showed they could compete with Cincinnati, anyway, when they downed the visiting Royals 108–104 in Leonard's coaching debut on December 29, but the good vibes didn't last. Chicago dropped eight of its next 10 to sink to 15-36, and as the losses mounted the attendance figures, already unimpressive, began shrinking even more. Soon, rumors of a possible shift of the franchise to Baltimore were being heard.

The most difficult and most galling stretch of all began with a two-point loss to the Pistons on January 25 at the Coliseum. That defeat marked the onset of a skid in which the Zephyrs were to lose 13 of 15 games to send their won-lost record plummeting to 19–47. Chicago simply lacked the experience, from the players to the coaches, to win the close ones. There was a 100–99 defeat at the hands of the champion Boston Celtics on January 29, a two-pointer to the San Francisco Warriors on February 5 and yet another two-point defeat the next night to the Los Angeles Lakers. The Zephyrs played the Lakers in L.A. again on February 8 and the Lakers won, 94–91; the two teams flew to Chicago and played the following evening at the Coliseum, and the Lakers won again, this time 107–106. On February 15 the Zephyrs lost at home to the Knicks 135–131 in double overtime; February 17 brought a 110–107 home-court loss to Boston. The team traveled to New York City to play the Syracuse Nationals at Madison Square Garden on February 19 and was "blown out" by eight; the two clubs met again on the 21st in Chicago, and the Zephyrs snapped an eight-game losing streak, 108–91.

Had he still been in baseball, Lane likely would have been able to swing a trade or two to land an experienced hand to provide some help for a struggling young team. But this was the NBA, not baseball. "In baseball," Lane explained, "almost anytime I sized up the situation, I had 25 major-leaguers and a raft of minor-leaguers who could be dealt.... Basketball is a five-man game. And so you carry maybe seven other players, some of whom could be regarded as regulars. That gives you 12 men to deal. But because of its very nature, basketball is a game where you have to protect your great players— the Terry Dischingers, the Walt Bellamys. Trading off a basketball star would hurt your team operation far more than trading off a baseball star."[11] The message, then, was clear: The Zephyrs would have to be built through the draft. Lane and his aides would not be able to miss on draft picks; they would have to get them right. And it was going to take time to see if they had made the right selections. Frank Lane had to be wondering whether or not he had the patience that this project surely was going to take.

Meanwhile, he continued to try to sell pro basketball to Chicago, which perhaps he was beginning to think might be too difficult a task even for him. When the ABL folded in January, he suggested that the NBA adopt the defunct league's three-point shot. "Just because the thought doesn't originate in our National Basketball Association doesn't mean it can't be a good idea. I feel we could add fan interest by giving premium points for long-distance baskets."[12] Yet while Lane talked of long-distance baskets, Dave Trager was taking and making long-distance phone calls. On March 5, he announced that he had been presented with "a very attractive offer" from the Baltimore Civic Center Association to move the team to Baltimore, beginning the following season (1963-64). Trager added that, under the offer's terms, he and his Chicago-based group would continue as the team's owners. Lane was available for questions during halftime of that night's home game against St. Louis, and he spoke of the Baltimore association's plans for radio–TV coverage and a guarantee to sell 3,000 season tickets—compared to the Zephyrs' total of 600 season tickets sold for '62–63. Lane also said a vote by the Zephyrs' board of directors would likely take place within a week, but he quickly pointed out that Trager owned 40 percent of the team, and that if he wanted to move the franchise the board would not stand in his way.[13]

At least the Zephyrs won the game that evening (paid attendance 1,560), downing the West Division's second-placers 116–93, as Bellamy scored 25 points and Dischinger 24 to more than offset the splendid play of the Hawks' Lenny Wilkens, who popped in 19 to lead St. Louis. In the individual points battle between the two forwards traded for each other on January 30, the Zephyrs' Barney Cable scored 16 points to 15 for Woody Sauldsberry.

Now only six games remained on the schedule, and the Zephyrs went out and equaled their longest winning streak of the season (three) by downing San Francisco on March 6 by 10 points and then edging the Celtics, 110–109, on March 8 in Chicago. The game with the Warriors was played at the new Baltimore Civic Center, and, while they didn't know it at the time, the Zephyrs were performing in what would be their new home in 1963–64. That became almost official when Lane, before the start of the March 12 matchup with Syracuse at the Coliseum, met with the press. "I think a decision already has been made to move the Chicago Zephyrs to Baltimore," said Lane, who, with his contract expiring soon, would not be moving east. "We just don't have any place to play here. That's our problem. We can't make money if we stay in the Coliseum because it's too small. We can't play in the International Amphitheatre after March 3, 1964, because they have a show booked in there, and the rental at the Stadium is too high. And that deal they've offered in Baltimore is tremendous."[14]

All that remained was for the rather routine matter of the vote of the Zephyrs' board of directors. Said Trager, perhaps a bit disingenuously: "I wouldn't want to bet either way on the result of the directors' vote." Then he added these words: "But I don't think pro basketball ever will 'go' in Chicago."[15] His top employee, Frank Lane, wasn't so sure. "You'll see the time, and pretty soon too, when Chicago's hockey club and its top collegiate basketball teams and [the Chicago pro basketball team] all are playing on the same night," Lane said. "And your Chicago papers will be giving the [main] headline to pro basketball." Pro hoops, he said, would someday be recognized as big league in Chicago. "Mark my words. It has to be. Chicago is a big-league sports town. And you guys will soon have to quit disagreeing with the rest of the country and admit that pro basketball is big league. Look at Los Angeles. The Lakers moved there from Minneapolis, and do you have any idea just how much profit they'll make in L.A. this season? A half a million! A half a million dollars' profit from a basketball operation. It floors you to think about it. Look at St. Louis. Pro basketball was a weak little sister when I was there running the Cardinals. But you know what Ben Kerner has been offered for the St. Louis Hawks? One and a half million dollars.

"Someday," Frank Lane predicted, "we'll have that kind of success story in Chicago."[16]

The Zephyrs fled for Baltimore, drafted West Virginia guard Rod Thorn and Idaho forward Gus Johnson in 1963 and became respectable in a hurry, reaching the 1965 West Division finals. In Chicago, a sportsman named Dick Klein landed yet another NBA expansion franchise, this in 1966, and named the team the Bulls. After two difficult seasons, everything began changing. A feisty coach from Weber State University in Utah named Dick Motta joined tenacious players like Jerry Sloan and Norm Van Lier and superb pros like Chet Walker and Bob Love to produce a team that began drawing five-digit crowds to Chicago Stadium. That particular group never won an NBA championship, but that same Rod Thorn, in his final important move as general manager of the Bulls, selected a guard from North Carolina named Michael Jordan with the third pick in the 1984 draft. Six NBA titles eventually followed, starting in 1991; a string of consecutive sellouts began in 1987 (it ended in 2000 at 610 games, third longest in league history); and, across Madison Street from the Stadium, a spectacular new arena, the United Center, was completed in 1994. A new sellout string continues unabated.

Frank Lane, as it turned out, was quite right.

11

Scouting for Titles
in Baltimore, 1965–1970

Lee MacPhail was on the line from Baltimore with an offer Frank Lane could not nor would not refuse. The Orioles' president and general manager asked Lane if he might be interested in joining the organization and working with Jim Russo, the club's top scout, reporting on opposing clubs and laying the groundwork for trades. Trades? Had he heard the word "trades"? Indeed he had. Lane leaped at the opportunity. Just like that, he was back where he belonged: in baseball.

MacPhail, whose father had brought Lane into baseball with the Cincinnati Reds three decades earlier, made the announcement on March 6, 1965. "Frank is a man with a great deal of experience and background in baseball," he said, "and we're glad to have him."[1] It had taken some 12 years, but Lane, who had turned down an offer in 1953 to become GM of the soon-to-be-transplanted St. Louis Browns, finally had made it to Baltimore. "My ultimate aim," Frank admitted to reporters, "is to own a ballclub, although I'd take a job as a general manager again. Not in Baltimore, however. The Orioles are well-fixed in that respect with Lee."[2]

Lane was to work closely with Russo, the "superscout" who had been with the Orioles since they were the Browns. Aggressive men both, they knew what the Orioles needed and were determined to get it for their bosses. Baltimore had won 97 games in 1964 and followed that up with 94 more wins in 1965, both times finishing third, a game back of second-place Chicago. The Orioles, like the White Sox, had succeeded mostly on the strength of their superb pitching — and the occasional punch provided by Brooks Robinson and Boog Powell. Russo and Lane pushed club president- "elect" Frank Cashen, newly promoted GM Harry Dalton and also MacPhail — who was preparing to leave the Orioles to be top aide for the new and virtually clueless commissioner, William Eckert — to pursue at all costs a big bat during the winter of '65–66.

At the winter meetings, held in Fort Lauderdale, Florida, the Oriole superscouts were thrilled to learn that a big bat indeed had been made available. During the meetings' first few days, former Orioles farm director Jim McLaughlin, now working for the Cincinnati Reds, handed his old pal Russo a note and said, "Take this to your people." On the note was written: "Pappas, Blefary and Baldschun for F. Robinson." Russo, excited, went to Dalton, Cashen and Orioles owner Jerry Hoffberger and showed them the missive from the Reds. That trio, however, decided that, because outfielder Curt Blefary had hit 22 homers and had just been named AL Rookie of the Year, the Orioles simply could not trade him — even if it meant no Frank Robinson.[3]

Russo and Lane could not believe what they were hearing. Didn't these people know who Frank Robinson was? "F. Robby" had been voted National League Rookie of the Year in 1956 and Most Valuable Player in 1961, when he led the Reds to the pennant by batting .323 with 37 home runs and 124 RBIs. For an encore, he then hit .342 the next season with 39 long ones and 136 runs batted in. During the 1965 season, he had scored 109 runs and collected 33 doubles, 5 triples, 33 home runs and 113 RBIs plus batting/on-base/slugging averages of .296/.386/.540. But he had just turned 30 in August, and Reds president Bill DeWitt said it was an "old 30." DeWitt also did not like the fact that Robinson had been caught carrying a concealed weapon late one night during the season. Those matters, plus the knowledge the Reds had blasted the ball all over NL playing yards and averaged a hair over 92 wins a year for the last four seasons— with nothing to show for it —convinced DeWitt and his staff that what the Reds needed most was a solid starting pitcher. And if getting one might cost a Frank Robinson, so be it.

Baltimore's best starter was Milt Pappas, who had been an Oriole mainstay since 1958, when he was 19. He was a lock to win 13 to 18 games every year with an ERA between 2.50 and 3.00. Still just 26, he had posted a 13–9 record and 2.60 ERA for Baltimore in '65. DeWitt wanted more than Pappas, however. He wanted a dependable right-handed reliever (like Baldschun) and a young, developing outfielder (like Blefary) to help replace Robinson. Enter the White Sox. GM Eddie Short tried to interest DeWitt in outfielder Floyd Robinson, a new F. Robby to replace Cincinnati's soon-to-be-gone F. Robby. The Chicago package also included two excellent pitchers: knuckleballing reliever Eddie Fisher, who was 15–7 with a 2.40 ERA and 24 saves in a then-record 82 games in '65, and starter Johnny Buzhardt, 13–8 with a 3.01 ERA in 1965 after posting marks of 2.42 and 2.98 in 1963 and '64 and 7–0 lifetime against the mighty New York Yankees.[4] But Floyd Robinson, 29, had slumped all the way to .265 in '65 (from .310, .312, .283 and .301 from 1961 through '64), and DeWitt was looking for someone younger, anyway. In addition, Short also asked for Chicago South Side native Jim O'Toole in the deal.

While Lane schmoozed DeWitt, his partner in the Colavito-for-Kuenn deal and the Gordon-for-Dykes managerial trade of 1960, Russo kept attempting to change the minds of his superiors—to no avail. They were not going to trade Curt Blefary. The meetings broke up, and the representatives of the various clubs headed home. On the flight to their hometown of St. Louis, Russo sat with Herk Robinson, the Reds' assistant farm director, who mentioned that his club most assuredly would consider a recent Orioles addition as a possible replacement for Blefary in the proposed deal for Frank Robinson.[5] The player was a young "on-the-verge" hitter, 22-year-old outfielder Dick Simpson. A 6–4, 180-pounder, Simpson had enjoyed a splendid season in the minors in 1965, and the Reds' Triple-A manager, Dave Bristol, had watched in admiration from Pacific Coast League dugouts and couldn't come up with enough superlatives to describe the kid. The Orioles had just traded first baseman/outfielder Norm Siebern to the California Angels earlier in the week for Simpson, who at Seattle in 1965 had put up some rather impressive numbers: 22 doubles, 12 triples, 24 homers, 79 RBIs, a .301 batting average and 29 stolen bases.

In the meantime, the Orioles had traded with the Phillies to get right-handed reliever Jack Baldschun. Baldschun, 29, had not been nearly as effective in '65 as in the two previous seasons. But the O's knew that the Reds wanted him, so on December 6 they sent to the Phils a rookie left-hander named Darold Knowles and veteran outfielder Jackie Brandt, now 31 and no longer a regular. Dalton and the rest of the Baltimore brass had agreed to make the deal with Cincinnati now that Blefary was not going to be included. The trade was announced on Dec. 9, 1965: Robinson to Baltimore for Pappas, Baldschun and Simpson. Unfortunately for Cincinnati, Pappas suffered through a rare off year in 1966: he finished 12–11, 4.29, partly because now he was pitching in tiny Crosley Field after working for years in spacious Memorial Stadium. As for the other new Reds, Baldschun's career continued its downward path and Simpson simply never made it. The Reds slipped all the way to seventh place, ending with a record of 76–84.

The Orioles, for their part, got off to a 12–1 start and, later, won 15 of 18 to lead the league by a game heading into the June 15 trading deadline. Frank Robinson was atop the AL in hitting at .350 and was tied with Boston's George Scott for the league lead in home runs (16). The O's were sitting pretty, yet Lane kept telling Russo, Cashen and Dalton that he was confident a deal with the White Sox could be completed, one that might well clinch the pennant right then and there. Chicago's infield had been decimated by injuries: Shortstop Ron Hansen was out for the season with a back injury and third baseman Pete Ward was sidelined by a hernia. The Sox had moved second baseman Don Buford to third, traded for Kansas City's Wayne Causey and placed him at second base and tried to get by with Triple-A shortstop Lee

Elia. Short kept asking Lane about the availability of Baltimore's Jerry Adair, who had lost his second-base job to rookie Davey Johnson and was unhappy. Short indicated to Lane that the White Sox, to land Adair, would be willing to trade a reliever — other than the resurgent Hoyt Wilhelm, whom Lane, as the reader has seen, would not have wanted anyway. The Sox had sinkerball specialist Bob Locker and hard-throwing rookie Dennis Higgins in the bullpen spelling Wilhelm and Fisher. Such an embarrassment of riches almost guaranteed a deal between the two clubs, and one was almost finalized during the exhibition season.

"I sat on the dugout bench with [O's manager] Hank Bauer for a half-hour during spring training one day," said Short. "We had a deal all set, and then it fell through." But now, on June 12 and with Chicago desperate for middle infield help, the Orioles sent Adair to the White Sox and received Eddie Fisher in return. Short represented the Sox at the trade announcement at Comiskey Park while Lane did the honors for the Orioles. Lane revealed that the Adair transaction originally had included several other players. "You [the White Sox] are getting the same guy," Lane said, "but we're getting somebody different."[6] Somebody better, too. Fisher, after a bit of a slow start in '66, was by this time back to 1965 form, having recorded a 2.29 ERA and six saves thus far and allowed 27 hits in 35 and one-third innings. Meanwhile, Adair had found himself in Bauer's doghouse and had emerged for just 17 games, during which he batted .288. After the trade, he was told by Short and manager Eddie Stanky the Chicago second-base job was his, but Adair ended up playing 75 games at shortstop as Elia was found wanting.

After the trade deadline, Lane headed to Mexico for some sun and more baseball. He wanted to check on two players in particular: Hector Espino, a slugging first baseman, and a left-handed-hitting catcher/first baseman from the Virgin Islands named Elrod Hendricks. "They were the class of the league, no question," Lane said a few years later. His reports back to Baltimore especially raved about Hendricks' unusual speed (for a catcher) as well as his quick bat, but the Orioles didn't seem interested. "I remember thinking the club might believe I was recommending him to justify my going to Mexico." Then, "after telling them about Hendricks, I said, 'And on the same club there's a kid who just might end up being the next Brooks Robinson.' I could see the Orioles thinking, 'If we listen to this guy Lane long enough, he'll have the whole Mexican League up here.'"[7] The "next Brooks Robinson" was Aurelio Rodriguez, who was to enjoy a lengthy big-league career, but he was signed by the California Angels — as was Hendricks. The latter, however, was left unprotected in the Rule 5 draft in December 1967 and, on the recommendation of both Lane and Earl Weaver, then an Orioles coach, finally was grabbed by Baltimore.

Meanwhile, up north, Eddie Fisher continued his fine pitching the rest of the season, helping to make Baltimore's run to the pennant that much easier (the O's finished 97–63, nine games ahead of runner-up Minnesota). He worked in 67 games, was credited with 19 saves, gave up 87 hits in 107 innings and finished the season with a 2.52 ERA. The big story, though, was Robinson, who had himself an MVP year, winning the Triple Crown by hitting .316 with 49 homers and 122 runs batted in — and the same number of runs scored. He had an on-base percentage of .410 and a remarkable slugging percentage of .637. Robinson also led the league in total bases (367) and, in the four-game World Series sweep of the Los Angeles Dodgers, he hit .286 with a triple and a pair of homers, one a two-run shot off Don Drysdale in the first inning of the opener — as Frank Lane and Jim Russo watched from Dodger Stadium seats so far from home plate that the two men must have thought they were in Pasadena.[8]

This marked the first time Lane had been involved in a World Series since 1940, when he was working for the Reds, that year's world champions. He had come close with the White Sox in 1955, the Cardinals in 1957 and the Indians in 1959, only to fall short. No one could stop this 1966 Baltimore club, with its pair of Gold Glovers on the left side of the infield (Brooks Robinson and Luis Aparicio), its young sluggers (Boog Powell and Curt Blefary), its fine young pitchers (led by Steve Barber, Wally Bunker, Dave McNally and Jim Palmer) and, of course, Frank Robinson. Frank Lane praised them all, but he had especially kind words for the little shortstop whom he had signed for the White Sox out of Venezuela years earlier. "My boy, Looie Aparicio, had a brilliant season at shortstop," Lane said. "He was hurting a lot, and [opposing baserunners] bumped him around. Still, they couldn't get him out of the game. This year, he'd get us the clutch hit. He would make the clutch defensive play."[9] Aparicio also stole 25 bases and batted .276, his best average since he hit .277 with Chicago in 1960.

Lane and Russo did not get much time to enjoy the world championship, for soon they were sitting down with Frank Cashen and Harry Dalton to discuss ways to make the Orioles even more formidable in 1967. Russo brought word that Chicago Cubs manager Leo Durocher had expressed major interest during the 1966 season in Baltimore power-hitting prospect Mike Epstein, a large (6–3, 230) first baseman then considered the top player in the minor leagues. Scouted heavily at Fairfax High School in Los Angeles and at the University of California-Berkeley, Epstein had signed with the Orioles and, in his first year in pro ball (1965), had slugged 30 home runs and hit .338 at Stockton in the California League. He was promoted to Triple-A

Rochester for the '66 season and responded by batting .309 with 29 homers and 102 RBIs. He was exactly the kind of young player Durocher wanted to get his rebuilding project underway. Leo had hoped to trade Ernie Banks for good prospects, but ownership would not allow it. He then tried to trade Ron Santo, but other teams were unwilling to part with real quality in return. So Durocher told the Orioles he would be willing to make sweet-swinging out-fielder Billy Williams available for the right package.

Lane and Russo could barely contain themselves when they reported this news to Cashen and Dalton at the winter meetings in Pittsburgh. Nor could manager Hank Bauer, who began scribbling lineups that included both Frank Robinson *and* Billy Williams. Billy had "slumped" in '66 to .278 with 29 homers and 91 RBIs, but still: Frank Robinson and Billy Williams in the same lineup? Lane, handling negotiations for the O's along with Dalton, proposed a 5-for-1 deal that Durocher and Cubs GM John Holland were willing to accept when they departed the Orioles' suite at 3 A.M. one morning after hours of give and take. The Orioles would send Epstein, 23; left fielder Curt Blefary, 23; right fielder Sam Bowens, 28; starting pitcher Tom Phoebus, 24, and reliever Eddie Watt, 25, to the Cubs.[10] Williams would head east to discover the joys of hitting third in a lineup that would have Frank Robinson in the cleanup spot and Brooks Robinson batting fifth.

However, shortly before Durocher and Cubs GM John Holland left the premises, Dalton expressed his opposition to the deal on the grounds that the Orioles were giving up too much. In addition to the manchild Epstein, Bal-timore would be surrendering Blefary, who had topped his rookie-year homer total of 22 in '64 with 23 more in '65; Bowens, a rookie star in '64 but now coming off a .210 season; Watt, who as a rookie the past season had gone 9–7 with a 3.83 ERA and 102 strikeouts and 44 walks in 145 and two-thirds innings; and Phoebus, 13–9 and 3.09 at Triple-A Rochester with 208 strikeouts in 200 innings.

According to Durocher, Lane immediately went on the attack. "Lane fought to make the deal," Leo wrote in his autobiography.[11] "He really fought for it. In front of all of us, he told Dalton, 'There's no way in the world you can sit here and not make that deal. You're going to get one of the four or five best left-handed hitters in the game, and he's young enough and he can run and he can field. How many times do you think that kind of player comes around?'"

So, with things up in the air, the teams agreed to meet the next day. When the Cub reps departed, it was Cashen's turn to express his doubts. "Let's not get in a hurry about moving Epstein," he said. "I have 400 Jewish box-seat holders who come to our ballpark. It would upset our budget if we piss them off and they didn't come out to the ballpark." Then it was Dalton's turn. "I don't think we can move Epstein. As far as I'm concerned, he's going to be a superstar."[12] He then placed a call to Orioles owner Jerry Hoffberger, who told his underlings he was unwilling to part with Epstein, who, he was certain, would become a great player and a terrific box-office attraction. The big boss had spoken. Billy Williams would not be an Oriole. For Russo and Lane, it was suddenly open season on their bosses. Said Russo: "If we get Billy Williams, the Jewish people will be just like everybody else — knocking the gates down to get in the ballpark and see this club play."[13] And Lane had this final shot for Dalton: "Boy, you're going to regret this," Frank told him. "Frank Robinson and Billy Williams in the same outfield, and you're letting it get away. I can't believe it."[14]

Williams might well have made a huge difference in the outcome of the 1967 American League pennant race, a wild affair in which just 1½ games separated the four contenders — Detroit, Chicago, Minnesota and Boston, the eventual winner — with one week to go. Where were the Orioles? They were in sixth place, 17 games back heading into the final week. What had happened? For one thing, physical maladies wreaked havoc on the pitching staff, and for another, Frank Robinson was out from June 27 through July 29 because of a concussion suffered in a collision at second base with White Sox infielder Al Weis. (Weis was less fortunate: He missed the rest of the season with a torn-up knee.) Some blame the loss of Robinson for the Orioles' failure in '67, but the truth is that, on the evening Frank went down, the O's were an unimpressive 32–35 and going nowhere. In addition, they were doing so without Mike Epstein, who had become a member of the Washington Senators.

Epstein had been blocked in Baltimore at first base by Boog Powell, another left-handed slugger who had homered 34 times the season before. Early on in 1967, Frank Lane came to the conclusion that the best landing spot for Epstein was Chicago — but the South Side, not the North Side. The White Sox, healthy again, were off to a good start but were dreadfully short on power. Although speedy, smooth-fielding Tommy McCraw seemed set at first base, the Sox, one would assume, happily would move him to the outfield to make room for a power guy like Epstein. Lane, acting as mouthpiece for Baltimore GM Harry Dalton, began talking trade with Chicago's Ed Short in early April. He was after one of the Sox's top three starting pitchers: Gary Peters, Joe Horlen or Tommy John. Apparently, Jerry Hoffberger had been convinced that getting pitching help made more sense than placing an "untouchable" tag on an untried rookie hitter. Lane, as he seemingly always did, brought the writers up to date with the progress of his discussions with Short. "Who could the White Sox get from Baltimore?" one scribe asked. Lane replied: "How about Mike Epstein? I can't make the final decision. But there's no law against the White Sox mentioning him. We want one of their top pitchers. Let them suggest names, Epstein included, if they're in a trading mood. We'll go on from there."[15]

Lane reappeared in Chicago in mid–May to talk some more with Short. Epstein had refused to be optioned to the minors earlier that month and was sitting at home in California. Short seemed unimpressed as Lane talked up Epstein's capabilities. A columnist approached and asked if the Orioles had received any solid offers for the left-handed swinger. "A while ago," he said, "I thought I could make a deal with Charlie Finley in Kansas City. Epstein and their pitcher, Catfish Hunter, would be the key men. But my Baltimore bosses stalled, and Finley took another look at Hunter — that guy's terrific — and withdrew him from the trade." What about the White Sox? "Well," Lane responded, "old Short here again has offered one of [Sox business manager] Rudie Schaffer's one-dollar steak sandwiches, and he only wants 10 pounds of prime rib in exchange."[16]

In the end, after all the talk and all the hype, Epstein wound up going to lowly Washington on May 29 along with lefty Frank Bertaina in exchange for left-hander Pete Richert, who would have several successful seasons in Baltimore. Epstein, meanwhile, finished his rookie year with nine homers, 29 RBIs and a .226 batting average. Two years later, under a new Senators manager — the immortal Ted Williams — Epstein blossomed, hitting 30 homers with 85 RBIs and a .278 batting average and .414 on-base percentage. However, he never again approached those numbers.

The entire Baltimore organization was determined never again to approach the embarrassment of its 1967 performance, which saw the Orioles finish 76–85 and in sixth place. Jim Palmer, 15–10 in 1966, was limited by arm trouble to nine games; Dave McNally pitched in only 24; Steve Barber, 10–6 and 2.30 in '66, couldn't find home plate and was traded to the Yankees in midseason. Such stalwarts as Luis Aparicio and right-fielder Russ Snyder were beginning to show their advancing years. "Little Looie" had dropped off to just 18 steals and a .233 batting average — and worse, because he was normally the Baltimore leadoff batter, to a .270 on-base percentage. Snyder, the team's other leadoff man, had slipped to .236 and .314. As the December winter meetings in Mexico City approached, the Orioles let it be known that Aparicio could be had. In return, they were asking for a solid leadoff batter and young pitching. Teams coming after the Orioles with offers for Aparicio included the Dodgers, Tigers, Yankees and White Sox.[17]

It wasn't long before Lane was busy chatting with his former publicity director, Ed Short, about an Aparicio deal. Lane and the Orioles' brass had long thought that Chicago's Don Buford was a better offensive player than his numbers showed. The former Southern Cal tailback, after hitting .336 at Triple-A Indianapolis with 41 doubles and 42 steals in 1963, had batted .262

as a White Sox rookie in 1964 but had posted a decent .337 on-base percentage. In 1965, Buford moved up to .283 and .358 and, in an August game against Baltimore in Chicago that summer, impressed the Orioles by leading off the first inning with a triple and then sprinting home on a popup to second baseman Bob Johnson in shallowest right field. The switch-hitter's batting averages the next two years were affected by the Sox's use of cold-storage baseballs and by their ordering groundskeeper Gene Bossard to keep the area in front of home plate at Comiskey Park soft, almost muddy. So Buford, though stealing 51 and 44 bases in '66 and '67, hit just .244 and .241 those two years but nonetheless had on-base marks 80 points higher than his batting averages. It was the Orioles' belief, too, that Buford belonged in the outfield, that his less-than-mediocre defensive play at second base and third base was affecting his offensive performance. Put him in the outfield, the Orioles figured, and Buford would hit around .290 and would become at least an adequate left fielder.

The White Sox, who probably should have won the pennant in '67 but instead lost the final five games of the season to 10th-place Kansas City and eighth-place Washington and finished fourth, three games out, wanted Aparicio mainly for his defense. Their shortstop, Ron Hansen, had not recovered totally from 1966 back surgery and had lost a shocking amount of range. Aparicio would be a major upgrade defensively at short, and, the Sox believed, would hit a lot closer to the .276 of '66 than the .233 of '67. Any kind of offensive improvement would be welcomed by manager Eddie Stanky, whose charges had batted just .225 as a team in '67.

Lane was there when the final details of the deal were completed. Aparicio, signed in Venezuela by Lane 15 winters before, was now party to a transaction that was sending Looie back to his original big-league organization. Joining him in the package were Snyder and minor-league first baseman John "Pineapple" Matias, a native of Hawaii. To Baltimore went Buford and two young right-handed pitchers, Bruce Howard and Roger Nelson. A week later, the White Sox, intent on adding offense, acquired former National League batting champion Tommy Davis from the Mets. The team also changed its television outlet from *WGN* to a fledgling station, *WFLD*, on the new *UHF* band. Soon, billboards all around town were conveying this message: "The Sox have traded for Aparicio, Davis and Channel 32." Unfortunately for Chicago, things didn't work out. The White Sox lost their first 10 games in 1968, Stanky was fired at midseason, Davis was hitting .194 at the All-Star break and the team stumbled home 67–95 and 36 games out of first place.

The Orioles, meanwhile, fell behind runaway Detroit early and were 43–37 at the All-Star break when Hank Bauer was fired and replaced by an irascible little fellow named Earl Weaver. The O's then went 48–34 in the second half and finished in second place at 91–71, a dozen games back of the Tigers. As Lane, Jim Russo and others in the Birds' front office had anticipated, Don Buford made himself right at home in Baltimore. With Chicago, he had started seven games in the outfield in four years. With the O's in 1968, he started 64 games in the outfield and played a total of 130 games, posting a .282 batting average and a .367 on-base percentage. In 1969, he became the everyday left fielder, playing alongside Paul Blair in center and Frank Robinson in right, and he improved to .291 (batting) and .397 (on-base). The Orioles romped to a 109–53 record before being shocked by the Mets in the World Series, then breezed to a 108–54 mark in 1970 and this time beat Cincinnati in a five-game Series. Buford slipped a bit to .277 but hit 17 homers, drew 109 walks and improved his on-base mark to .406. And then, in 1971, he hit .290 with a career-best .413 on-base percentage and 19 home runs, also a career high, and scored 99 runs for the third straight season. That Baltimore got more out of Don Buford than did Chicago is both obvious and understandable.

When Lane wasn't busy advising on or laying the foundation for trades, he was mesmerizing sportswriters with stories about the old days or turning in scouting reports on players from opposing clubs. Sometimes the reports would be rather unfavorable, like this one: "The only reason this guy is used is because nine players are required."[18] His scouting job took him to ballparks in both leagues, and he also used his time on the road to garner support for various pet causes. Years earlier, he had campaigned successfully for mandatory head protection for batters and had campaigned, unsuccessfully, for the awarding of two bases instead of one for a hit batsman. In 1962, he also argued for a "major-league" umpiring staff rather than having American and National League umps and their respective, and quite different, strike zones.[19] (He got his wish in 2000.)

Lane began a new crusade in 1967, becoming an advocate of a rule change proposed by Connie Mack in 1906 and championed in 1961 by GM Dewey Soriano of the Pacific Coast League's Seattle Rainiers.[20] Lane went from camp to camp in the spring of 1967 and 1968, trying to sell the idea of a "designated pinch hitter" who would be selected before the game and would bat for the starting pitcher (and his successors, if any) throughout the game — unless, of course, he himself were lifted for a pinch hitter. The "designated pinch hitter" was needed, Lane told anyone who would listen, because low-scoring games, beloved in the '40s and '50s when they were rarities, had become so commonplace that the sport was becoming dull. Also, he pointed out, "by giving a pinch batter the status of a regular, many great players would remain around longer. Under this system, guys like Ted Williams and Joe DiMaggio could have prolonged their careers by a few years and hyped attendance."[21] The American League adopted the rule in 1973.

Another of his ideas also had to do with aiding the pitiful offensive output of AL hitters, whose composite batting average in 1967 had been just .236. Lane disagreed with Paul Richards, then the Atlanta Braves' GM, who had suggested that the distance between home plate and the pitching rubber be increased by two to three feet. Instead, he preached, lower the mound from 15 inches to 10. That would maintain the traditional home-to-rubber distance at 60 feet 6 inches, enable hitters to follow the ball much better and, he said, "make a world of difference in bringing the bat back into baseball."[22] And indeed, after "The Year of the Pitcher" in 1968, the mound was lowered to 10 inches in both leagues.

The Orioles, who did not mind low-scoring games because their defense and starting pitching surpassed everyone else's, boasted three 20-game winners in Jim Palmer, Dave McNally and Mike Cuellar as the brass headed for the Biltmore Hotel in Los Angeles for the 1970 winter meetings. Even so, their goal was to add more pitching. At the top of their "most wanted" list was fireballing Mets right-hander Nolan Ryan, at that time still honing the skills that would make him a legend. Lane was given the assignment of discussing with the Mets the possibilities for a deal in advance of his bosses' arrival on the scene. Adding to the potential for a blockbuster deal, the Orioles had decided to put Frank Robinson on the block.

"A few years back," Lane said in 1978,[23] "when I was with Baltimore and Nolan Ryan was with the Mets, I was trying to trade Frank Robinson for Nolan Ryan — 'cause he had a *great* arm. Well, [Mets manager] Gil Hodges didn't come to the convention in Los Angeles, but Whitey Herzog and Bob Scheffing were there, representing him. And Herzog and Scheffing would've done the deal, but they put me on a phone in the next room with Gil Hodges back in New York. And he said, 'I don't want Robinson. I think he's more interested in being a manager.' I said, 'I *know* he's not, because I already told him that if he's a manager he'd have to take a hell of a cut in salary.' He was getting $140,000 from us. But Hodges didn't want him around.

"And in the course of the conversation, Gil said, 'Frank, don't feel too badly about not getting Nolan Ryan. He's a .500 pitcher.' I said, 'Well, you're just trying to make me feel good.' 'No,' he said, 'he's a .500 pitcher.' And he was exactly right." Indeed, despite all the 300-plus strikeout seasons and all the no-hitters and near-no-hitters, through the 1978 season, the 11th season of his career, Ryan's lifetime won-lost record was 151–145, an average W-L mark of 14–13. For his 26-year career, his final record was 324–292, an average of 12–11. So Gil Hodges was right: Ryan was a .500 pitcher. But he surely was an exciting .500 pitcher.

In any case, Lane had tried to get the deal done for Cashen, Dalton & Co., but he couldn't help it that Gil Hodges was distrustful of Frank Robinson. So Ryan, the number one target on the Orioles' trade list, remained in New York — until the following winter, when he was dealt to the California Angels. In the meantime, the Orioles on December 1, 1970, traded pitcher Tom Phoebus and two lesser players in a deal that netted them their number two target: San Diego's Pat Dobson. (The trade worked out quite well: Dobson went 20–8 in 1971, McNally was 21–5, Palmer 20–9 and Cuellar 20–9, making the O's the first team since the 1920 White Sox with four 20-game winners.)

A month after the winter meetings had ended, Frank Lane's phone rang. The caller was Milwaukee Brewers owner Allan "Bud" Selig. "We want you to come to Milwaukee," Selig said, "and run our baseball operation." Lane was 74, more than twice the age of his soon-to-be new boss. But suddenly, he was feeling like he was 44 again. Frank Lane was on his way to Brew Town.

12

Making Bud Wiser in
Milwaukee, 1971–1972

Frank Lane was a week shy of his 75th birthday on January 25, 1971, when his new boss, Allan "Bud" Selig, just 36 years old, introduced him as the Milwaukee Brewers' new "director of baseball operations"—apparently so as not to confuse those in the media who might have thought Lane was to be in charge of the Brewers' basketball or football operations. Frank, for the first time, would be running an expansion baseball team (though he had been at the helm of a fledgling NBA team). It would be a new experience for him, while having Lane around and watching him in action would be a new experience for Selig. "I will tell you," he remembered, "it was some kind of education for a young guy like me, just coming into the game of baseball, to be with Frank."[1]

The Brewers essentially were a third-year expansion club that had gotten its start in Seattle in 1969. As the Seattle Pilots, they finished 64–98 and had played their home games before seemingly private audiences. The next spring, with the ballclub headed for bankruptcy court, Selig and his investors in Milwaukee agreed to buy the Pilots and move them to Wisconsin. The change in location didn't improve the club's play, as the new Brewers ended up 65–97. Hence the call for Lane and a series of front-office changes, one of them the arrival of a new farm director, Bob Quinn, 34, the son of former Milwaukee Braves and Philadelphia Phillies general manager John Quinn and brother-in-law of Roland Hemond, who was then in his first year as Chicago White Sox GM. His dad would have been able to fill in Bob about Lane's colorful manner of speech, but if he hadn't, the younger Quinn soon got an example. If, for instance, one had not completed a task requested by Lane or had messed up in some other manner, it was best not to go to Frank to seek his understanding. "If you're looking for sympathy," he would say, "it's right there in the dictionary between 'shit' and 'syphilis.'"[2]

So the language had remained the same, as had his old telephone skills. As an indication that this was so, Lane made three trades during his first week on the job. Said Selig: "I was not surprised at all. That was Frank. I used to kid Frank that he thought he got paid by the number of deals he made."³ In the first one, just three days after he accepted the job, Lane sent Wisconsin native Gene Brabender, a big right-hander, to the California Angels for outfielder Bill Voss, a son of southern California. Two days later, he sent outfielder Bob Burda to the Cardinals for a minor-league pitcher and also, to show his boss that he meant to earn his salary, he exchanged catchers with the Royals the same day, trading Carl Taylor and getting Ellie Rodriguez — and, by far, the best of the deal. In April, he pilfered left-hander Marcelino Lopez from Baltimore and outfielder Johnny Briggs from the Phillies, and in July he landed three players from St. Louis, most notably the Cuban-born outfielder Jose Cardenal. By July, the Brewers' regular lineup contained only two players who had been regulars on the 1970 club: center fielder Dave May and left fielder Tommy Harper, the team's third baseman in '70. The starting rotation had also been overhauled and now featured two rookies: Bill Parsons, who was to win 13 games, and Jim Slaton, who would win 10.

The turnover in personnel had little effect, though. At season's end, the Brewers had a 69–92 record, safely ensconced in the American League West Division cellar. Lane's touch as a master trader was a tad tarnished by the deal that sent left-hander Al Downing to the Dodgers for outfielder/first baseman Andy Kosco, who had slipped from 19 homers and 74 RBIs for L.A. in 1969 to eight and 27 in '70. Downing, a former Yankee and the 1964 AL strikeout king, had split 1970 between Oakland and Milwaukee, posting a 5–13 record (2–10 with the Brewers). Lane figured his pitching was his strong point and that power was what Milwaukee needed. Kosco, after a fast start, did not provide it, finishing the season with 10 homers, 39 RBIs and a .227 batting average. Downing, meanwhile, won 20 games for the Dodgers and registered a 2.68 ERA.

Even so, there had been highlights in 1971, some of them amusing. The defending division champion Minnesota Twins found nothing funny, though, about their 7–2 Opening Day loss to the Wisconsin visitors, who roughed up 24-game winner Jim Perry and his associates for 12 hits, including a double and home run by Kosco. Marty Pattin pitched a complete game for the first of his 14 wins in 1971. The home opener, likewise, was a rousing success, as 40,566 poured into County Stadium and saw a 4–3 triumph over the Angels, a victory saved by the lefty Lopez, who retired the final six California hitters in succession. After a while, victories became more difficult to come by for manager Dave Bristol's club. On June 20, the Brew Crew stood at 22–38. Then, from June 20 through June 29, came a stretch of nine victories in 11 games, and Milwaukee was 31–40. The next evening brought a doubleheader defeat at the hands of Chicago, and the Brewers were back in fadeout mode.

Not that there wasn't fun along the way. Selig remembered spending home games seated behind the home-plate screen, learning from Lane the intricacies of the game as well as Frank's newest curse words of choice. "We did not have skyboxes in those days," Selig remembered. "He and I sat behind home plate, and I finally had to move him out to left field, because his language left a fair amount to be desired." After all, the current commissioner of baseball pointed out, "this was where our season-ticket customers sat."[4]

There was the Friday night in Kansas City (May 21), when the Brewers held a 4–1 lead after 4½ innings. Rain was falling as Royals catcher Jerry May came to bat. With the winds howling and the rain beginning to pour down, May struck out. Plate umpire Hank Soar than called for the Municipal Stadium infield to be covered. After a while the rain subsided and the grounds crew removed the tarp, but just then the rains returned, with the same force as before. Soar, who was also the crew chief, waited a little more than an hour and then called off the game, which would have to be replayed later in the season. Remarkably, Lane kept his silence for the time being, but when a close call went against the Brewers the next evening, he could no longer hold his peace. "I can't get over the rainout," he said. "That game should have been permitted to go on. It cost us a victory." Then, when asked about AL umpiring in general, he said, "There are only three sound umpires in the league." When he got wind of Lane's remarks, Soar reacted: "I hope he gets fined. He's just a showboat. Always has been, always will be. I looked for him and I wanted to see him so I could give him a piece of my mind." Lane's response: "He can't afford to give anybody a piece of his mind. He won't have that much left."[5] His Brewers had a less humorous response: They fashioned a 12–0 romp on May 22 as Pattin five-hit the Royals, followed by a 4–0 whitewash job the next day by Parsons, who threw a four-hitter in the series finale. Pattin and Parsons had a few more shutouts in them before the season was completed. Oakland sensation Vida Blue led the AL (and the majors) in shutouts with eight, Mel Stottlemyre of New York and Wilbur Wood of Chicago both had seven and Wood's teammate, Tom Bradley, fired six. But next in line was Pattin with five and Parsons and Jim Slaton with four apiece.

The Lane-Soar scrap escalated a bit during the summer when "Frantic Frank" called for the establishment of umpiring schools, where aspiring arbiters would get training from veteran major-league umpires and where umps already in the big leagues would get a refresher course or two—not only in positioning and rules and other topics, but also in on-field behavior. Lane believed the umpires had become too powerful, unwilling to let managers and players speak their mind and make their point. "A manager or player," he said, "can't open his mouth before he's thrown out. They won't even let anyone holler from the bench." Furthermore, he added, "there are two attitudes in the calling of plays—one for the contending clubs and the other for the teams at the bottom. If you belong to the have-nots, the umpires have a 'so-what' attitude. 'If in doubt, call 'em out.' That's their credo. That crack that [umpire] Jim Honochick made, calling the Brewers 'a bunch of raga-muffins,' is typical of how they feel. But we're one-twelfth of the league, and we pay our share of their salaries. So we should get the same shake as everyone else."[6]

In between blasts at the men in blue, Lane was keeping the press busy with a flurry of deals, all designed to improve the club. All they seemed to do, however, was weaken the other clubs—and the Brewers. On May 11, he sent two pitchers (John Gelnar and Jose Herrera) to Detroit for Jim Hannan, a teammate of Carl Yastrzemski at Notre Dame who had experienced some success in Washington a few years earlier, and also traded outfielder Ted Savage to the Royals for backup man Tom Matchick. Then came three pre-deadline deals: Outfielder Floyd Wicker went to the Giants for utility infielder Bobby Heise; first baseman Mike Hegan was sold to Oakland; and 1970 Brewers early-season home-run hero Danny Walton went to the Yankees for two outfielders, Bobby Mitchell and Frank Tepedino, who never were able to stay long in the big leagues.

"I knew Tepedino when he was in the Baltimore organization," said Lane, the former Orioles superscout. "They put him on the draft-eligible list when he was just 18, never dreaming anyone would take him. But the Yankees simply stole him and put him on the roster. He turned out to be an outstanding hitter (.300 and 16 homers at Triple-A Syracuse in 1969), just like the Orioles knew he could become. He has an excellent bat and he'll hit some home runs in Milwaukee."[7] He hit two, as it happened, and that "excellent" bat produced a .198 average in 53 games. The following March 31, Lane sold him back to the Yankees.

"Frantic Frank" almost made another move before the deadline. He had a chance to land troubled Angels outfielder Alex Johnson, who had won the AL batting title the year before (.329 average, 14 homers, 86 RBIs). Unfortunately, he had never gotten along too well with teammates or managers, had difficulty remembering to run out groundballs and invariably treated flyballs as potential dangers to be avoided at all cost. Angels manager Lefty Phillips was asked to compare him to the often controversial National League star, Richie Allen. "Once you get Richie Allen on the field," Phillips said, "your problems are over. When Johnson gets on the field, your problems are just beginning."[8] Still, Lane gave serious thought to the idea of trading for Johnson and was encouraged to at least make an attempt by Dave Bristol, for whom Johnson had played well at Cincinnati in 1968 and '69. But already in 1971, Johnson had been benched four times and suspended once. Angels GM Dick Walsh, most experts figured, should have been willing to practically give him away. Instead, he was asking Lane for Tommy Harper, Milwaukee's best every-day player. By June 15, with Johnson hitting only .262 with one home run and 16 RBIs, Lane's interest in a deal had reached its lowest point. And when Harper hit two doubles and a homer to beat Baltimore that evening, the inter-est level sank further. Walsh tried once more, at 10 minutes before midnight, but Lane said no. "Walsh called me a coward," Frank said. "Just say I'm a happy coward."[9]

Nothing Lane did could help the offense, not even the hiring of his old friend and Milwaukee native Harvey Kuenn as the new hitting instructor. The best indication of that was the four-game series July 9–11 at Chicago's Comiskey Park the weekend before the All-Star break. In the four games, the Brewers held the White Sox to just nine runs and yet lost three out of four. Joe Horlen topped Milwaukee's Jim Slaton 4–1 on Friday night, and, on Sat-urday, Rick Reichardt's single with two out in the ninth beat the usually invin-cible relief specialist Ken Sanders, 4–3. (Sanders led the AL in saves with 31 and appearances with 83 and finished with a 1.91 ERA.) On Sunday, Marty Pattin threw a four-hitter and struck out 10 in outdueling Tommy John 1–0 in the opener, but Wilbur Wood defeated Bill Parsons 1–0 in Game 2 on Ed Herrmann's fifth-inning homer. Milwaukee was heading to the break with a 37–48 record.

A skid of 10 losses in their next 13 games sent the Brewers' record plum-meting to 40–58, and the Brew Crew fell 20 games under .500 for the first time on August 20, when Joe Niekro edged Parsons, 3–2, in Detroit. Right about that time is when Lane, weary of one offensive failure after another, promised himself the Brewers would have at least a modicum of run-scoring potential in 1972. He had his eyes on Boston, where GM Dick O'Connell had told him he'd be more than willing to discuss the availability of big first base-man George Scott come the off-season. The two men agreed to keep the phone lines open and also to meet at the World Series. A deal, a large one, was quite possible.

It rained in Baltimore on October 10, enough so that Game 2 of the 1971 World Series between the Orioles and Pittsburgh Pirates had to be postponed until the next afternoon. This was a situation made for Frank Lane, the news-paperman's friend. Lane went into conference with his Boston counterpart, O'Connell, and convinced him of the news value of completing a deal now, with writers and broadcasters from everywhere hanging around the hotel lobby with little to do. A couple of hours later, the Brewers and Red Sox called a press conference and announced a deal involving 10 players. Milwaukee gave up one of the league's best pitchers in Pattin, plus right-hander Lew

Krausse, Tommy Harper and minor-league outfielder Pat Skrable. In return, Lane received six players, chief among them George Scott and former Cy Young award winner Jim Lonborg, both veterans of the 1967 World Series. The very thought forced folks back in Wisconsin to take notice: The Brewers suddenly had two players who actually had played in a World Series. Also coming from Boston were outfielders Billy Conigliaro and Joe Lahoud, backup catcher Don Pavletich and promising lefty Ken Brett, still just 22.

Noted Selig some 40 years afterward: "The 10-player trade was a very important trade.... It gave us a lot of credibility. [With it] Frank began to set us up for greater days to come."[10] He had told the *Milwaukee Journal*'s Bob Wolf basically the same thing in 1976. "I'd have to call it the best deal we've made. Considering what we got in the deal, and the ultimate byproducts of it, you might say it was the making of the franchise. Pattin and Harper were actually the only real talent we had, and we were fortunate enough to market them into something worth a whole lot more. We got Scott, certainly one of the best first basemen in baseball, and we ultimately used Lonborg and Brett to get Don Money, one of the best third basemen in baseball, from Philadelphia.... All in all, I can't begin to measure the importance of the Boston deal to this ballclub."[11]

The next stop for Lane was Phoenix and the winter meetings. Having traded Pattin and Krausse to Boston, he now looked to replenish his pitching inventory — especially with the team preparing to switch to the AL East in advance of the Washington Senators' rebirth as the Texas Rangers. Lane had his eye on a 25-year-old right-hander named Jim Colborn, who had fared well as a Cubs rookie in 1970 but, with a numbers problem on the Chicago staff, spent '71 at Tacoma in the Pacific Coast League. There he was 8–9 with a 3.92 ERA, certainly an acceptable earned-run average for that hitter-happy league. Most impressive were his 109 strikeouts and 31 walks in 124 innings as a starter and reliever. Along with Colborn (7–7, 3.11 ERA in '72 and 20–12, 3.18, in '73), Lane asked for Earl Stephenson, 24, a lanky left-hander for the bullpen. The Cubs in turn asked for Jose Cardenal, who had hit just .254 the final two months of the '71 season after coming over from St. Louis. Lane agreed but got the Cubs to add to the package center fielder Brock Davis, a onetime Astros prospect who had managed only .256 at Tacoma in '71 but had stolen 28 bases. The deal was made, and a few days later, so too was another one with the Orioles, who traded reserve outfielder Curt Motton to Milwaukee for pitcher Bob Reynolds. Lane, who remembered Motton from his days as a hot-shot prospect in Baltimore, hoped the 32-year-old would provide help off the bench. (He was 1-for-6 as a Brewer before being dispatched to the Angels.)

The performance of the 1972 Brewers pitching staff was quite creditable:

Lonborg was excellent at 14–12 and 2.83, Parsons won 13 games and Sanders and Frank Linzy were effective relievers. Despite Lane's efforts to improve the attack, however, Milwaukee still wound up hitting just .235 as a team, only six points higher than the 1971 Brewers, belted fewer home runs (104–88) and scored fewer runs as well (534 in '71 to 493 in '72) in six fewer games—a brief players' strike wiped out the season's first week. Even big George Scott batted just .266, though he did sock 20 homers (second on the club to Johnny Briggs' 21) and drove in a team-leading 88 runs. But this club was anemic right from the beginning, when, after winning the opener, the Brew Crew dropped 10 of 12. The hitting was at its most feeble during a period from April 25 through May 6. In that rather inglorious stretch, the Brewers lost to the Angels, 3–1 and 4–1, and to Oakland, 5–1 and 2–1, before erupting for a 3–1 dismantling of Oakland, Ken Brett getting the win. There followed a 7–0 defeat handed to them by the Twins' Bert Blyleven and 4–0 and 2–0 losses to Nolan Ryan and Andy Messersmith of the Angels.

While the scoreboard operator stocked up on NoDoz, Frank Lane, watching his team prove it could finish last in the AL East as well as the AL West, tried to find ways to keep his mind occupied. His chief interest—after firing manager Dave Bristol and replacing him with former Milwaukee Braves All-Star catcher Del Crandall—seemed to lie in the mysterious scoreboard at Comiskey Park. The 1972 White Sox, bolstered by the addition of former National League slugger Richie Allen—now to be known as Dick—were pounding pitchers in Chicago but not having quite the same success on the road. The difference in wins and losses was quite startling, in fact. When manager Chuck Tanner's White Sox completed a four-game sweep of Lane's Brewers on June 11, Chicago was 24–4 at home and 6–14 on the road. Their overall record of 30–18, though, was still only good for second place in the AL West, where Oakland was rolling at 33–14. The huge discrepancy in Chicago's home and road records made Lane suspicious. So did the fact that the Sox's top three home run hitters—Allen (11 through June 11), Bill Melton (six) and Carlos May (five)—had hit 18 of their 22 homers at home.

"I'm convinced they have someone up in the scoreboard stealing signs," Lane said after the White Sox had rallied in the ninth to capture Sunday's series finale, 5–4. "There shouldn't be that much difference between a club's hitting at home and away. But I don't blame them. When I was here [in Chicago], we had someone up there. In fact, I went out to look [Saturday], but they saw me coming. And unless you catch them red-handed, it's the hardest thing in the world to prove."[12] Lane had been down this road before, starting in 1949 in Cleveland, when he realized that Bill Veeck's Indians, managed by Lou Boudreau, were stealing and relaying signs from their scoreboard. In Kansas City six years after that, Boudreau, by then managing the A's, had set up a system for getting the catcher's signs—a system discovered by Lane. The White Sox, using an elaborate scheme set up by Lane, stole opponents' signs from the Comiskey Park scoreboard in 1955. And Veeck, when he owned the Sox, did the same in 1960. Lane, many years later, talked freely about Comiskey Park's cheating center-field scoreboard.

"In '55," he began, "we were almost certain they were stealing our signs in Kansas City, Detroit and Cleveland. So I said to George Kell and Bob Kennedy, 'Those sons of bitches are getting our signs.' So either Kell or Kennedy, or both, said, 'Well, why don't *we* do it?' So I got hold of Del Wilber, who I had picked up as a bullpen coach. I gave him a pair of binoculars and put him up in the scoreboard."

The board in those days, Lane explained, showed just the uniform numbers of the pitchers and catchers of the Sox game in progress. Chicago catcher Sherm Lollar's number was 10. "The pitcher," Lane said, "might've been 32 or whatever the hell it was, but Lollar's number was the key. Now Wilber, up in the scoreboard, would get the catcher's sign. If it was a fastball, the scoreboard operator would 'wiggle' the 'one'—if it was a curveball, they'd wiggle the zero. Now, not everybody would use the signs. Fox wouldn't take the signs; Minnie wouldn't take the signs. I think the only two guys who took them were Kell and Kennedy. And on the first homestand of, oh, eight to 10 days, those two just wore it out. And we're getting ready to go on the road and Kennedy says, 'Geez, Frank, why don't we do this on the road?' I said, 'You bastard, what do you think I'm gonna do? Sit out in the bleachers with a sparkler?'

"Now since then, they have done it here. Veeck, I know, will laugh and say no. Tanner wouldn't admit it. But I said to Chuck, 'Tanner, you bastard, we're gonna change our signs around and one of your guys is gonna get killed'—which could happen. But he used the board (in '72), and it didn't hurt the White Sox's hitting, either. See, I had signed Tanner back in '59. He had about 35 days to go to get his pension. He had a bad leg, but I signed him anyway and brought him to Cleveland. So I told him, 'You son of a bitch. I got you your pension, and now you're gonna steal our signs?' He laughed. And he never did admit it. But he never denied it, either."[13]

Two months later, Lane was back in Chicago for two more Brewers-White Sox games, both won by the hosts, 2–1 and 8–6. "They're still getting signs from somewhere," Lane charged. "Tanner swears nobody is passing them from the scoreboard, but what difference does it make how they do it? They're 44–14 at home and batting .280, and 20-32 on the road, hitting 6 and seven-eighths. There's got to be an explanation."[14] He didn't have an explanation a week later, either, when someone asked him why, with an allegedly improved ballclub in 1972, the Brewers had a worse record (43–69) than they had after the same number of games in 1971, when they were 48–64. "When you look at the personnel," he said, "there's no comparison. The hitting is improved ... our pitching has held up but has been inconsistent. We're better on defense and have better depth. Still, we're losing."[15]

Lane likely had an idea of what would happen when the season was over, that Selig had plans for a front-office shakeup that would take him out of the GM's chair. Before the season came to a close, though, there were some final highlights for Frank to enjoy. As he used to say, "Anytime we'd beat the Yankees one game it was like beating somebody else three."[16] No, these 1972 Yankees were hardly the Yankees who terrorized the American League in the '50s. But they were still the New York Yankees, so when the Brewers beat New York 7–2 on September 19 at County Stadium (paced by Parsons' pitching and homers by George Scott and John Briggs) and followed that with a 4–1 win over the Yanks (Briggs homered again and drove in three), Lane had to be wearing a smile. And when the Brewers closed the campaign in New York on October 2–3–4 by sweeping a three-game series — 6–1 behind Ken Brett, 3–2 behind Skip Lockwood and 1–0 on Lonborg's three-hitter — one could expect Lane to have been downright giddy.

If he was, the giddiness did not last. At a press conference the next day in Milwaukee, Bud Selig announced that (a) Lane was out as general manager and would become the club's superscout, and that (b) he was being replaced by former big-league pitcher Jim Wilson, whom Lane had brought in the year before as director of scouting. Also, top scout Jim Baumer, first signed out of high school by Lane for the White Sox in 1949, was to get Wilson's old job, and Al Widmar, a former pitcher acquired by Lane in the Sherm Lollar deal 20 years before, was taking over as director of player development. Everyone made the proper comments. Said Wilson: "The first thing I thought was, how do you replace a legend? Frank Lane is just that — a legend." [17] Added Selig: "I'd like to make it clear that this restructuring is in no way a criticism of Frank Lane or minimizes the outstanding work he has done for the club over the last two seasons.... He has a position with us as long as he wants one."[18] Even Lane seemed pleased. "I won't have to worry about all that office work," he said. "This will leave me free to go where the hell I should go — and that's on the road."[19]

If there was disappointment in the realization that the GM chair at County Stadium likely was the last such one in which he would sit, Lane didn't show it. He answered the questions like the seasoned veteran he was. No, he had *not* been fired. "If I had been fired," he said, "I would have been on a plane to Acapulco instead of catching planes to the playoffs and World Series." And no, he wasn't discouraged by the just-completed season. "I liken myself to an expectant grandfather, waiting for the birth. I think we are going to give birth to a very fine baseball club and organization, and I want to be present at the [big event]."[20]

Almost 40 years later, Bud Selig gave Frank Lane his final job review. "Frank was great to work with. I know I had heard all of the stories about 'Trader Lane' and how bombastic he was and everything else, but I never found that of him. Frank was a pleasure to work with. He got along great with everyone. He had a great sense of humor.... He was a character and really a very interesting guy. I know my family loved Frank. I cannot say enough about him."[21]

13

Closing It Out with the Cowboy, 1974–1979

It wasn't long before Frank Lane had resigned from his rather powerless position with the Brewers, knowing full well that Milwaukee could have been his final stop in baseball. He was 76 now, after all, and employers generally are not wont to hiring 76-year-olds. This, however, was Frank Lane, a man who still had plenty to offer a baseball operation. His former boss at Baltimore, Harry Dalton, was well aware of it, too. Dalton had left the Orioles to take the general manager's position with Gene Autry's California Angels in 1972. Certainly, if he wanted it, there would be a spot for Lane on Dalton's new board of strategy.

For the time being, though, he took a job in December 1973 as a special assistant in the front office of the Texas Rangers. There he was reunited with two former comrades: the Rangers' new manager, Billy Martin, and a new front-office employee named Jimmy Piersall. Between stories of their old Cleveland days, that trio, along with the Rangers' flamboyant owner, Bob Short, managed to get some work done, despite the occasional arguments. Wrote Washington columnist Mo Siegel: "Tapes of their meetings—Martin, Lane, Piersall and Short all in the same room at the same time — would have made the Nixon Watergate tapes sound like a Billy Graham broadcast."[1] However, a Fort Worth industrialist, Brad Corbett, bought the club from Short in April 1974, and then the fun really began. Corbett, 34 at the time, had made millions through his plastic pipe and tubing company and seemed bent on becoming the latest of the George Steinbrenner-Ray Kroc-Ted Turner-type baseball club owner — the kind who figured a baseball team is run the same way as one's business. If the team gets off to a slow start, there is little thought given to the reality that the schedule lasts six months and not six weeks (or days). It's time to start firing first the hitting or pitching coaches and then, of course, the manager. If a high-priced hitter is batting only .225 after 20 games, why, it's time to unload him or, at the very least, bench him. And do the benching yourself: don't *suggest* the manager bench him; *tell* the manager to bench him.

Corbett vowed to pay top dollar for players, improve Arlington Stadium and, in general, make it worthwhile to be a Rangers fan. The 1974 team, spurred on by veteran right-hander Fergie Jenkins' 25 wins and by Jeff Burroughs' MVP season, went 84–76 and finished second in the AL West, five games behind Oakland. Everything began unraveling the following year, though, and with the Rangers shuffling along at 44–51 in July, Corbett decided Martin had to go — and with him, his two most trusted coaches: ex-Yankee teammate Charlie Silvera and pitching coach Art Fowler. "He wants to call the shots," Martin said of Corbett. "One year in baseball, and all of a sudden he's a genius."[2] It wasn't long before Corbett was depending as much upon his son, with whom the father spent many evenings going over newspaper sports sections and baseball record books, than his own front-office aides. (Brad Jr. was 11 years old in 1975.) Lane, for one, soon was questioning Corbett's sanity. "Having him run a baseball team," Frank said, "is like giving a 3-year-old a handful of razor blades."[3]

By 1977, the year he went through four different managers, Corbett was taking to the airwaves, ostensibly to announce that the Rangers were for sale but actually just to blow off steam. Texas, a terrific offensive club, was having trouble pitching and catching the baseball. "I've got players that I'd put complete confidence and faith in, and I've found that those players just don't give a damn. They don't care about anything but drawing a paycheck. They are dogs on the field and off the field."[4] The next year, Corbett called a press conference to announce that "there *might* be a chance we will get [the Angels'] Nolan Ryan tomorrow."[5] He didn't get Ryan, but two weeks later, Corbett got angry — angry enough to kick open the clubhouse door after a 2–1 loss to Kansas City. "At first he didn't say anything," reported first baseman Mike Hargrove, "but he was breathing mighty heavy." Then Corbett began: "It's incredible to me that this team — with all its talent — has scored 153 runs fewer [actually 63] than Kansas City. We've got to start playing with some pride." The reaming continued for several minutes before Corbett departed the scene.[6]

Lane had departed Texas by then, having taken up Harry Dalton on his offer to join him with the Angels, who had finished dead last in the AL West in 1975. His base again was to be Chicago, the place where it had all begun almost 30 years before. Now, as a superscout and an adviser to Dalton, he was to cover American League teams and players at Comiskey Park when the White Sox were in town, and then cover National League teams and players at Wrigley Field when the Cubs were home. The job would keep him in the sunshine — and, at times perhaps, in the spotlight — and would enable him to once again visit with influential columnists and writers, off of whom he could bounce his latest thoughts and opinions about the "grand old game."

He'd had much fun doing so during the '60s; now he'd have to add new material to his repertoire, even though the old material was funny then and remains rather comedic today. For one, there was his commentary on Cubs owner P.K. Wrigley's decision to hire an athletic director in the early '60s to go along with his so-called College of Coaches. The duties of the AD, retired Air Force colonel Bob Whitlow, seemingly began and ended with sitting behind home plate and charting pitches. Lane's take: "The Cubs are improving. Now they have an athletic director whose job it is to chart every pitch. Now Wrigley has all sorts of records proving that his players strike out on the 2–2 pitch instead of the 3–2 pitch."[7]

Lane also had ripped baseball's leadership for allowing *CBS* to purchase the Yankees in 1964. "Baseball," he said, "is a personal game. When I was with the White Sox, if we won, the fans would stand outside and cheer us. When we lost, they'd boo me or Chuck Comiskey and they'd ask who we planned to trade next. Can you imagine Yankee fans searching all over New York to boo 43 *CBS* vice presidents?"[8]

On the other hand, Lane was pro-establishment when it came to player-owner relations. He had little use for Marvin Miller, executive director of the players' union, because he believed Miller was in it for himself. In March of 1970, when there was talk of a possible strike by the players, Lane remarked: "It certainly isn't going to hurt Miller if the players go on strike. While they're going hungry, Miller will merely open up another office and handle the milk-wagon drivers or car washers or someone else. The players are taking all the risks. Miller is going to get all the credit. If the players give Miller enough rope, he'll take credit for the bases being 90 feet apart and the grass being green.... The greatest thing the players have going for them is that the owners are the most enthusiastic fans that baseball has. The players don't need Miller."[9]

All this had come about as the result of Curt Flood's January 1970 $1 million lawsuit against major-league baseball. Flood, the $90,000-a-year center fielder of the St. Louis Cardinals, had been traded to the Philadelphia Phillies but refused to report, setting in motion his crusade to eliminate baseball's reserve clause, which he compared to slavery. If he lost the case, which eventually he did, Flood said he would retire from the game and fall back on his artistic skills to make a living. He already had painted portraits of Martin Luther King Jr. and "Gussie" Busch, among other subjects. Lane wished him luck: "You know that the $100-a-week fan, who is sitting up there wondering if his two tickets deprived a kid of a pair of shoes, isn't so worried about Curt Flood being sold into bondage. And Flood sure as hell better be twice as good as Rembrandt if he's going to quit baseball and devote his time to painting."[10]

The columnists and baseball writers who knew him best loved passing the time with him in the press boxes of the American and National leagues. "A guy once asked me," one reporter said, "why I spend so much time with Lane. I told him I can learn more from Lane in two minutes than I can in two days from any other baseball man."[11] They especially enjoyed chatting with Frank during the winter meetings as well as just before and after the old June 15th trading deadline. They knew he would give them the latest information on trade talks — those of his team and those of everyone else's. There were times, though, when work had to be done and even Lane had to leave the writers behind and get on the phone with other deal-makers. He was just learning the Angels' personnel in early December 1975 when Harry Dalton asked him to meet with the Yankees to see if they'd be willing to deal slugging speedster and right fielder Bobby Bonds, who had hit 32 home runs and also stolen 30 bases for New York in 1975. The Angels had hit all of 55 home runs in '75, a total that Billy Martin had found amusing. "The Angels," Billy said, "could take batting practice in a hotel lobby and not break anything."[12] The presence of Bonds, if Dalton and Lane could land him, would end such talk. Dalton assigned Lane to shadow Yankee GM Gabe Paul at the winter meetings in Hollywood, Florida, to determine if indeed Bonds was on the block and to convince Paul that the offers he was hearing from other clubs could not match California's. The Angels' offer was too good for the Yankees to pass up: pitcher Ed Figueroa (16–13, 2.90 ERA in '75) and center fielder Mickey Rivers (.284, 13 triples, 70 steals) for the 29-year-old Bonds, who had hit just .270 but with an on-base percentage of .375.

Paul and Lane shook hands on the deal, and Dalton and Angels manager Dick Williams announced it to the media. And then, the same day, Lane met with Bill Veeck, who had just gained control of the White Sox for the second time. The Angels, seeking more power, took third baseman Bill Melton off Veeck's hands for first baseman Jim Spencer, expendable because California already had a lefty-swinging first baseman in Bruce Bochte. Melton, former AL home run king, had hit 33 homers in both 1970 and '71 but, slowed by back trouble and pained too by the constant, grinding criticism of Sox broadcaster Harry Caray, had hit just 15 long ones in 1975. He was happy to be getting out of Chicago, maybe more happy than Dalton and Williams were to be adding his bat and that of Bonds. "It took us 26 weeks to hit 55 home runs last season and 10 hours to pick up 47 in one day here," said Dalton, laughing. Added Williams: "Maybe now we can break some windows."[13] They didn't break many. The '76 Angels hit 63 home runs, eight more than the year before, and improved their record only slightly, from 72–89 to 76–86. Melton never did get going, finishing at .208 with six homers. Bonds, after hitting .354 with six home runs and 24 RBIs through the Angels' first 30 games, slumped steadily thereafter until his season ended on August 8, when he had surgery to repair a broken hand. Mickey Rivers and Ed Figueroa, meanwhile, helped the Yankees win their first pennant in a dozen years.

Next came the first off-season of free agency, what Curt Flood had dreamed of just a few years before. Players could now play out their contracts and then sell themselves to the highest bidder. Angels owner Gene Autry advised Harry Dalton that the checkbook was wide open, so Dalton sized things up and happily noted that the free-agent "class" included two players his organization had developed in Baltimore: outfielder Don Baylor and second baseman Bobby Grich. He signed Baylor to a six-year, $1.6 million contract; Grich signed a five-year, $1.35 deal. And former Oakland star Joe Rudi got the fattest pact: five years, $2 million. Fans were startled by the "huge" numbers, but making the proper signings in free agency was just another way to rapidly improve a ballclub — without having to give up any ballplayers. Surely the Angels would be improved in 1977. They had two standout starting pitchers, Frank Tanana and Nolan Ryan (but admittedly not much to go with them). Offensively, they had Grich, Rudi and Baylor joining a healthy Bobby Bonds. Grich was moving to his original position, shortstop, because the Angels already employed a fine second baseman, Jerry Remy. That they were dangerously short on pitching was not lost on Dalton, who was reminded of that fact time and time again by Frank Lane.

The first pitcher to arrive after the 1977 season began, in a May 11 deal for Bruce Bochte, was lefty reliever Dave LaRoche, who had first come up to the big leagues as an Angels rookie in 1970 and had enjoyed success in Anaheim as well as Cleveland. Next, in June, Dalton picked up onetime big winner Gary Nolan from the Reds for a minor-leaguer. (Nolan, it soon became obvious, was finished.) Finally, on June 15, right-handers Don Kirkwood and John Verhoeven plus minor-league infielder John Flannery were dealt to the White Sox for lefty Ken Brett, the result of weeks of bargaining between Lane and Bill Veeck. Brett had been superb in 1976, going 10–12 with a 3.28 ERA and only five home runs allowed in 203 innings. Thus far in '77, the older brother of George Brett was 6–4 but his ERA was up to 5.01. Obviously, Lane and Dalton were confident that Brett would put together a strong finish. "Frank Lane should get credit for the Brett deal," Dalton said. "He did most of the negotiating with Veeck. We've been after Brett for months. We've scouted him in eight games. He's throwing well."[14]

So were the staff aces. Tanana was off to a 10–2 start and Ryan opened 8–4, but then key injuries began ruining California's season. Grich's lasted until June 8, when the club was 26–26; within a week, he had undergone season-ending back surgery. Rudi suffered a fractured right thumb on June 26 when he was hit by a Nellie Briles fastball in Texas. He, too, was lost for the season. The Angels were 35–33 at the time of Rudi's mishap, and they were 39–42 at the halfway mark, when Dalton fired manager Norm Sherry and replaced him with third-base coach Dave Garcia. Changing managers didn't help. Despite solid years from Bobby Bonds (37 homers, 115 RBIs, 41 stolen bases), Baylor (25 homers, 75 RBIs, 26 steals), Tanana (15–9, 2.54) and Ryan (19–16, 2.77, 342 strikeouts in 299 innings), the Angels ended up 74–88. That did not faze Autry, however. He gave Dalton and new front-office chief Buzzy Bavasi, moving up the coast from San Diego, the go-ahead to spend more. Introduced on November 21 at Anaheim Stadium was ex–Minnesota Twins outfielder Lyman Bostock, whose .336 batting average in 1977 was second in the AL only to teammate Rod Carew's .388. Bostock signed for five years for a total of $3 million. Later that same day, Dalton bid the Angels farewell and accepted an offer to become the Milwaukee Brewers' general manager.

With the winter meetings in Honolulu just over a week away, Bavasi, new both to the American League and to the Angels, suddenly was in a bind. Enter Frank Lane. Dalton had told Bavasi that if he needed someone to carry the ball for him, Lane was his man. So off to Hawaii flew the Angels' delegation, headed nominally by Bavasi but in actuality by Lane, who knew exactly what the ballclub needed. Within just a few days, Lane acquired it. First he stunned the convention by trading Bonds to the White Sox with swift 21-year-old rookie outfielder Thad Bosley and 18-year-old pitcher Richard Dotson — the Angels' first-round amateur draft pick the previous June — for young right-handers Chris Knapp and Dave Frost and catcher Brian Downing. Knapp had gone 12–7 as a rookie in '77, Frost had spent the year at Triple-A Iowa and Downing, though hitting .284, had lost the starting catcher's job to Jim Essian and had played in just 69 games. Next day, Lane gave up second baseman Jerry Remy — expendable now with Bobby Grich set to move back to second base and young Rance Mulliniks taking over at shortstop — for $150,000 and right-hander Don Aase, 23, who as a Boston Red Sox rookie had posted a 6–2 record and 3.12 ERA in 13 starts. Bavasi, meanwhile, made a deal with his son Peter, a vice president with the Toronto Blue Jays, that brought ex–Dodger Ron Fairly back to southern California and also signed Boston outfielder Rick Miller, a terrific defensive player, as a free agent — for the $150,000 received in the Aase-Remy deal. Most observers agreed that these were sensible moves — except for the Bonds trade, which had people scratching their heads and/or making jokes about the Angels' front office.

"It was highway robbery," Detroit senior scout Jack Tighe said. "Bill Veeck hasn't lost his touch." Added one AL manager: "I'm going to tell Gene Autry he ought to fire Buzzy Bavasi for making that deal." Even Harry Dalton moved quickly to distance himself from any blame for his former club's surprising trade. "I don't want to start any controversy," he said, "but I want to make this clear: It wasn't *my* deal."[15]

No, it wasn't. But he was one of the people who in a roundabout way had forced it, in Frank Lane's view. In his Chicago hotel room six months later, Lane provided his version of why the trade — which eventually proved to be heavily in the Angels' favor — had to be made.

"I wanted arms," he began. "We needed pitching last season too, so Dalton went out and signed Rudi, who isn't worth a shit right now — he's hitting .185 and he has a five-year contract worth about $2 million. He signed Grich, who had a bad back. And he isn't hitting — never was that good a hitter. But he's a second baseman, and we needed pitching. So Dalton signed two outfielders and a second baseman. Then two of them got hurt, and Dalton says, 'Well, we've got our two best guys in the hospital.' Finally, I told him, 'Harry, change your tune. For Christ's sake, even if they're *not* in the hospital, they're not pitchers.' See, Dalton's been so used to having a bunch of guys around him suckin' his ass— it's shocking. I said, 'For Christ's sake, Harry, you know bleepin' well I'm not gonna yes you.' But he's surrounded himself with about five guys from Baltimore, and they're going around saying, 'We're all right. We've got this, we've got that....' And finally I told one of the 'yes' men, 'Don't give me that shit. If we're that good, how come we're down around fifth or sixth place?' Unless you're 1-2-3, you can't talk in terms of having a good ballclub."[16]

He smiled when reminded of the reaction to the Bonds deal. "When we made that deal, Bill [Veeck] and [White Sox VP] Roland Hemond were howling to the writers about how they had fleeced Lane. To start with, if Buzzy Bavasi doesn't OK the deals, I don't make them. But I recommend them, and I told Buzzy, 'This is what we need. We need pitching.' But anyway, they were all busy saying Veeck fleeced me. And they asked me, and I said, 'Yeah, he fleeced me — he's too smart for me. But I needed pitching, and if Bonds hadn't had that good a year, we wouldn't have been able to get the two young pitchers and Downing.' Which is true."[17]

Hemond, serving as a messenger from his boss Veeck, had visited with Lane in the stands at the World Series in Los Angeles two months earlier. Veeck and Hemond knew the Angels needed a catcher and were aware of Lane's admiration for Downing, who had given it all he had ever since his first game in the major leagues, a May 31, 1973, contest with Detroit. Downing, with the host Sox up 10–2 in the sixth, subbed for Bill Melton at third base and sprinted after a pop foul and dived into the dugout in hopeless pursuit. A broken bone here, a few bruises there, and Downing was out for two full months. On his second at-bat after returning, he drilled an inside-the-park homer to center field off Mickey Lolich in Tiger Stadium for his first hit in the big leagues.

"I wanted Downing," Lane said as he recalled his October 1977 in-game visit with Hemond. "I knew Downing had a questionable arm, but I liked his gung-ho stuff. They'd give us Downing — if we'd give them Bosley, a young pitcher and Mulliniks, our young shortstop. I said, 'What the hell are you talking about?'"[18] Sure, Lane wanted Downing, but not at that cost. Yet that mini-conference set in motion the process that eventually yielded the Bonds deal.

By June 1978, the Angels already had the edge in the trade. Bonds, who had hit only two home runs for the slow-starting White Sox in the first six weeks, had been traded to Texas by Veeck, who was unwilling to pay Bonds' big salary ($178,000) during what was going to be a bleak season on the South Side. Bosley had been promoted to Chicago over the Memorial Day weekend (and was 7 for his first 14), but Knapp was pitching well in the Angels' rotation and Downing — who for a time was on the Angels' all-time home run leader until being passed by Tim Salmon and Garret Anderson — had settled in as first-string catcher. California, however, was spinning its wheels, unable to get rolling, even with all the new additions. The biggest disappointment had been Lyman Bostock, a sure .300 hitter who had left Chicago on May 31 after a three-game series with the White Sox in a 1-for-16 slump and carrying a .209 batting average. That night, with Lane watching from the Comiskey Park press box, the Sox had pounded the Angels, 17–2, to sweep the series and extend California's losing streak to five games. It was Dave Garcia's final night on the job. Former Angels star shortstop Jim Fregosi asked for and received his release from the Pittsburgh Pirates and went to work immediately as Garcia's successor. Bostock also went to work, collecting 13 hits in his first 23 at-bats under Fregosi and fulfilling Garcia's prediction made to Lane just days before: "Bostock will hit. He's always hit. He'll start soon."

"That's the tough thing," Lane said. "If Bostock gets those 13 hits for Dave, Dave's still our manager. You lose your job because someone else doesn't do his job. And I can't blame Dave for not motivating Bostock. He was right: He was going to start hitting. But Dave was not a motivator. So he wasn't going to bother Bostock. He'd never bother anybody. I'd say, 'Are you worried about hurting the players' feelings? Think about our feelings. Think about Gene Autry's.' He'd say, 'They'll be all right, they'll be all right.' But there are times you have to put on the act. And I often begged Dave, 'Go out there and get thrown out of the goddamn ballgame. It won't change the umpire's decision, but it will change the opinion the players have of you.'

"Dave is a very knowledgeable baseball man. You'd sit down with him and talk and you'd marvel at his knowledge of the game — and players. But there's more to managing a baseball team than knowledge. Very few Harvard professors would make good managers. You have to be able to motivate. That's where Billy Martin ... Earl Weaver ... those little bastards—that's where they come in. They get 'em stirred up—get 'em off their dead duff. Because if your manager's fighting for you, goddamn it, you're gonna fight too."[19]

Fregosi was a fighter as well as having been an outstanding ballplayer, Gene Autry's favorite. Autry believed he could be as successful as a manager as he had been as a player. In any case, he was the right answer as far as Bostock was concerned. As soon as Fregosi assumed command, Bostock embarked on a 14-game hitting streak and, when that was halted for one game, he collected hits in the next five, a surge that upped his batting average to .279. The rest of the ballclub did not respond instantly; in fact, the Angels fell to 36–36 after a fifth consecutive defeat, this one the opener of a four-game series with Kansas City in Anaheim. In the series' second game, though, with the Angels down 4–1 in the seventh, Rudi came off the bench to drill a two-out grand slam and California won, 5–4. Knapp improved to 8–6 the next night as Grich's home run paved the way to a 9–5 triumph. One day later, Dave Frost, just up from Triple-A Salt Lake City, threw eight innings of three-hit ball and Ron Fairly's two-run, two-out single off Al Hrabosky in the home eighth gave California a 3–1 victory and left the Angels and Royals tied for second place in the West, a game behind Texas.

At the All-Star break, the Angels (45–40) were in first place, leading Kansas City by one game and Texas by 2½. By August 1, the Royals were back on top by four games, but then the Halos put together a string of nine victories in 11 games to close the gap to a single game. California's four losses in the next five games should have meant big trouble, but the Royals matched the futility of the Angels.

Baltimore came to town August 18–20 for a three-game series. In the opener, Knapp gave up back-to-back homers in the fourth to Doug DeCinces and Eddie Murray but gave nothing after that, and Baylor's two-out solo homer in the ninth off Scott McGregor won it, 3–2. Rick Miller's RBI single with two gone in the seventh snapped a 3–3 tie and gave Paul Hartzell a 4–3 decision over Jim Palmer before 38,870 in Saturday night's matchup. Ryan and Dennis Martinez went at it on Sunday in a game that was scoreless until Baylor's bloop two-out double scored Miller in the 14th. Now the Angels and Kansas City were in a virtual tie for the AL West lead.

The final visitors on the homestand were the New York Yankees, who split a pair of games. Kansas City, meanwhile, was losing two of three in Chicago, so when the Angels arrived in Boston on Thursday night, the 24th, they were leading the division by a half-game. Three straight losses to the Red Sox while the Royals were dropping two of three at Texas meant Kansas

City was back on top by a half-game. It also meant that Frank Lane would be spending the next few days trying to pry loose White Sox right-hander Steve Stone, a 15-game winner in '77 and 10–10 so far this season with a subpar club.

Lane had gone to watch Stone pitch Saturday night against Cleveland and had come away impressed, "Stoney" having worked seven innings of six-hit, two-run baseball. "There's no question we have to have another starting pitcher if we're going to win this thing," Lane told reporters. "Nolan Ryan has a pulled rib muscle, and he isn't even with the club on our [Eastern] trip. Frank Tanana has been pitching for a year with a sore arm." As for Stone, said Lane, "Anyone would like to have a pitcher like that. He knows what he's doing." Stone, a free agent at season's end and well aware that the Angels were trying to get him before the August 31 deadline for setting postseason rosters, said he'd welcome the warmth of Anaheim. "The Angels would be my absolute No. 1 choice. I think they have a good shot at the pennant. It would be nice to play a part in it."[20]

However, Stone went nowhere, as it happened, and after splitting their next 10 games it appeared the Angels had the same destination. On Friday, September 8, when the Royals arrived in Anaheim for a four-game series, Kansas City had a 2½-game lead, which became 3½ when the Royals rolled 9–7 in the opener. Now, it was up to two of Frank Lane's youthful, local December acquisitions, Don Aase (from Orange) and Dave Frost (of Long Beach), to stem the tide. In front of 41,511 at "The Big A," Aase worked eight scoreless innings and won 3–2 in Game 1 of a twi-nighter, while Frost went the full nine innings and topped K.C. ace Dennis Leonard, 4–2, in the night-cap. Don Baylor's first-inning grand slam started the Angels and Nolan Ryan toward a 13–3 rout the next day, and just like that, the Royals' lead was again just a half-game.

California got no closer. Kansas City won five straight after departing Anaheim and 10 of 12 to go up by five games with eight to play. That was it. The Angels, who ended the season in Chicago, finished second at 87–75 and they also finished without one of their stars. Lyman Bostock was shot to death in nearby Gary, Indiana, on the morning of the season finale.

Bostock's murder brought a tragic ending to the season, and for a time the mood throughout the organization was somber. Eventually, though, the realization set in that 1978 had been the franchise's best year yet and that a championship was close. Vacationing in Mexico, a vindicated Frank Lane was sitting in the sun, smiling.

The Angels' main addition in 1979 was seven-time AL batting champion and 12-time All-Star Rod Carew, Bostock's former teammate with the Twins.

Carew, at age 33 and coming off his second straight hitting crown, did not come cheaply. The Angels gave up two top minor-league prospects—lefty Brad Havens and catcher Dave Engle—right-hander Paul Hartzell, a staff regular the previous two seasons, plus the key to the deal: 24-year-old outfielder Kenny Landreaux. The Twins were not going to make the deal unless Landreaux was in it. Off went Landreaux to the Twin Cities, and the left-handed hitter had a better year than Carew. He batted .305 with 27 doubles, 5 triples, 15 homers, 83 RBIs and 10 steals. But Buzzy Bavasi, Jim Fregosi, Frank Lane and Gene Autry figured that this was Rod Carew. If you have a chance to get him, you do whatever it takes to get him. So they did. Earlier, at the winter meetings, Bavasi had left Lane with Twins boss Cal Griffith to see if a deal could be worked out for Minnesota right fielder Darnell "Disco Dan" Ford. Lane and Griffith, who had been doing these sorts of things since the '50s, soon had a trade to announce: Ford to the Angels for two former high draft picks, infielder Ron Jackson and catcher Danny Goodwin.

The team opened the season on fire, a 10-game April winning streak staking the Angels to a 12–3 start. They put together both a six-game win skein and a five-gamer in May as they built a four-game lead over Kansas City. But then, after getting swept in successive three-game series by Texas and the Royals, some concerns began developing. It was June 28, and California had dropped a half-game back of both Kansas City and Texas. Consternation quickly departed, though, thanks to a stretch of 13 victories in 16 games leading up to the All-Star break. First the Angels swept three at K.C., then they came home and won three in a row from Oakland before dropping the series finale. California took two of three from both Baltimore and Boston before the Yankees came into town for the final three games (July 13–15) before the break.

On Friday night before 41,805, the Angels won 6–1 as Brian Downing and Dan Ford each collected three hits and Nolan Ryan took a no-hitter into the ninth before Reggie Jackson's one-out single broke it up. A turnout of 41,693 on Saturday night saw the Yanks take a 6–2 lead into the eighth, but homers by Don Baylor and Joe Rudi off Rich Gossage closed the gap to 6–4. It was 7–4 when the Angels came up to bat in the ninth, but singles by Carney Lansford and Ford gave Baylor a chance, and he took advantage. His second homer of the night and 23rd of the season tied the game at 7–7. Finally, in the 12th, against previously unbeaten Yankee reliever Ron Davis (8–0), Downing opened with a double, took third on Rudi's bunt and scored on Merv Rettenmund's single to right. For those 40,739 fans seeking more thrills on Sunday, they had come to the right place. Dave Frost gave up a pair of two-run homers in the first two innings (to Chris Chambliss and Jim Spencer), but he and Jim Barr threw zeros the rest of the way while Bobby Grich (4–

for-5) went to work against lefty Ron Guidry. In the seventh, Grich's two-run double cut the New York lead to 4–3, and in the ninth, with a man on and two out, Grich took Guidry deep for a game-ending home run. The 5–4 triumph gave the Angels a two-game edge on Texas and a five-game lead on Kansas City.

A stretch of eight defeats in nine games knocked California out of first in the AL West on August 30, a half-game behind the Royals. Then, however, came nine wins in the next 10 games, and the Angels were back on top by four. With California's lead at three entering the series, the Halos and Royals split four games in Kansas City September 17–20, but a Royals victory at Oakland and an Angels loss to Texas on Friday night the 21st in Anaheim cut the lead to two. But then, with Frank Lane watching approvingly from a luxury suite at "The Big A," Chris Knapp and Dave Frost delivered, in succession, two of the year's most clutch performances. Knapp went the route on Saturday afternoon before 33,730 people, allowing just five Rangers hits and one walk to win 3–1, and Frost then threw a complete-game six-hitter on Sunday (attendance: 40,631), striking out five and walking no one for a 6–1 triumph, his 16th of the season. The lead was back up to three games, and now the Royals were coming to town for three games, two of which they had to win to remain alive. They never had a chance. Nolan Ryan pitched a five-hitter and struck out eight and Ford drove in all the home team's runs in a 4–3 victory Monday night before 40,423. Finally, Downing went 3-for-3 with two RBIs and Frank Tanana, making only his 17th start of 1979, matched Ryan with a route-going five-hitter of his own to beat K.C., 4–1, and clinch the division title. Gene Autry immediately began paying homage to his *second* champion. After all, his horse "Champion" would always be his first.

That the Angels went on to lose to Baltimore three games to one in the American League Championship Series could not diminish the joy of the 19-year-old franchise's first trip to the postseason. The team had been built with Autry's money, which had been spent wisely, for the most part, by Harry Dalton and Buzzy Bavasi, who were able to put 1979 AL MVP Don Baylor, Bobby Grich, Joe Rudi, Rick Miller and, most recently, Rod Carew in Angel uniforms. It had been built through the continued development of the farm system, which had turned out Carney Lansford, Frank Tanana and rookie reliever Mark Clear, among others. And it had been built through some shrewd trades, several of them made by the grandest trader of all, "Frantic Frank" Lane. For, while the Angels would not have won the division without Baylor (36 homers, 139 RBIs, .296), Grich (30/101/.294), Lansford (19/79/.287) and Carew (.318, .419 on-base percentage), they also most assuredly would not have won without Ford (21/101/.290), Frost (16–10, 3.57, 239 and one-third innings) and, most of all, Downing (.325, 12, 75, .418 OBP).

Downing, as it turned out, spent 13 seasons with his hometown team and wound up writing his name all over the franchise's record book. As the 2013 season begins, he is third on the club's all-time list in home runs, runs batted in, runs scored, base hits, extra-base hits, doubles, total bases, games played and sacrifice flies. He also ranks second in bases on balls and first in hit by pitches. One could say that he was Frank Lane's contribution to Anaheim. Maybe not as memorable as Walt Disney's, but a contribution nonetheless.

As for Lane, when the World Series was over, he called Gene Autry to say that retirement was knocking loudly because this was the right way to go out — as a winner. Truth be told, he had planned to retire after the 1979 season, anyway. He had said so back in June 1978, to that young interviewer at the Bismarck Hotel. "What I've told Gene," he said then, "is that I'll work this year and next year, and then I'm going to retire. But I don't know what I'd do if I retired. Get up in the morning, and then how am I going to kill the day? Of course, someone may kill me first."[21]

Dead or alive, "The Trader" had made his last trade.

Epilogue

The news came over the radio that morning in March 1981. Frank Lane, the controversial and colorful baseball executive who had transformed the White Sox, Cardinals and Indians from also-rans into contenders, had passed away in Richardson, Texas, at age 85. He had suffered a broken hip some months earlier in his Chicago hotel room and recuperated in a Chicagoland rest home before being moved to the Dallas area by his only child, daughter Nadi. "Dad just never perked up since the accident," she said. "And his health was rapidly failing."[1]

It was a sad day for baseball, although some in the game, perhaps understandably, weren't exactly crying their eyes out. In his autobiography, Bobby Bragan, who lived in the Dallas–Fort Worth area and was asked by then-commissioner Bowie Kuhn to represent him at Lane's funeral, seemed to take special delight in the fact that only eight people attended. On hand were Bragan, a minister, a Dallas city council member, Lane's second wife, his daughter, her husband and their two children. "Had I not received Kuhn's request," Bragan wrote, "I would never have gone to Lane's funeral. But as it turned out, I was glad I did. I drove to the cemetery and looked around for the large crowd I expected to be in attendance at Lane's services. There was none."[2] (One person who had wanted to be there was Bill Veeck, who was unable to travel at the time because of health issues of his own.)

Among the ballplayers, managers and front-office personnel of the 1950s and early '60s, there weren't many lukewarm feelings toward "Frantic Frank" Lane. They either liked him or disliked him. There was no middle of the road. It's understandable that players might not like a man who could and did trade them at the drop of a hat, a man with whom they had to negotiate contracts every winter, a man who on occasion would rip into them from his seat — whether that be on the roof of old Busch Stadium, the first row of boxes at Yankee Stadium or in the upper deck at old Comiskey Park. And yet some, such as Jimmy Piersall, the great defensive center fielder acquired for Cleveland by Lane in December 1958 and himself one of the game's great characters, liked him as a person and truly enjoyed his "act."

"Lane second-guessed the world. He would've second-guessed the pope,"

Piersall said, laughing. "He used to sit up in the right-field upper deck at Comiskey Park when he was general manager of the White Sox, and he'd scream at his own players. He'd scream at George Kell: 'You're too goddamn old!' Or at Sam Mele: 'Why'd I get you for?' I used to listen to him, and I'd holler back up at him, and then I'd throw salt tablets up to him."[3] He knew Lane was always thinking pennant and of ways to make his club better. "What he did was give himself a chance to win something," Piersall said. "He put a good club together [at Cleveland] in '59. He just made a mistake on the manager [Joe Gordon]."

Perhaps Lane's biggest fan was Minnie Minoso, who played for him for seven seasons, five in Chicago and two in Cleveland. Frank called Minnie "my son," while Minnie called Lane his "Papa Number Two." One reason for that was the way Lane took care of Minoso's financial affairs. "Minnie didn't trust banks or anything else," Chicago broadcaster Jack Brickhouse remembered. "One time he slid into second base and they had to hold the game up because the slide had jarred his money belt loose. He was wearing a money belt! And he had about $3,000 on him."[4] Thereafter, Lane became Minoso's banker as well as his boss. Even so, the two had their moments. Often in 1951, Minoso played right field against left-handed pitching, enabling Paul Richards to use right-handed hitters Bob Dillinger at third and Don Lenhardt in left. That meant Minoso might get an earful from Lane, seated in the right-field upper deck, if Minnie misplayed a ball or failed in the clutch offensively. "Once I dropped a flyball," Minnie said, "and he yelled, 'Hey Minoso! I'm gonna send you back to goddamn Cuba to cut sugar cane!'" Minoso turned and hollered back at his boss: "Here! You're so good, you come out here and play!" But, Minnie added, "He really did treat me like a son. I knew I could trust him."[5]

Another Frank Lane fan was White Sox outfielder Jim Rivera. "He'd go on the road with us," Rivera remembered, "and if we won a series—swept it, [or] won three out of four—Frank would buy dinner for the ballclub. I had a lot of general managers, in the majors and the minors, but he was the only one I liked."[6] Not that Lane didn't have an occasional barb for "Jungle Jim." Rivera drove up to Comiskey Park one morning in a new white Eldorado. Lane sized up the situation and barked, "There are too many .260 hitters in this league driving around in Cadillacs."[7] However, as Rivera later pointed out, "Frank had a white Cadillac, too. I don't remember if it was an Eldorado or not, but it was white. Guess it bothered him that a .260 hitter was driving the same kind of car as the general manager of the ballclub."[8] Rivera, nominally the regular right fielder during much of Lane's tenure in Chicago, often heard it from Frank during weekday afternoon home games, when Lane invariably watched from the right-field upper deck. "He hollered at me all the time," Rivera said. "We'd be up to bat, and I might be batting with two on and two out, something like that, and I might strike out. And then, as I'd be running out to my position, Frank would holler down, 'What's the matter? Can't hit anymore?'" Then there might be a comment about guys driving Cadillacs who shouldn't be, and then all would be forgotten.[9]

"On rainy days or nights," Rivera continued, "I remember he'd come into the clubhouse after the game, and if your shoes were soaked through, he'd tell ya, 'Go get yourself a new pair of spikes at such-and-such a store — have them put it on my bill.' He'd do those kinds of things for the ballplayers. That's the way he was." He didn't forget those players, either. On the night of September 22, 1959, even though Rivera's home run had been a key blow in Chicago's pennant-clinching 4–2 triumph over Lane's second-place Indians at Cleveland, "I remember Frank coming into our clubhouse and congratulating his former players — me, Nellie [Fox], Sherm [Lollar], Billy [Pierce], Dick Donovan."[10] He also congratulated those who hadn't actually played for him but whom he had signed to their first pro contracts: Luis Aparicio, center fielder Jim Landis, right fielder Jim McAnany, catchers Johnny Romano and Earl Battey, first baseman Norm Cash, pitchers Barry Latman and Rodolfo Arias, infielder Sammy Esposito plus two September call-ups: first baseman Ron Jackson and outfielder Joe Hicks.

Lane did something else for Rivera that Jim would not forget. The White Sox had released Rivera, then 38, in early June 1961. Lane, then with Kansas City as GM under Charlie Finley, told the boss he wanted to sign the former Chicago South Side favorite. Finley, a White Sox fan who'd grown up in Gary, Indiana, and had seen Rivera play any number of times, was all for it. Finley saw it as a good public-relations move. Lane saw it as something else. "He didn't sign me right away," Rivera recalled. "I was getting some offers to do some scouting, but Frank knew I needed just a couple more months or so to get my 10 years in for the pension. So he signed me, and I got to play a little, too — a lot more than I had the year before [165 plate appearances versus just 20 in 1960]."[11]

Vic Power, Lane's first baseman at Cleveland, hit .312 in 1958. Lane believed that Power, who with Kansas City had hit .319 and .309 in successive seasons before (1955-56) but had slumped to .259 in 1957, had the talent to hit .300 every year. So, the GM challenged him. If Power hit .300 in '59, Lane would buy him a new car. Power went out and had a fine season and was particularly steady in the second half, as the Indians battled the White Sox for the AL lead. After games of June 28, he was batting .296. At the close of Sunday action for the next eight weeks, his batting averages read .301, .300, .301, .305, .305, .303, .302 and .301. At the close of the ninth week, which ended with the pennant-deciding four-game sweep by Chicago on August 28–30, Power was still at .301. No doubt a bit dispirited, Power then went into an 8-for-56 skid and finished at .289.

"Oh, baby, I was so mad," Power told author Larry Moffi. Lane, however, knew what Power had done while the race was at its most heated. He called Power into his office. "He told me, 'Listen, Vic, sometimes you didn't hustle enough; if you had hustled more, you could have hit .300. Sometimes you didn't sleep enough; if you went to bed earlier, you could have hit .300.' He got me nearly crying. But after he finished, you know what he did? He threw the keys to me. He gave me the car anyhow. I went home to my wife and told her the same thing: 'Listen, sometimes you didn't cook for me. Sometimes I had to take care of the kids at 4 in the morning when you were sleeping. If you could've done more, I could've hit .300.' She was about to cry when I threw the keys to *her*. Then she got dressed and we went for a ride, baby. It was a Pontiac station wagon — white, with red inside. Oh, I enjoyed that station wagon. I brought it back to Puerto Rico. 'Trader Frank' Lane? He was a pro, baby."[12]

Not that a supporter like Power didn't ever disagree with Lane. "We had a lot of players coming and going," he said, "but the biggest mistake he made was trading Colavito. We didn't have anyone to take his place. I even batted cleanup a lot of the time [in 1960]. I had 84 RBIs, which was my career best, but I wish someone else on the team had more, because we needed it. We had a lot of good hitters, but no RBI men."[13]

In June of 1955, before the days of the amateur draft, the finest players just out of college and high school traveled to big-league ballparks to work out in front of the various teams' farm directors, top scouts and general managers. A left-handed-hitting second baseman named Grover "Deacon" Jones, a recent graduate of Ithaca (N.Y.) College with a B.S. degree in physiotherapy, had made stops at Yankee Stadium, Connie Mack Stadium in Philadelphia, Milwaukee County Stadium and a few more. He had been working out at Comiskey Park for two days and now he found himself sitting in the office of Frank Lane, with White Sox manager Marty Marion on hand as well. The Sox, with two bonus babies already on the roster (first baseman Ron Jackson from Western Michigan and outfielder Bob Powell from Michigan State), were not going to add a third and thus could only offer Jones $4,000 to sign. If a prospect received anything above that amount — Jackson, for instance, had pocketed $80,000 in June '54 and Powell, earlier in June '55, had been given $36,000 — he would be forced to spend two years with the major-league club before he could be sent to the minors. The not-very-well-kept secret of the period was that some of the best players received $4,000 and also took home gifts of various kinds.

Jones, whose playing career was cut short by a severe shoulder injury but who made a name for himself as a batting instructor for several big-league clubs, was a bit intimidated by Lane's presence. "Finally," Jones related, "Lane spoke. 'OK, Jones, I want to sign you. What do you want?' Now you've got to appreciate the fact that here I am, a young, punk kid, scared ... and Lane's a very tough guy. I told him, 'Well, I'd like to have a car.' And he said, 'What kind of car?' 'Well, one like Marty Marion's.' And Marty had this new black Ford convertible, and he'd only had it a week. And Lane says, 'Marty, give him your car.' And he did."[14]

The side of Lane shown in the preceding vignettes would likely be dismissed out of hand as fictional by his critics. That's probably because their experiences with the man were seldom positive. Bobby Bragan, for one, almost felt relieved to be fired as Cleveland manager in July 1958. On that day, he told reporters what it was like working under Lane: "When I walked into the clubhouse, there was Frank Lane. When I stepped into the airport limousine, there was Frank Lane. I walked out to the batting cage, and there was Frank Lane again."[15] Bragan also made it obvious that his ringing public endorsement of Lane's hiring by the Tribe in November 1957 had been nothing but a lie. Wrote Bragan: "My heart sank at the thought, and damn near plunged from sight, when I read who [Hank] Greenberg's replacement would be — the notorious Frank Lane. 'Trader' Lane, everybody called him. The man who became famous because he made changes just to shake things up, with no plan really in mind. Lane had been general manager of the Cardinals.... I didn't think it was any accident that St. Louis had quickly dropped from contention in the National League."[16] Apparently Bobby wasn't paying attention to the NL standings while he was managing the Pirates in 1956 and '57, when the Cardinals, under Lane's leadership, improved from seventh place in 1955 to fourth in '56 and to first place at the All-Star break in '57 before finishing a close second.

It is obvious he couldn't have been paying too much attention during the 1959 World Series between the Chicago White Sox and his Dodgers (he had managed their Triple-A Spokane club that season). Wrote Bragan: "I also remember [White Sox manager] Al Lopez inserting Minnie Minoso for defensive purposes in one game and Minnie making a great catch to save a run."[17] First, a .300 hitter like Minoso certainly would have been in the starting lineup for an offensively challenged team like the 1959 White Sox; second, and a bit more important, Minnie was not a member of the 1959 White Sox.

Just as critical of Lane was Rocky Colavito, who battled with "Frantic Frank" over salary each off-season before The Trade With Detroit. "I can look back now," he told author Terry Pluto, "and see that Lane had a vendetta against me. In our contract talks, he lied to me in 1957. Then he just downgraded everything I did. He tried to blame me for not winning the pennant in 1959 because, he said, I had a slump in September." (In fact, Rocky's slump began before that. He was hitting .292 on July 14, but he finished the season at .257. In 20 games in September, he batted .207 with three home runs.) "Lane kept dwelling on my strikeouts, but I never struck out 100 times in a season, which is really good for a power hitter."[18] Opening Day 1960 was one opener Colavito never forgot. He went 0-for-6 in his new team's 4–2, 15-inning victory over his former team, striking out four times, flying out softly and grounding into a double play. "It was the worst game of my career," he said. "I never struck out four times in a game before or after that. Every time I came to the plate, I wanted to make Frank Lane eat every bad word he'd said about me."[19] The next day, Rocky blasted a three-run homer off Jim Perry and the Tigers beat the Indians again. The Tribe would miss Colavito's power in a big way that season. Said Cleveland pitcher Mudcat Grant: "You want to know why Lane traded Rocky? That's easy. Lane was an idiot."[20]

Stan Musial was another who had little use for Lane. Eleven years after Frank had traded Red Schoendienst and was rumored to be trading Musial too, Lane was scouting for Baltimore, "Stan the Man" was the new GM of the Cardinals and Schoendienst was their manager. One day, Musial and Schoendienst were sitting near the front of the bus that was to take the Cardinals from their hotel to the ballpark. Frank stepped onto the bus and grabbed a seat, hoping to ride along — a fairly common practice among baseball men. Musial, however, still wouldn't forgive or forget. He got up, walked over to Lane and said, "Get the hell out of here. Get off our bus." Lane complied.[21]

Gus Zernial was forced off the White Sox bus after Lane completed the three-team trade that put Minnie Minoso in a Chicago uniform. Zernial had hit .318 as a 1949 rookie and had followed up by batting .280 and setting a club record with 29 home runs the next season. "I thought ... the White Sox had a young nucleus that could develop into a contending team," he said. "However, Frank Lane liked to trade anyone who shared the limelight with him. So he made me part of that big deal."[22] "Ozark Ike" ended up leading the AL in homers (33) and RBIs (129). Meanwhile, the Sox did become contenders — without Zernial.

They would not have done so without Chico Carrasquel, the All-Star shortstop from Venezuela. Chico had no Colavito-class disputes with Lane, but sometimes he simply couldn't figure him out. "My best year was 1954," he told author Danny Peary. "I scored 106 runs and I hit 12 homers — I'd hit a total of nine my first four seasons. When I was a rookie in 1950, I didn't steal any bases, but in '51, under Paul Richards, I stole 14, double the seven I had in 1954, my next-highest total. After the '53 season, I asked Frank Lane for a raise. He said I should hit more home runs. So after I hit those 12 home runs in '54, I went to see Lane and reminded him of what he said. But now he said that I didn't steal enough bases!"[23]

Frank Lane's biggest boosters, besides fans of the Chicago White Sox, were the members of the media. This was understandable, since he treated them with respect, was a veritable gold mine of ideas for reporters needing off-day stories, and understood they had a job to do. After all, he once had been one of them, having worked in his younger days on the sports staff of the *Cincinnati Commercial Tribune*. He talked about his relationship with the media one day toward the end of his career. "I'd never give a damn if I was misquoted. The worst thing that could happen," he added, grinning, "was if they *didn't* quote me. But I never lied to them. When I couldn't tell them the truth, I wouldn't tell them anything." Also, he said, he never flaunted his position or power. "Just because you have the title of general manager doesn't make you God Almighty. I mean, I could be wrong. They still put erasers on pencils. But the sportswriter, the broadcaster, they're seeing your ballclub every day. [If they criticize your club], what are you gonna tell them? 'What the hell do you know?' But they *do* know."[24]

Sometimes they knew even when they didn't. One writer passed along word to *The Sporting News* in early March 1955 that Lane, then with Chicago, was about to land third baseman Jim Finigan (a .302 hitter for the Athletics as a rookie in '54) and pitcher Arnie Portocarrero for veteran third baseman George Kell, infielder/outfielder Stan Jok, 19-year-old catching prospect Earl Battey and pitchers Mike Fornieles and Connie Johnson. There was nothing to it, but Lane didn't mind. "That didn't come from me," he said. "The writers never took the trouble to ask me. They'd throw in any names they wanted. They figured that someday, sooner or later, I'd get around to it, because I was making quite a few deals, and sometimes what they guessed ahead of time would come true. And they always figured I was making deals because I was a compulsive dealer, that I couldn't wait to make the next deal. But every deal I made, I thought it out and, if I thought it wouldn't help us, I wouldn't make the deal." [25]

Joe Falls, the longtime Detroit columnist, might have wondered if Lane had really meant that, but he was one of those writers who gave thanks daily for Frank. "I wonder," he wrote in 1972, when Lane was GM at Milwaukee, "how many of us sportswriters, especially baseball writers, guys who make a living in the business, really appreciate this man. It seems as if Frank Lane has been around forever. He's been in baseball ever since I began covering the sport. It seems as if you see him everywhere. He's in the hotel lobbies. He's at all the conventions. He comes up to the press rooms. It seems as if he has a new job every 30 minutes. He is always around. And he is always talking baseball. OK, there's a need for the Marvin Millers ... the Bowie Kuhns and even the Curt Floods. But thank heaven there is still a Frank Lane in our presence, and long may he wave."[26]

One wonders if "Frantic Frank" could operate in today's game as a general manager — or, indeed, if he even would have the desire to do so. "He would feel stifled if he still were a general manager," C.C. Johnson Spink wrote in 1979. And Lane agreed: "Baseball's become a silly business — the most un-businesslike business in the world."[27] Jimmy Piersall's belief mirrored that of Spink — that Lane would feel constricted in the world of sports agents, no-trade clauses, free agency and long-term contracts — no longer able to pick up the phone and make an eight-player deal without consulting anyone's agent. "He wasn't a businessman — he was a baseball man," Piersall said. "His job was to get players. Today he couldn't be a general manager. No, he couldn't operate today. After all the years he operated his way, I don't think he'd have the patience."[28]

Still, here was a man whose hyperactive mind produced so many ideas for improving the product; surely he would conceive of ways to exist and succeed in 21st-century baseball. "I'm sure," Roger Kahn declared recently, "he would've adjusted to the frenetic world of baseball today."[29] Commissioner Bud Selig agreed: "Frank would have had to change a little bit to survive in the front office of today's game, because life itself has changed so much. [But] I think Frank was smart enough that he could have made the necessary adjustments."[30]

Lane had adjusted before, after all. He ran ballclubs in four different decades. He had outworked and outsmarted older men as well as younger men. He had done it before; he likely could have done it again. In any case, Lane left behind a body of work that puts him at or near the top of the list of baseball's most colorful and successful front-office chiefs. "In the winter, he was like [George] Steinbrenner, only better," said Piersall, referring to the bombastic, bullying former New York Yankees boss who dominated the winter meetings from the late '70s until the '90s with his often-outrageous free-agent signings. "Steinbrenner couldn't carry Lane's jock. They'd go to the winter meetings, there'd be a bunch of player movement, and he'd be right in the middle of everything. He's the most colorful general manager of all time. Nobody close to him."[31]

Rest assured that Frank Lane would heartily endorse that last statement, too. Proof of that would be a response he gave Falls and his fellow Detroit scribe, Jim Hawkins, in a long-forgotten pregame baseball quiz at Milwaukee's County Stadium. For their paper's weekly feature, Lane was asked to give one-name responses to the writers' questions. The final four went like this:

"Who was the best baseball player you ever saw?"

"Ty Cobb."

"Who was the best manager you ever saw?"

"Joe McCarthy."

"The best team you ever saw?"

"I'd have to pick the old Yankees ... the era of Ruth and Gehrig, definitely."

"The best general manager?"

"I would say ... because you see, the facilities that a man has ... you see, I had jobs where..."

"One name, Frank, one name."

"Well, the fellow who had to do the most with the least was Frank Lane."[32]

THE END

Appendix I: The Best and Worst of Frank Lane

The Five Best Trades

1. **White Sox send catcher Joe Tipton to Athletics for second baseman Nelson Fox (October 19, 1949).** A backup catcher for an eventual Hall-of-Famer, team sparkplug and 1959 American League MVP.
2. **White Sox send veteran catcher Aaron Robinson to Detroit for pitcher Billy Pierce and $10,000 (November 10, 1948).** Lane's first deal. Pierce, then 21, went on to start three All-Star Games, and amass 211 victories and post two 20-win seasons.
3. **White Sox land outfielders Minnie Minoso and Paul Lehner in three-team (Indians and A's), seven-player trade in which Lane gives up outfielders Gus Zernial and Dave Philley (April 30, 1951).** Minnie, a rookie, electrified Chicago and ushered in the "Go-Go" era.
4. **Indians trade outfielder Larry Doby to Tigers for outfielder-first baseman Tito Francona (March 21, 1959).** Doby was at the end; Francona, just 25, hit .363 with 20 homers as the Indians fell just short of the White Sox in the run for the pennant.
5. **Angels trade outfielders Bobby Bonds and Thad Bosley and minor-league pitcher Richard Dotson (then 18) to the White Sox for catcher Brian Downing and pitchers Chris Knapp and Dave Frost (December 5, 1977).** Lane, as Angels superscout, negotiated the deal that brought two keys to California's 1979 division title (Frost, who won 16 games, and Downing, who went on to hit 222 home runs in an Angels uniform). Bonds was gone from Chicago by May '78.

The Five Worst Trades

1. **Indians trade first baseman Norm Cash to the Tigers for infielder Steve Demeter (April 12, 1960).** Cash, whom Lane had signed out of college in 1955, hit .361 with 41 home runs in 1961 and ended with 377 career homers. Demeter had two hits in 23 major-league at-bats.
2. **Indians trade right fielder Rocky Colavito to the Tigers for outfielder Harvey Kuenn (April 17, 1960).** Trading Colavito, the 1959 AL home run champ and a

179

Cleveland folk hero, for the '59 AL batting champ soured many northern Ohioans on baseball for years to come.

3. **Cardinals send reliever Hoyt Wilhelm to Indians for the waiver price (September 21, 1957); Indians send Wilhelm to the Orioles for the waiver price (August 23, 1958).** Lane twice unloaded the almost-unhittable knuckleball king because he had grown weary of passed balls.

4. **Cardinals send center fielder Bill Virdon to Pirates for center fielder Bobby DelGreco and pitcher Dick Littlefield (May 17, 1956).** Virdon, 1955 NL Rookie of the Year, went on to an outstanding career. DelGreco simply could not hit, although his sensational catches helped knock the Braves out of first place on the '56 season's final weekend.

5. **Indians trade outfielder Roger Maris, first baseman Preston Ward and pitcher Dick Tomanek to Kansas City for first baseman Vic Power and shortstop Woodie Held (June 15, 1958).** Power and Held were dangerous hitters, and Power was a perennial Gold Glove winner, so it's difficult to criticize this one — except that the Maris then warming Cleveland's bench turned into the Maris who hit 61 homers in '61.

Appendix II: Lane's Major League Transactions

KEY: (A) = American League; (N) = National League;
(AA) = American Association; (PCL) = Pacific Coast League;
(IL) = International League; (SA) = Southern Association;
(TL) = Texas League; (ML) = minor-league player.

As Chicago White Sox GM

11/10/48—C Aaron Robinson to Detroit for P Billy Pierce and $10,000.

11/15/48—OF Taffy Wright to Philadelphia (A) for cash.

12/2/48—P Frank Papish to Cleveland for P Bob Kuzava and P Ernie Groth.

12/14/48—OF Jim Delsing to New York (A) for OF-1B Steve Souchock.

12/48—Purchased C Ray Berres from Milwaukee (AA) and named him pitching coach.

1/12/49—C Mike Tresh to Cleveland for cash.

1/17/49—Purchased P Bill Bevens from New York (A); returned to NY 3/28/49.

1/26/49—1B Tony Lupien to Detroit for waiver price.

4/15/49—1B Ralph Weigel to Washington for cash.

5/7/49—IF Don Kolloway to Detroit for OF Earl Rapp.

5/16/49—Purchased P Ed Klieman from Washington.

6/2/49—Signed IF Jim Baumer to bonus contract.

6/8/49—Purchased 1B Charlie Kress from Cincinnati.

6/11/49—OF Earl Rapp and cash to Oakland (PCL) for OF Catfish Metkovich.

6/27/49—Signed P Gus Keriazakos to bonus contract.

7/12/49—P Al Gettel to Washington for cash.

7/13/49—Purchased C Eddie Malone from Chicago (N).

7/21/49—Purchased P Mickey Haefner from Washington.

8/4/49—IF Bobby Rhawn and cash to Chicago (N) for OF Johnny Ostrowski.

8/5/49—P Alex Carrasquel to Buffalo (IL) for P Luis Aloma.

9/13/49—Signed P Jack Bruner to bonus contract.

9/26/49—Purchased C Bill Salkeld from Boston (N).

9/30/49—IF Fred Hancock, ML P Charlie Eisenmann and $25,000 to Brooklyn for ML SS Alfonso "Chico" Carrasquel.

9/30/49—Purchased P Ken Holcombe from Sacramento (PCL).

10/19/49— C Joe Tipton to Philadelphia (A) for 2B Nelson Fox.

12/14/49— P Ed Klieman to Philadelphia (A) for 3B Hank Majeski.

2/2/50— Purchased 1B Herman Reich from Chicago (N) on waivers.

2/9/50— Purchased C Phil Masi from Pittsburgh.

4/16/50— P Marino Pieretti to Cleveland for waiver price.

4/25/50— Sold 1B Charlie Kress to St. Louis (N).

5/26/50— Fired manager Jack Onslow and replaced him with coach Red Corriden.

5/29/50— Purchased OF Marv Rickert from Pittsburgh.

5/31/50— 2B Cass Michaels, P Bob Kuzava and OF Johnny Ostrowski to Washington for 1B Eddie Robinson, P Ray Scarborough and 2B Al Kozar.

6/27/50— Purchased C Gus Niarhos from New York (A).

6/28/50— Sold C Eddie Malone to New York (A).

6/30/50— Purchased OF Mike McCormick from Oakland (PCL).

7/1/50— Sold P Jack Bruner to St. Louis (A).

7/5/50— Purchased P Lou Kretlow from St. Louis (A) on waivers.

7/31/50— Purchased C Sam Hairston from Indianapolis Clowns (Negro American League) and assigned him to Colorado Springs (Western League).

8/2/50— Purchased 1B Bob Boyd from Memphis Red Sox (Negro American League) and assigned him to Colorado Springs (Western League).

8/8/50— P Mickey Haefner to Boston (N) for cash.

8/18/50— P Max Surkont to Boston (N) for cash.

9/11/50— OF Herb Adams to Cleveland for cash.

10/10/50— Named Paul Richards as manager.

11/16/50— Drafted P Harry Dorish from Toronto (IL) and IF Joe DeMaestri from Birmingham (SA).

12/10/50— P Ray Scarborough and P Bill Wight to Boston (A) for OF Al Zarilla, P Joe Dobson and P Dick Littlefield.

12/11/50— OF Mike McCormick to Washington for OF Ed Stewart.

3/5/51— Signed C/OF J.W. Porter to bonus contract.

4/30/51— Leg 1: Philadelphia (A) sent P Lou Brissie to Cleveland for OF-IF Minnie Minoso, C Ray Murray and P Sam Zoldak; Leg 2: White Sox traded OF Gus Zernial and OF Dave Philley to Philadelphia (A) for Minoso and OF Paul Lehner.

5/15/51— P Bob Cain to Detroit for P Saul Rogovin.

5/16/51— Purchased 3B Bob Dillinger from Pittsburgh.

5/29/51— P Bob Mahoney to St. Louis (A) for waiver price.

6/4/51— Leg 1: White Sox sent 3B Hank Majeski to Philadelphia (A) for IF Kermit Wahl; Leg 2: White Sox sent Wahl, OF Paul Lehner and cash to St. Louis (A) for OF Don Lenhardt.

6/28/51— Purchased OF-IF Bert Haas from Sacramento (PCL).

7/22/51— C Joe Erautt to Seattle (PCL) for C Bud Sheely.

7/23/51— Purchased OF Jim Rivera from Seattle (PCL) for September 30 delivery.

7/31/51— Purchased OF Ray Coleman from St. Louis (A) on waivers.

8/30/51— Purchased P Ross Grimsley (Sr.) from Montreal (IL) in Brooklyn organization.

8/31/51— Purchased P Connie Johnson from St. Hyacinthe (Provincial League) for $6,500.

9/20/51—Purchased 1B Rocky Nelson from Pittsburgh on waivers.

10/10/51—P Marv Rotblatt, P Jerry Dahlke, P Dick Duffy, SS Jim Baumer and P Bill Fischer to Seattle (PCL) for P Marv Grissom and P Hector "Skinny" Brown.

10/16/51—Purchased OF Don Nicholas from Mobile (SA) in Brooklyn organization.

10/24/51—IF Floyd Baker to Washington for SS Willie Miranda.

11/13/51—P Randy Gumpert and OF Don Lenhardt to Boston (A) for P Chuck Stobbs and IF Mel Hoderlein.

11/19/51—Drafted OF George Wilson from Boston (A) organization.

11/27/51—Leg 1: C Gus Niarhos, OF Jim Rivera, 1B Gordon Goldsberry, P Dick Littlefield and IF Joe DeMaestri to St. Louis (A) for C Sherm Lollar, IF Tom Upton and P Al Widmar. Leg 2: White Sox sent Upton to Washington for IF Sam Dente.

12/6/51—1B Rocky Nelson to Brooklyn for ML 3B Hector Rodriguez.

3/13/52—Purchased P Bill Kennedy from St. Louis (A).

5/3/52—OF Jim Busby and IF Mel Hoderlein to Washington for OF Sam Mele.

5/5/52—Purchased P Jim Suchecki from Pittsburgh on waivers.

5/8/52—OF George Wilson to New York (N) for $25,000.

5/22/52—Purchased P Dixie Howell from New York (N) and assigned him to Memphis (SA).

6/15/52—OF Al Zarilla and SS Willie Miranda to St. Louis (A) for OF Tom Wright and 3B Leo Thomas.

6/16/52—P Ken Holcombe sold to St. Louis (A) on waivers.

6/28/52—Purchased SS Willie Miranda from St. Louis (A) on waivers.

7/28/52—OF Ray Coleman and ML C/OF J.W. Porter to St. Louis (A) for OF Jim Rivera and C Darrell Johnson.

8/22/52—Released C Phil Masi.

8/27/52—Purchased P Hal Hudson from St. Louis (A) on waivers.

9/1/52—Player to be named later (P Howie Judson) to Cincinnati for OF Hank Edwards.

10/13/52—Purchased P Bob Keegan on condition from Syracuse (IL).

10/16/52—SS Willie Miranda and OF Hank Edwards to St. Louis (A) for P Tommy Byrne and IF Joe DeMaestri.

12/6/52—P Chuck Stobbs to Washington for P Mike Fornieles.

1/20/53—IF Dixie Upright and $25,000 to St. Louis (A) for IF Freddie Marsh.

1/27/53—1B Eddie Robinson, IF Joe DeMaestri and OF Eddie McGhee to Philadelphia (A) for 1B Ferris Fain and ML IF Bob Wilson.

2/9/53—P Marv Grissom, P Hector "Skinny" Brown and P Bill Kennedy to Boston (A) for 3B Vern Stephens.

3/7/53—Purchased P Earl Harrist from St. Louis (A) on waivers.

3/18/53—Purchased P Gene Bearden from St. Louis (A) on waivers.

5/3/53—Sold IF Sam Dente to Cleveland.

5/12/53—Purchased OF Allie Clark from Philadelphia (A) on waivers.

5/12/53—Purchased P Sandy Consuegra from Washington.

5/23/53—P Earl Harrist to Detroit for waiver price.

6/11/53—Sold P Tommy Byrne to Washington.

6/13/53—P Lou Kretlow, C Darrell Johnson and $65,000 to St. Louis (A) for P Virgil Trucks and 3B Bob Elliott.

7/20/53—3B Vern Stephens to St. Louis (A) for waiver price.

8/25/53—Purchased IF Connie Ryan from Philadelphia (N) on waivers.

9/1/53—Purchased IF Neil Berry from St. Louis (A) on waivers.

9/17/53—Purchased P Jack Harshman from Nashville (SA).

10/8/53—3B Hector Rodriguez to Toronto (IL) for P Don Johnson.

11/30/53—Purchased C Carl Sawatski from Chicago (N) on waivers.

12/8/53—Purchased IF Cass Michaels from Philadelphia (A).

12/10/53—P Saul Rogovin, 3B Rocky Krsnich and IF Connie Ryan to Cincinnati for OF Willard Marshall.

2/5/54—OF Sam Mele and IF Neil Berry to Baltimore for OF Johnny Groth and IF Johnny Lipon.

3/27/54—OF Tom Wright to Washington for OF Kite Thomas.

4/18/54—IF Johnny Lipon to Cincinnati for IF Grady Hatton.

5/10/54—Purchased 3B Stan Jok from Philadelphia (N) on waivers. Assigned to minors.

5/23/54—IF Grady Hatton and $100,000 to Boston for 3B George Kell.

5/24/54—Signed 1B Phil Cavarretta as a free agent.

5/29/54—C Red Wilson to Detroit for C Matt Batts.

6/11/54—Leg 1: White Sox sent P Gus Keriazakos to Washington for P Sonny Dixon. Leg 2: White Sox traded P Sonny Dixon, OF Bill Wilson and $20,000 to Philadelphia (A) for P Morrie Martin and OF Eddie McGhee.

6/15/54—Signed Western Michigan U. 1B Ron Jackson to $80,000 bonus contract.

7/25/54—Sold P Tom Hurd to Boston.

8/16/54—Signed P Bob Cain as free agent.

9/4/54—SS Jim Baumer to Pittsburgh for IF Jack Phillips.

9/7/54—Purchased P Dick Donovan from Atlanta (SA).

9/21/54—Purchased P Leo Cristante from Milwaukee organization.

9/30/54—Purchased 3B Bill Serena from Chicago (N) on waivers.

12/6/54—C Matt Batts, IF Freddie Marsh, P Don Johnson and P Don Ferrarese to Baltimore for C Clint Courtney, IF Jim Brideweser and P Bob Chakales.

12/6/54—1B Ferris Fain, IF Jack Phillips and P Leo Cristante to Detroit for 1B Walt Dropo, OF Bob Nieman and P Ted Gray.

12/14/54—Signed C Del Wilber as a free agent and named him bullpen coach.

1/4/55—Signed P Al Brazle as a free agent.

2/10/55—Purchased OF Lloyd Merriman from Cincinnati.

4/16/55—Sold OF Lloyd Merriman to Chicago (N).

5/9/55—Signed 3B Vern Stephens as a free agent.

5/30/55—Purchased IF-OF Bob Kennedy from Baltimore on waivers.

6/6/55—P Harry Dorish to Baltimore for C Les Moss.

6/7/55—OF Johnny Groth, C Clint Courtney and P Bob Chakales to Washington for OF Jim Busby.

6/8/55—Purchased P Dixie Howell from Memphis (SA).

6/8/55—Signed Michigan State OF Bob Powell to $36,000 bonus contract.

6/15/55—Purchased P Harry Byrd from Baltimore on waivers.

7/16//55 — Purchased OF Gil Coan from Baltimore.

7/26/55 — Purchased IF Bobby Adams from Cincinnati.

8/2/55 — Purchased P Al Papai from Oklahoma City (TL) for Sept. 1 delivery.

8/2/55 — Purchased SS Buddy Peterson from San Diego (PCL) for Sept. 1 delivery.

8/26/55 — OF Gil Coan to New York (N) for OF Ron Northey, then at Minneapolis (AA).

As St. Louis Cardinals GM

11/22/55 — Drafted P Billy Muffett from Chicago (N) organization.

12/4/55 — Purchased P Ellis Kinder from Boston on waivers.

1/31/56 — P Brooks Lawrence and ML P Sonny Senerchia to Cincinnati for P Jackie Collum.

3/30/56 — OF Pete Whisenant to Chicago (N) for OF Hank Sauer.

4/10/56 — P Frank Smith to Cincinnati for waiver price.

5/1/56 — P Paul LaPalme to Cincinnati for IF Milt Smith.

5/5/56 — P Luis Arroyo to Pittsburgh for P Max Surkont.

5/10/56 — IF Alex Grammas and OF Joe Frazier to Cincinnati for IF Chuck Harmon.

5/11/56 — P Harvey Haddix, P Stu Miller and P Ben Flowers to Philadelphia for P Murry Dickson and P Herm Wehmeier.

5/14/56 — IF Solly Hemus to Philadelphia for IF Bobby Morgan.

5/17/56 — OF Bill Virdon to Pittsburgh for OF Bobby DelGreco and P Dick Littlefield.

5/28/56 — C Dick Rand and cash to Pittsburgh for C Toby Atwell.

6/4/56 — Signed P Jim Konstanty as a free agent.

6/4/56 — Sold P Max Surkont to Boston.

6/14/56 — 2B Red Schoendienst, OF Jackie Brandt, C Bill Sarni, P Dick Littlefield and IF Bobby Stephenson to New York (N) for SS Alvin Dark, OF/1B Whitey Lockman, C Ray Katt and P Don Liddle.

6/26/56 — Purchased IF Grady Hatton from Boston.

7/4/56 — Sold C Toby Atwell to Philadelphia.

7/11/56 — Sold P Ellis Kinder to Chicago (A) on waivers.

7/30/56 — Purchased 1B Rocky Nelson from Brooklyn on waivers.

8/1/56 — Sold IF Grady Hatton to Baltimore.

10/1/56 — Sold P Gordon Jones to New York (N).

10/2/56 — 3B Stan Jok and cash to Toronto (IL) for P Lynn Lovenguth.

11/19/56 — OF Rip Repulski and IF Bobby Morgan to Philadelphia for OF Del Ennis.

12/11/56 — P Jackie Collum, P Tom Poholsky, C Ray Katt and ML P Wally Lemmers to Chicago (N) for P Sam Jones, P Jim Davis, C Hobie Landrith and IF/OF Eddie Miksis.

2/26/57 — OF/1B Whitey Lockman to New York (N) for P Hoyt Wilhelm.

4/20/57 — OF Bobby DelGreco and P Eddie Mayer to Chicago (N) for OF Jim King.

4/21/57 — Signed C Walker Cooper as a free agent.

5/10/57 — IF Chuck Harmon to Philadelphia for OF Glen Gorbous.

5/14/57 — Sold P Bob Smith to Pittsburgh.

5/23/57 — Signed P Von McDaniel of Hollis, Oklahoma, to $50,000 bonus contract.

6/4/57 — P Jim Davis to New York (N) for waiver price.

6/20/57— Signed P Bob Miller of St. Louis' Beaumont High School to bonus contract.
8/31/57— Purchased OF/1B Irv Noren from Kansas City on waivers.
9/19/57— IF/OF Eddie Miksis to Baltimore for waiver price.
9/19/57— Purchased P Morrie Martin from Baltimore.
9/19/57— Purchased P Bob Kuzava from Pittsburgh.
9/21/57— Sold P Hoyt Wilhelm to Cleveland.

As Cleveland Indians GM

12/2/57— Drafted OF Gary Geiger off of St. Louis Cardinals' Omaha roster.
12/4/57— P Early Wynn and OF Al Smith to Chicago (A) for OF Minnie Minoso and IF Fred Hatfield.
1/29/58— Purchased 1B Mickey Vernon from Boston on waivers.
2/18/58— P Hank Aguirre and C Jim Hegan to Detroit for P Hal Woodeshick and OF/C J.W. Porter.
2/25/58— ML P Pete Mesa to Washington for IF Milt Bolling.
3/26/58— Purchased P Chuck Churn from Boston on waivers.
3/27/58— IF Milt Bolling and P Vito Valentinetti to Detroit for P Pete Wojey and $20,000.
4/1/58— OF Gene Woodling, OF/IF Dick Williams and P Bud Daley to Baltimore for OF Larry Doby and P Don Ferrarese.
4/3/58— Purchased P Steve Ridzik from San Francisco.
4/23/58— IF Fred Hatfield to Cincinnati for P Bob Kelly.
5/18/58— Purchased IF Fred Hatfield from Cincinnati.
6/7/58— Purchased P Jim Constable from San Francisco on waivers.
6/12/58— SS Chico Carrasquel to Kansas City for SS Billy Hunter.
6/15/58— OF Roger Maris, 1B Preston Ward and P Dick Tomanek to Kansas City for 1B Vic Power and SS/OF Woodie Held.
6/26/58— Fired Bobby Bragan as manager and replaced him with Joe Gordon.
7/2/58— Purchased P Morrie Martin from St. Louis on waivers.
7/12/58— Sold P Jim Constable to Washington on waivers.
8/4/58— Purchased 3B Randy Jackson from Los Angeles.
8/23/58— Sold P Hoyt Wilhelm to Baltimore for waiver price.
10/13/58— IF Larry Raines and OF Dave Pope to Toronto (IL) for P Bobby Tiefenauer.
10/27/58— C/OF J.W. Porter to Washington for IF/OF Ossie Alvarez.
11/20/58— P Don Mossi, P Ray Narleski and IF/OF Ossie Alvarez to Detroit for 2B Billy Martin and P Al Cicotte.
12/2/58— 2B Bobby Avila to Baltimore for P Russ Heman and $30,000.
12/2/58— OF Gary Geiger and 1B Vic Wertz to Boston for OF Jimmy Piersall.
1/23/59— C Earl Averill to Chicago (N) for P Johnny Briggs and OF Jim Bolger.
3/21/59— OF Larry Doby to Detroit for OF Tito Francona.
4/11/59— 1B Mickey Vernon to Milwaukee for P Humberto Robinson.
5/4/59— 3B Randy Jackson to Chicago (N) for P Bob "Riverboat" Smith.
5/7/59— Sold P Steve Ridzik to Chicago (N).
5/16/59— P Humberto Robinson to Philadelphia for IF Granny Hamner.

5/23/59—Sent IF Fred Hatfield and $10,000 to Los Angeles for IF Jim Baxes.

5/25/59—P Hal Woodeshick and C Hal Naragon to Washington for C Ed FitzGerald.

6/6/59—OF Jim Bolger and cash to Philadelphia for 3B Willie Jones.

6/29/59—Purchased OF Elmer Valo from Seattle (PCL).

7/1/59—Sold Willie Jones to Cincinnati.

7/30/59—Purchased P Jack Harshman from Boston on waivers.

9/1/59—Purchased OF Chuck Tanner from Minneapolis (AA).

12/6/59—OF Minnie Minoso, C Dick Brown, P Don Ferrarese and P Jake Striker to Chicago (A) for 3B Bubba Phillips, C Johnny Romano and 1B Norm Cash.

12/15/59—P Cal McLish, 2B Billy Martin and 1B Gordy Coleman to Cincinnati for 2B Johnny Temple.

1/8/60—IF Ray Webster to Boston for P Leo Kiely.

1/20/60—Purchased 1B Bob Hale from Baltimore on waivers.

3/16/60—C Russ Nixon and OF/1B Jim Marshall to Boston for C Sammy White. (Trade cancelled when White decided to retire.)

4/5/60—P Leo Kiely to Kansas City for P Bob Grim.

4/12/60—1B Norm Cash to Detroit for IF Steve Demeter.

4/17/60—OF Rocky Colavito to Detroit for OF Harvey Kuenn.

4/18/60—P Herb Score to Chicago (A) for P Barry Latman.

4/29/60—Purchased OF Pete Whisenant from Cincinnati.

5/12/60—Purchased OF Johnny Powers from Baltimore on waivers.

5/15/60—OF Pete Whisenant to Washington for IF Ken Aspromonte.

5/18/60—Sold P Bob Grim to Cincinnati.

6/2/60—OF Johnny Powers to Pittsburgh for C Hank Foiles.

6/2/60—Sold P Bobby Tiefenauer to St. Louis.

6/13/60—C Russ Nixon and OF Carroll Hardy to Boston for P Ted Bowsfield and OF Marty Keough.

7/26/60—C Hank Foiles to Detroit for C Red Wilson and IF Rocky Bridges.

7/29/60—Purchased P Don Newcombe from Cincinnati.

7/30/60—Sold P Johnny Briggs to Kansas City.

8/3/60—Manager Joe Gordon to Detroit for manager Jimmy Dykes.

8/4/60—Third-base coach Jo Jo White to Detroit for third-base coach Luke Appling.

8/9/60—Purchased IF Joe Morgan from Philadelphia.

9//2/60—Sold IF Rocky Bridges to St. Louis.

12/3/60—OF Harvey Kuenn to San Francisco for P Johnny Antonelli and OF Willie Kirkland.

As Kansas City A's GM

1/24/61—OF Russ Snyder and OF Whitey Herzog to Baltimore for IF Wayne Causey, 1B Bob Boyd, C Clint Courtney and P Jim Archer.

1/25/61—P Johnny Briggs and P John Tsitouris to Cincinnati for P Joe Nuxhall.

1/31/61—Purchased C Joe Pignatano from Los Angeles (N).

3/30/61—P Howie Reed and cash to Los Angeles (N) for P Ed Rakow.

4/12/61—P Dick Hall and OF-IF Dick Williams to Baltimore for P Jerry Walker and OF Chuck Essegian.

4/28/61 — Signed IF Dagoberto "Campy" Campaneris as amateur free agent.

5/3/61 — Sold OF Chuck Essegian to Cleveland.

6/1/61 — OF Bill Tuttle to Minnesota for IF Reno Bertoia and P Paul Giel. (Giel was returned to Minnesota for cash payment.)

6/8/61 — 1B Marv Throneberry to Baltimore for OF Gene Stephens.

6/9/61 — Signed OF Jim Rivera as a free agent.

6/10/61 — Sold 1B Bob Boyd to Milwaukee.

6/10/61 — P Ray Herbert, P Don Larsen, 3B Andy Carey and OF Al Pilarcik to Chicago (A) for P Bob Shaw, P Gerry Staley, OF Wes Covington and ML OF Stan Johnson.

6/14/61 — P Bud Daley to New York (A) for P Art Ditmar and OF/IF Deron Johnson.

6/19/61 — Fired Joe Gordon as manager and replaced him with OF Hank Bauer.

6/19/61 — Signed P Fred Norman as amateur free agent.

7/2/61 — OF Wes Covington to Philadelphia for OF Bobby DelGreco.

7/21/61 — Purchased P Mickey McDermott from St. Louis.

7/21/61 — Sold P Ken Johnson to Cincinnati.

7/31/61 — P Gerry Staley and IF Reno Bertoia to Detroit for P Bill Fischer and IF Ozzie Virgil (Sr.).

As Milwaukee Brewers GM

1/28/71 — P Gene Brabender to California for OF Bill Voss.

2/2/71 — C Carl Taylor to Kansas City for C Ellie Rodriguez.

2/4/71 — Purchased OF Joe Nossek from St. Louis.

2/10/71 — P Al Downing to Los Angeles for OF Andy Kosco.

3/26/71 — Sold IF Fred Stanley to Cleveland.

4/5/71 — P Roric Harrison and ML P Marion Jackson to Baltimore for P Marcelino Lopez.

4/5/71 — P Wayne Twitchell to Philadelphia for OF Pat Skrable.

4/22/71 — P Ray Peters and OF/1B/C Pete Koegel to Philadelphia for OF/1B John Briggs.

5/11/71 — P John Gelnar and P Jose Herrera to Detroit for P Jim Hannan.

5/11/71 — OF Ted Savage to Kansas City for IF Tom Matchick.

6/1/71 — OF Floyd Wicker to San Francisco for IF Bobby Heise.

6/7/71 — OF Danny Walton to New York (A) for OF Bobby Mitchell and OF/1B Frank Tepedino.

6/14/71 — Sold 1B Mike Hegan to Oakland.

6/30/71 — Purchased P Floyd Weaver from Tucson (PCL).

7/8/71 — C Phil Roof to Minnesota for C Paul Ratliff.

7/29/71 — IF Ted Kubiak and ML P Charlie Loseth to St. Louis for OF Jose Cardenal, P Bob Reynolds and IF Dick Schofield.

10/10/71 — P Marty Pattin, OF/IF Tommy Harper, P Lew Krausse and ML OF Pat Skrable to Boston for 1B George Scott, P Jim Lonborg, P Ken Brett, OF Billy Conigliaro, OF Joe Lahoud and C Don Pavletich.

10/22/71 — IF Tom Matchick and C Bruce Look to Baltimore for 3B Mike Ferraro.

12/3/71 — OF Jose Cardenal to Chicago (N) for P Jim Colborn, P Earl Stephenson and OF Brock Davis.

12/9/71 — P Bob Reynolds to Baltimore for OF Curt Motton.

1/26/72— OF Andy Kosco to Oakland for OF Tommie Reynolds.
2/8/72— ML IF Chico Vaughns to Philadelphia for IF Bobby Pfeil.
3/20/72— Sold IF Bobby Pfeil to Boston.
3/26/72— ML P Rich Stonum to St. Louis for P Frank Linzy,
3/29/72— Sold P Marcelino Lopez to Cleveland.
3/31/72— Sold OF/1B Frank Tepedino to New York (A).
5/26/72— OF Curt Motton to California for P Archie Reynolds.
6/20/72— OF Bill Voss to Oakland for IF Ron Clark.
6/29/72— Purchased OF Ollie Brown from Oakland.
7/28/72— IF Ron Clark and C Paul Ratliff to California for IF Syd O'Brien and C Jose Azcue.
9/13/72— Purchased P Chuck Taylor from New York (N).

Among the Deals Recommended and/or Negotiated While Superscout with Baltimore Orioles

12/9/65— P Milt Pappas, P Jack Baldschun and ML OF Dick Simpson to Cincinnati for OF Frank Robinson.
6/12/66— IF Jerry Adair and ML OF John Riddle to Chicago (A) for P Eddie Fisher.
5/29/67—1B Mike Epstein and P Frank Bertaina to Washington for P Pete Richert.
11/29/67— SS Luis Aparicio, OF Russ Snyder and ML 1B John Matias to Chicago (A) for IF Don Buford, P Bruce Howard and P Roger Nelson.

Among the Deals Recommended and/or Negotiated While Superscout with Texas Rangers

12/5/74— P Don Stanhouse and IF Pete Mackanin to Montreal for OF Willie Davis.

Among the Deals Recommended and/or Negotiated While Superscout with California Angels

12/11/75— OF Mickey Rivers and P Ed Figueroa to New York (A) for OF Bobby Bonds.
12/12/75—1B Jim Spencer and OF Morris Nettles to Chicago (A) for 3B Bill Melton and P Steve Dunning.
6/15/77— P Don Kirkwood, P John Verhoeven and ML IF John Flannery to Chicago (A) for P Ken Brett.
12/5/77— OF Bobby Bonds, OF Thad Bosley and ML P Richard Dotson to Chicago (A) for C Brian Downing, P Chris Knapp and P Dave Frost.
12/4/78— 3B Ron Jackson and C Danny Goodwin to Minnesota for OF Dan Ford.
2/3/79— OF Ken Landreaux, C Dave Engle, P Paul Hartzell and P Brad Havens to Minnesota for 1B Rod Carew.

Appendix III

Five Rules of Trading

1. "Don't cry about a bad deal. Walk away from it and go on to the next one. The worst thing a general manager can do after a bad deal is to stand pat."
2. "Never be concerned with what the player does that you just traded away. Be concerned only with the one you're getting in return."
3. "Never try to outfox the other club. Give its officials credit for intelligence."
4. "Never trade a young, established pitcher. When you've got a gem, keep it and protect it."
5. "If I can be right 65 percent of the time in getting what I want, I consider that a good percentage."

— From *The Sporting News*, June 15, 1960

Chapter Notes

Preface

1. *Sports Illustrated*, 8/26/68.
2. *Chicago Tribune*, 3/20/81.
3. Lane's comments on Veeck are taken from taped interview with the author, 6/7/78.
4. Jim Enright ed., *Trade Him!* (Chicago: Follett, 1976), p. 28.
5. Electronic interview with Allan "Bud" Selig, 2/21/12.

Chapter 1

1. Vanderberg, Bob. *Sox: From Lane and Fain to Zisk and Fisk* (Chicago: Chicago Review Press, 1982), p. 3.
2. *Ibid.*, p. 4.
3. *Chicago Tribune*, 8/23/75
4. Vanderberg, *Sox*, p. 3.
5. *Ibid.*, p. 356.
6. From taped interview with Frank Lane, 6/7/78.
7. *Ibid.*
8. Vanderberg, *Sox*, p. 5.
9. *Ibid.*
10. *Ibid.*
11. *Sport* magazine, April 1952.
12. *Chicago Tribune*, 5/27/50.
13. *Sport* magazine, April 1952.
14. Enright (ed.), *Trade Him!* p. 259.
15. *Sport* magazine, April 1952.
16. Arch Ward. *The New Chicago White Sox* (Chicago: Regnery, 1951), p. 32.
17. *Ibid.*, pp. 5–6.

Chapter 2

1. From taped interview with Frank Lane, 6/7/78.
2. *The Sporting News*, 12/20/50.
3. Vanderberg, *Sox*, p. 62.
4. *Ibid.*, pp. 6–7.

5. *Ibid.*, p. 7.
6. *Ibid.*, p. 63.
7. *Ibid.*, p. 355
8. *The Sporting News*, 6/20/51.
9. From taped interview with Frank Lane, 6/7/78.
10. Vanderberg, *Sox*, p. 62.
11. *Sport* magazine, April 1952.
12. Vanderberg, *Sox*, p. 357.
13. *Sport* magazine, April 1952.
14. *Chicago Tribune*, 6/14/52.
15. Vanderberg, *Sox*, p. 12.
16. From taped interview with Frank Lane, 6/7/78.
17. *Chicago Tribune*, 7/18/77.
18. Vanderberg, *Sox*, p. 139.
19. Vanderberg, Bob. *Minnie and The Mick: The Go-Go White Sox Challenge the Fabled Yankee Dynasty, 1951–1964*. South Bend: Diamond Communications, 1996, p. 34.

Chapter 3

1. *The Sporting News*, 12/18/52.
2. Photocopy of Frank Lane letter to Nelson Fox on official club stationery, dated 12/11/52.
3. *Chicago Tribune*, 1/28/53.
4. *The Sporting News*, 2/4/53.
5. *Sport* magazine, July 1953.
6. Vanderberg, *Minnie and the Mick*, p. 41.
7. Vanderberg, *Sox*, p. 10.
8. *Ibid.*, p. 11.
9. *Ibid.*, p. 11.
10. *Ibid.*, p. 12.
11. *Ibid.*, p. 12.
12. *Ibid.*, p. 66.
13. *Ibid.*, p. 66.
14. *Ibid.*, p. 14.
15. UPI report, 8/3/53.

16. Vanderberg, *Sox*, p. 16.
17. *Sport* magazine, June 1955.
18. *Sport* magazine, August 1954.
19. *Chicago Tribune*, 5/24/54.
20. *Ibid.*
21. Vanderberg, *Sox*, p. 66.
22. *Chicago Tribune*, 7/4/54.
23. *Sport* magazine, June 1955.
24. *Chicago Tribune*, 8/28/54.
25. *Ibid.*
26. From taped interview with Frank Lane, 6/7/78.

Chapter 4

1. Phone interview with Frank Lane, July 1978.
2. *The Sporting News*, 12/8/54.
3. *The Sporting News*, 12/15/54.
4. From taped interview with Frank Lane, 6/7/78.
5. Chicago tied the American League record for most runs in one game, set by Boston in 1950 against St. Louis. Texas broke the record with its 30–3 rout of Baltimore in 2007.
6. Vanderberg, *Sox*, p.75.
7. From taped interview with Frank Lane, 6/7/78
8. Vanderberg, *Sox*, p. 8.
9. Vanderberg, *Sox*, p. 8.
10. *Chicago Tribune*, 8/29/55; the Lane quotations in this and next four paragraphs are taken from "In the Wake of the News" column.
11. Vanderberg, *Sox*, p. 15.
12. *Ibid.*, p. 15.
13. *Ibid.*, pp. 15–16.
14. *The Sporting News*, 9/2/55.
15. Vanderberg, *Sox*, p. 16.
16. *Chicago Tribune*, 9/24/55.
17. Baseballinwartime.com, Gary Bedingfield.
18. Vanderberg, *Sox*, pp. 15–16.
19. *Chicago Tribune*, 9/24/55.
20. *Ibid.*
21. *Chicago Tribune*, 9/25/55.
22. *Chicago Tribune*, 9/26/55.

Chapter 5

1. *Sports Illustrated*, 3/5/56.
2. *Ibid.*

3. *Ibid.*
4. *Saturday Evening Post*, 6/23/56.
5. Correspondence from Roger Kahn, December 2011.
6. *Sport* magazine, August 1956.
7. Rains, Rob. *The St. Louis Cardinals: The 100th Anniversary History*. New York: St. Martin's Press, 1992. p. 137.
8. *Ibid.*, p. 137.
9. *The Sporting News*, 5/23/56.
10. Saturday Evening Post, 6/23/56.
11. *Sports Illustrated*, 5/28/56.
12. *The Sporting News*, 5/23/56.
13. Vecsey, George. *Stan Musial: An American Life*. New York: Ballantine Books/ESPN Books, 2011. p. 220.
14. *Ibid.*, p. 220
15. *Sports Illustrated*, 8/26/68.
16. AP report, 11/20/56.
17. *The Sporting News*, 12/5/56.
18. Boyd, Brendan C., and Harris, Fred C. *The Great American Baseball Card Flipping, Trading and Bubble Gum Book*. Boston: Little, Brown. 1973. p. 69.
19. AP report, 3/28/62.
20. *Sports Illustrated*, 8/26/68.
21. *The Sporting News*, 9/11/57.
22. AP report, 9/17/57.
23. *Ibid.*
24. *The Sporting News*, 10/2/57.
25. Vecsey, *Musial*, p. 221.
26. *The Sporting News*, 10/2/57.
27. *Sports Illustrated*, 10/7/68.

Chapter 6

1. Cleveland Plain Dealer, 11/13/57.
2. *Ibid.*
3. *Ibid.*
4. *Ibid.*
5. From taped interview with Frank Lane, 6/7/78.
6. *Cleveland Plain Dealer*, 12/1/57.
7. Vanderberg. *Sox*, p. 83–84.
8. *Cleveland Plain Dealer*, 12/5/57.
9. *The Sporting News*, 1/6/79.
10. *Cleveland Plain Dealer*, 12/8/57.
11. *Ibid.*
12. *Ibid.*
13. Bragan, Bobby. *You Can't Hit the Ball with Your Bat on Your Shoulder*. Ft. Worth: The Summit Group, 1992. p. 223.
14. *Sports Illustrated*, 3/17/58.

15. Moffi, Larry. *This Side of Cooperstown.* Iowa City: University of Iowa Press, 1996. p. 59.

16. Pluto, Terry. *The Curse of Rocky Colavito.* New York: Simon & Schuster, 1994. p. 36.

17. *Cleveland Plain Dealer,* 6/5/58.

18. Bragan. *You Can't Hit the Ball,* p. 226.

19. Moffi. *This Side of Cooperstown,* p. 244.

20. *Cleveland Plain Dealer,* 6/16/58.

21. *Cleveland Plain Dealer,* 4/11/59.

22. From taped interview with Frank Lane, 6/7/78.

23. Coolquotes.com

24. Baseball Biography Project, "Hoyt Wilhelm," Mark Armour, bioproj@sabr.org

25. Vanderberg. *Sox,* p. 151.

26. Pluto. *The Curse,* p. 38.

27. Binkley, Jim, and Eisenhammer, Fred. *Baseball's Most Memorable Trades.* Jefferson, N.C.: McFarland, 1997. pp. 110–111.

28. *Ibid.,* p. 116.

Chapter 7

1. *Cleveland Plain Dealer,* 11/21/58.

2. *Ibid.*

3. Vignette taken from taped interview with Frank Lane, 6/7/78.

4. Pluto, *The Curse,* p. 63.

5. From taped interview with Frank Lane, 6/7/78.

6. Vanderberg, Bob. *'59: Summer of the Sox.* Champaign: Sports Publishing Inc. 1999. p. 65.

7. *Cleveland Plain Dealer,* 6/16/59

8. Lane quotes in this and next paragraph from *Sports Illustrated,* 7/27/59, pp. 31, 56, 57.

9. Vanderberg. *'59 Summer.* p. 120.

10. Vanderberg. *Sox,* p. 14.

11. *Chicago Tribune,* 8/31/05.

12. *Sports Illustrated,* 10/5/59.

13. *Ibid.*

14. *Chicago Tribune,* 6/27/66.

15. *Sports Illustrated,* 10/5/59.

16. *Chicago Tribune,* 8/31/05.

Chapter 8

1. *Cleveland Plain Dealer,* 12/4/59.

2. *Cleveland Plain Dealer,* 12/6/59.

3. *Cleveland Plain Dealer,* 12/7/59.

4. *Chicago Tribune,* 8/31/05.

5. *Cleveland Plain Dealer,* 12/10/59.

6. *Cleveland Plain Dealer,* 12/16/59.

7. *Ibid.*

8. *Sports Illustrated,* 7/27/59.

9. *Cleveland Plain Dealer,* 12/16/59.

10. *Ibid.*

11. *Cleveland Plain Dealer,* 12/17/59.

12. Binkley and Eisenhammer. *Most Memorable Trades,* p. 111.

13. *Ibid.,* p. 112.

14. *Ibid.*

15. Pluto. *The Curse,* p. 54.

16. Binkley and Eisenhammer. *Most Memorable Trades,* p. 113.

17. *Ibid.,* p. 114.

18. *Chicago Tribune,* 8/31/05.

19. Pluto. *The Curse,* p. 49.

20. *The Sporting News,* 6/8/60.

21. Binkley and Eisenhammer. *Most Memorable Trades,* p. 118.

22. *Chicago Tribune,* 8/31/05.

23. Binkley and Eisenhammer. *Most Memorable Trades,* p. 115.

24. *Cleveland Plain Dealer,* 1/5/61.

Chapter 9

1. From taped interview with Bob Elson, The Drake Hotel, Chicago, 1979.

2. Peterson, John E. *The Kansas City Athletics: A Baseball History, 1954–1967.* Jefferson, N.C.: McFarland, 2003. p. 124.

3. *Chicago Tribune,* 1/7/65.

4. *Ibid.*

5. UPI report, 2/2/61.

6. AP report, 1/10/61.

7. *Ibid.*

8. AP report, 1/18/61.

9. AP report, 2/17/61.

10. *Ibid.*

11. AP report, 2/25/61.

12. AP report, 1/6/61

13. *Sports Illustrated,* 6/5/61.

14. *Ibid.*

15. *Ibid.*

16. AP report, 1/18/61.

17. Peterson. *Athletics,* p. 136.

18. AP report, 5/25/61.

19. *Chicago Tribune,* 6/10/61.

20. From taped interview with Frank Lane, 6/7/78.

21. From phone interview with Frank Lane, July 1978.
22. Peterson. *Athletics,* p. 136.
23. *Ibid.,* p. 139.
24. *Ibid.,* p. 138.
25. *Sports Illustrated,* 6/5/61.
26. *Chicago Tribune,* 8/23/61.
27. AP report, 6/17/61.
28. *Chicago Tribune,* 6/20/61.
29. *Chicago Tribune,* 1/7/65.
30. *Chicago Tribune,* 8/24/61.
31. *Chicago Tribune,* 8/24/61
32. *The Sporting News,* 1/9/65.
33. *Chicago Tribune,* 8/28/61.
34. *Chicago Tribune,* 10/9/63.
35. *Chicago Tribune,* 1/7/65.
36. *Chicago Tribune,* 1/6/65.
37. *Chicago Tribune,* 6/65.
38. *Sports Illustrated,* 8/26/68.
39. *Chicago Tribune,* 1/8/65.
40. *Ibid.,* 1/8/65.

Chapter 10

1. Hareas, John. *Washington Wizards: A Colorful Tradition.* NBA.com, 2011.
2. *Chicago Tribune,* 4/26/62.
3. *Chicago Tribune,* 5/8/62.
4. UPI report, 5/9/62.
5. *Chicago Tribune,* 3/25/69.
6. *Ibid.,* 2/7/63.
7. Hareas. *Wizards.*
8. UPI report, 12/20/62.
9. *Chicago Daily News,* 10/26/62.
10. *Chicago Tribune,* 12/29/62.
11. *Chicago Tribune,* 12/20/62.
12. *Chicago Tribune,* 1/9/63.
13. *Chicago Tribune,* 3/6/63.
14. *Chicago Tribune,* 3/13/63.
15. *Chicago Tribune,* 3/13/63.
16. *Chicago Tribune,* 2/7/63.

Chapter 11

1. New York Times, 3/7/65.
2. UPI report, 3/7/65.
3. Russo, Jim. *SuperScout.* Chicago: Bonus Books, 1992. pp. 53–55.
4. *Chicago Tribune,* 6/27/66.
5. Russo. *SuperScout,* pp. 55–56.
6. *Chicago Tribune,* 6/13/66.
7. *The Sporting News,* 3/21/70.
8. Russo. *SuperScout,* p. 94.

9. *Chicago Tribune,* 10/10/66.
10. Durocher, Leo, with Linn, Ed. *Nice Guys Finish Last.* Chicago: University of Chicago Press, 1975. p. 371.
11. *Ibid.,* p. 371.
12. Russo. *SuperScout,* p. 91.
13. *Ibid.,* p. 91.
14. Durocher, *Nice Guys,* p. 372.
15. *Chicago Tribune,* 4/9/67.
16. *Ibid.,* 5/19/67.
17. *Ibid.,* 11/27/67.
18. *Sports Illustrated,* 8/26/68.
19. *Sport* magazine, May 1962.
20. *Sports Illustrated,* 4/5/93.
21. *Chicago Tribune,* 4/26/68.
22. *The Sporting News,* 4/20/68.
23. From taped interview with Frank Lane, 6/7/78.

Chapter 12

1. Electronic interview with Allan "Bud" Selig, 2/21/12.
2. Pluto. *The Curse,* p. 37.
3. Selig interview, 2/21/12
4. *Ibid.*
5. *The Sporting News,* 6/21/71.
6. *Ibid.,* 7/24/71.
7. *The Sporting News,* 6/26/71.
8. Baseball Biography Project, "Alex Johnson," Mark Armour, bioproj@sabr-org
9. *The Sporting News,* 7/3/71.
10. Selig interview, 2/21/12.
11. Enright (ed.), *Trade Him!.* pp. 81–82.
12. *The Sporting News,* 7/1/72.
13. Following three paragraphs from Lane interview, 6/7/78.
14. *Chicago Tribune,* 8/17/72.
15. *The Sporting News,* 9/2/72.
16. Vanderberg. *Sox,* p. 8.
17. *The Sporting News,* 10/21/72.
18. *Ibid.*
19. *Chicago Tribune,* 10/6/72.
20. *The Sporting News,* 10/21/72.
21. Selig interview, 2/21/12.

Chapter 13

1. Enright, ed. *Trade Him!* p. 155.
2. AP, 7/22/75.
3. *Chicago Tribune,* World Series section, story by Phil Rogers, 10/26/10.
4. AP, 7/5/77.

5. *Chicago Tribune*, 6/11/78.
6. *Sports Illustrated*, 8/7/78.
7. *Chicago Tribune*, 12/18/64.
8. *Ibid.*, 12/18/64.
9. *Ibid.*, 3/26/70.
10. *Ibid.*, 3/26/70.
11. *Sports Illustrated*, 8/26/68.
12. *The Sporting News*, 12/27/75.
13. *Ibid.*
14. *The Sporting News*, 6/25/77.
15. *Ibid.*, 12/24/77.
16. From taped interview with Frank Lane, 6/7/78.
17. Lane interview, 6/7/78.
18. Lane interview, 6/7/78.
19. Lane interview, 6/7/78.
20. *Chicago Tribune*, 8/27/78.
21. Lane interview, 6/7/78.

Epilogue

1. *Chicago Tribune*, 3/20/81.
2. Bragan. *You Can't Hit the Ball*, p. 226.
3. *Chicago Tribune*, 8/31/05.
4. Vanderberg. *Sox*, p. 354.
5. Minoso, Minnie with Fagan, Herb. *Just Call Me Minnie*. Champaign: Sagamore Publishing, 1994. p. 77.
6. Phone interview with Jim Rivera, 11/28/11.
7. *Chicago Tribune*, 9/3/80.

8. Phone interview with Jim Rivera. 11/28/11.
9. *Ibid.*
10. Interview with Jim Rivera at U.S. Cellular Field, Chicago. 11/17/11.
11. *Ibid.*
12. Moffi. *This Side of Cooperstown*, pp. 103–104.
13. Peary, Danny. *We Played the Game.* New York: Hyperion, 1994. p. 478.
14. Vanderberg. *Sox*. p. 241.
15. Pluto. *The Curse*. p. 37.
16. Bragan. *You Can't Hit the Ball*, p. 222.
17. *Ibid.*, p. 244.
18. Pluto. *The Curse*. p. 46.
19. *Ibid.*, p. 57.
20. *Ibid.*, p. 49.
21. Vecsey. *Stan Musial*. p. 221.
22. Peary. *We Played the Game*. p. 167.
23. *Ibid.*, p. 229.
24. From taped interview with Frank Lane, 6/7/78.
25. Lane interview, 6/7/78.
26. *The Sporting News*, 5/13/72.
27. *The Sporting News*, 1/6/79.
28. *Chicago Tribune*, 8/31/05.
29. Kahn correspondence, December 2011.
30. Electronic interview with Commissioner Bud Selig, 2/21/12.
31. *Chicago Tribune*, 8/31/05.
32. *The Sporting News*, 5/13/72.

Bibliography

Books

Binkley, Jim, and Eisenhammer, Fred. *Baseball's Most Memorable Trades.* Jefferson, N.C.: McFarland, 1997.

Boyd, Brendan C., and Harris, Fred C. *The Great American Baseball Card Flipping, Trading and Bubble Gum Book.* Boston: Little, Brown, 1973.

Bragan, Bobby, as told to Jeff Guinn. *You Can't Hit the Ball with Your Bat on Your Shoulder.* Ft. Worth: The Summit Group, 1992.

Corbett, Warren. *The Wizard of Waxahachie.* Dallas: Southern Methodist University Press, 2009.

Durocher, Leo, with Ed Linn. *Nice Guys Finish Last.* Chicago: University of Chicago Press, 1975.

Enright, Jim (ed.) *Trade Him! 100 Years of Baseball's Greatest Deals.* Chicago: Follett, 1976.

Kahn, Roger. *Memories of Summer.* New York: Hyperion, 1997.

Miller, Jeff. *Down to the Wire.* Dallas: Taylor, 1992.

Minoso, Orestes, with Herb Fagan. *Just Call Me Minnie: My Six Decades in Baseball.* Champaign, Ill.: Sagamore, 1994.

Moffi, Larry. *This Side of Cooperstown.* Iowa City: University of Iowa Press, 1996.

Peary, Danny. *We Played the Game: 65 Players Remember Baseball's Greatest Era, 1947–64.* New York: Hyperion, 1994.

Peterson, John E. *The Kansas City Athletics: A Baseball History, 1954–1967.* Jefferson, N.C.: McFarland, 2003.

Pluto, Terry. *The Curse of Rocky Colavito.* New York: Simon & Schuster, 1994.

Rains, Rob. *The St. Louis Cardinals: The 100th Anniversary History.* New York: St. Martin's Press, 1992.

Reichler, Joseph L. (ed.). *The Baseball Encyclopedia.* 9th Edition. New York: Macmillan, 1985.

Russo, Jim. *Super Scout.* Chicago: Bonus Books, 1992.

Vanderberg, Bob. *Sox: From Lane and Fain to Zisk and Fisk.* Chicago: Chicago Review Press, 1982.

Vanderberg, Bob. *Minnie and The Mick: The Go-Go White Sox Challenge the Fabled Yankee Dynasty, 1951–1964.* South Bend: Diamond Communications, 1996.

Vanderberg, Bob. *'59: Summer of the Sox.* Champaign, Ill.: Sports Publishing Inc., 1999.

Vecsey, George. *Stan Musial: An American Life.* New York: Ballantine Books/ESPN Books, 2011.

Veeck, Bill, with Ed Linn. *Veeck as in Wreck.* New York: Putnam's, 1962.

Veeck, Bill, with Ed Linn. *The Hustler's Handbook.* New York: Putnam's, 1962.

Ward, Arch. *The New Chicago White Sox.* Chicago: Regnery, 1951.

Newspapers

Chicago Daily News, Chicago Sun-Times, Chicago Tribune, 1948–2005
Cleveland Plain Dealer, 1957–61
St. Louis Post-Dispatch, 1957
Milwaukee Journal, 1971–72
The New York Times, 1954–65
The Sporting News, 1949–90

Periodicals

Saturday Evening Post, "I'm Here to Win a Pennant," by Frank Lane (as told to Roger Kahn). June 23, 1956.
Sport magazine. April 1952, July 1953, August 1954, May 1955, June 1955, August 1956, May 1962, December 1978.
Sports Illustrated. March 5, 1956; May 28, 1956; March 17, 1958; July 27, 1959; Sept. 7, 1959; Sept. 14, 1959; Oct. 5, 1959; April 11, 1960; April 25, 1960; May 23, 1960; June 6, 1960; June 5, 1961; June 26, 1961; Aug. 26, 1968; Oct. 7, 1968; April 12, 1971; Aug. 7, 1978; April 5, 1993.

Web Sites

Baseball Almanac
Baseball in Wartime
Baseball Library
Baseball-Reference.com
Basketball-Reference.com
Bioproj@sabr.org
Coolquotes.com
NBA.com
Retrosheet.org

Index